The
1945–2005
A complete Record

TONY WAGTAR

PARKBENCH PUBLICATIONS

Published in Great Britain by Parkbench Publications,
PO Box 1081, Belfast BT1 9EP

A CIP catalogue record for this title is available from the
British Library

ISBN 978-0-9555756-9-3

Designed and typeset by Bookcraft Ltd,
Stroud, Gloucestershire
Printed and bound in Great Britain by
CPI Antony Rowe, Eastbourne

J'ACCUSE

Fool that I am, several years ago, I decided to write a football book. As an unknown writer, I predictably found difficulty in attracting any of the mainstream publishers who will not entertain any would-be authors unless they have a cookery programme on Channel Four. Consequently, I found myself traversing the route of vanity (or self-subsidy) publishing. I thus found myself having to invest quite a large sum into my book. I then wrote another football book and again I chose a more 'competitively priced' so-called vanity publisher.

When a third project of mine again failed to attract the attention of the bandwagon-jumping major publishers, I then made the decision to bypass publishers and do it all myself. I formed my own publishing company which if nothing else allowed me to be in complete control of my product. However, self-publishing has proved to be as bitter an experience as making use of the vanity publishers was. For a start, when one opts to self-publish, one is compelled to pay for a minimum of ten ISBN numbers, even if one only wishes to publish one title. Anyhow, let me bore you with the following hard luck story.

When one produces a new book, one knows that its only major opportunity of achieving substantial sales is if it is accepted for stock by one of the two major British book wholesalers, Gardners Books, or its poor cousin, Bertrams Books. I have sent several titles to these wholesalers, all without success. The result of their rejection is that book retailers such as Border Books and WH Smith will almost certainly not order copies for their stores if the items are not held in stock by the major wholesalers. One's chances of accumulating sales are thus at the mercy of a handful of individuals, namely Alan Street and Gail Harbour of Gardners. To what extent they scrutinise the sales potential of the titles is questionable, especially when they issue the same, standard customised letter with their rejection of the new titles.

Waterstones at least to their credit will study the new title, irrespective of the decision of the wholesalers, though I guess that Waterstones rarely stock books that are not also held in stock by the wholesalers. Waterstones can also be commended in that they do make public the email addresses of all their stores and new authors are given a fair hearing and able to place their books in various shops, unlike WH Smiths and Border Books whose shops appear to hide behind invisible email addresses.

What is so important then about having one's title held in stock by the wholesalers? The scenario is that many shops are more inclined to order perhaps half a dozen copies of one's book on a sale or return basis from the wholesalers with the result that one's publication will be considerably more conspicuous on the shop shelves and able to attract attention. When the books are not held in stock, they are designated as 'special orders' which means that all shops are forced to order copies as a firm sale and are clearly much more reluctant to invest in many copies which are not available on a sale or return basis. The problem is that stores like Waterstones will order a small handful of copies and it becomes more difficult to attract the attention of the book-shop browser if one has two books with only the spine showing on the shop shelf. If one's books are ordered in greater quantity, the chances are that one will be placed in a face-up position which renders it more eye-catching. The likes of Waterstones will state that they don't shift copies of my books as quickly as some other books, but how many of my books have been displayed in a prominent position in the shop? My titles are always liable to struggle when they are competing on a non-level playing field.

What is even more frustrating is that when one receives sales via the Nielsen Book-Data site, the source of the orders is not disclosed by the two main wholesalers. How on earth is a new publisher supposed to monitor the progress of their marketing attempts when one is forbidden from discovering who has actually ordered the books that are being delivered to the wholesalers. I have sent Gardners emails about my concerns. They have been less than helpful. They confirm my worst suspicions that the new publisher has little or no opportunity of thriving in a celebrity-driven book trade. I mean, one can hardly move in a book shop without knocking over a celebrity kiss and tell piece of trash. Book retailers appear to pander to the lowest common denominator by stocking a plethora of unimaginative celebrity books. What chance has the new publisher or writer of competing in a market where there is saturated coverage of books by famous non-writers, many of whose best-selling titles are in fact ghost written. It is my humble opinion that if Charles Dickens or William Shake-speare were starting out on the road to literary acclaim today, their chances of success would be thwarted by any absence from Big Brother or any of the other reality tv bullshit. The British bookbuying public are being nourished on a diet of junk food celebrity books when the cutting edge and thought-provoking works of some new authors are being elbowed aside.

Then of course there is the equally frustrating avenue of attempting to attract the attention of the media, whose patronage or lack of it can be instrumental in deter-mining the sales potential of one's new title. I have submitted many books to various radio stations and other media outlets. I take the view that if the book is not reviewed, it should be returned. Review copies should only be free if they actually are reviewed. Depressingly, not all in the media have the integrity to agree, even if one has submitted a stamped addressed envelope for the book's return, if it is not worthy of review. Again, the lack of celebrity status or one's failure to be seen in the right restaurants and winebars usually condemns one to a failure to obtain many reviews. Disc jockeys love nothing more than a yarn with a well-known person in an attempt at networking with them and moving in entertainment circles. They are less favourably disposed towards a clever nonentity. It is indeed a remarkable achievement that almost 100 Waterstones shops have stocked my titles when they have been operating in a virtual vacuum of publicity. I could employ a publicist, but paying someone £1000 to achieve maybe 200 extra sales is scarcely a worthwhile investment.

My advice to any would-be author or new publisher is have a re-think before you embark on the literary world. Your chances of success or fulfilment lie somewhere between nil and zero. In the meantime, for all the individuals and parties who may choose to take umbrage at this preface, then to quote, the Duke of Wellington, "sue and be damned."

Lots of love
Tony Wagtar, talented loser

1ST TEST: at Brisbane; November 29, 30, December 2, 3, and 4 1946; Australia won the toss

AUSTRALIA: 645

Barnes	c Bedser	b Wright	31	(46–2)
Morris	c Hammond	b Bedser	2	(9–1)
Bradman*		b Edrich	187	(322–3)
Hassett	c Yardley	b Bedser	128	(428–4)
Miller	lbw	b Wright	79	(465–5)
McCool	lbw	b Wright	95	(599–7)
Johnson	lbw	b Wright	47	(596–6)
Tallon	lbw	b Edrich	14	(629–8)
Lindwall	c Voce	b Wright	31	(645)
Tribe	c Gibb	b Edrich	1	(643–9)
Toshack	not out		1	

Extras: 29

Wright 5–167; Edrich 3–107

ENGLAND: 141

Hutton		b Miller	7	(10–1)
Washbrook	c Barnes	b Miller	6	(25–2)
Edrich	c McCool	b Miller	16	(56–4)
Compton	lbw	b Miller	17	(49–3)
Hammond*	lbw	b Toshack	32	(121–6)
Ikin	c Tallon	b Miller	0	(56–5)
Yardley	c Tallon	b Toshack	29	(134–7)
Gibb		b Miller	13	(136–8)
Voce	not out		1	
Bedser	lbw	b Miller	0	(136–9)
Wright	c Tallon	b Toshack	4	(141)

Extras: 16

Miller 7–60; Toshack 3–17

ENGLAND: 172

Hutton	c Barnes	b Miller	0	(0–1)
Washbrook	c Barnes	b Miller	13	(33–3)
Edrich	lbw	b Toshack	7	(13–2)
Compton	c Barnes	b Toshack	15	(62–4)
Hammond*		b Toshack	23	(65–5)
Ikin		b Tribe	32	(112–7)
Yardley	c Hassett	b Toshack	0	(65–6)
Gibb	lbw	b Toshack	11	(114–8)
Voce	c Hassett	b Tribe	18	(143–9)
Bedser	c &	b Toshack	18	(172)
Wright	not out		10	

Extras: 25

Toshack 6–82

The first Ashes contest since 1938 was horribly one-sided, not that the Australians were complaining, as Miller and Toshack shared eighteen wickets between them.

AUSTRALIA won by an innings and 332 runs to lead the series 1–0.

2ND TEST: at Sydney; December 13, 14, 16, 17, 18, and 19 1946; England won the toss

ENGLAND: 255

Hutton	c Tallon	b Johnson	39	(88–2)
Washbrook		b Freer	1	(10–1)
Edrich	lbw	b McCool	71	(148–5)
Compton	c Tallon	b McCool	5	(97–3)
Hammond*	c Tallon	b McCool	1	(99–4)
Ikin	c Hassett	b Johnson	60	(234–9)
Yardley	c Tallon	b Johnson	25	(187–6)
Smith	lbw	b Johnson	4	(197–7)
Evans		b Johnson	5	(205–8)
Bedser		b Johnson	14	(255)
Wright	not out		15	

Extras: 15

Johnson 6–42; McCool 3–73

ENGLAND: 371

Hutton	hit wicket	b Miller	37	(49–1)
Washbrook	c McCool	b Johnson	41	(118–2)
Edrich		b McCool	119	(327–6)
Compton	c Bradman	b Freer	54	(220–3)
Hammond*	c Toshack	b McCool	37	(280–4)
Ikin		b Freer	17	(309–5)
Yardley		b McCool	35	(366–8)
Smith	c Hassett	b Johnson	2	(346–7)
Evans	st Tallon	b McCool	9	(369–9)
Bedser	not out		3	
Wright	c Tallon	b McCool	0	(371)

Extras: 17

McCool 5–109

AUSTRALIA: 659 for 8 declared

Barnes	c Ikin	b Bedser	234	(564–6)
Morris		b Edrich	5	(24–1)
Johnson	c Washbrook	b Edrich	7	(37–2)
Hassett	c Compton	b Edrich	34	(96–3)
Miller	c Evans	b Smith	40	(159–4)
Bradman*	lbw	b Yardley	234	(564–5)
McCool	c Hammond	b Smith	12	(595–7)
Tallon	c &	b Wright	30	(617–8)
Freer	not out		28	
Tribe	not out		25	

Extras: 10

Edrich 3–79

It was business as usual as Don Bradman's six and a half hour stint yielded a huge total. Sid Barnes also recorded his highest first-class score with 234 of his own.

AUSTRALIA won by an innings and 33 runs to lead the series 2–0.

3RD TEST: at Melbourne; January 1, 2, 3, 4, 6, and 7 1947;
Australia won the toss

AUSTRALIA: 365

Barnes	lbw	b Bedser	45	(108–2)
Morris	lbw	b Bedser	21	(32–1)
Bradman*		b Yardley	79	(188–4)
Hassett	c Hammond	b Wright	12	(143–3)
Miller	c Evans	b Wright	33	(192–6)
Johnson	lbw	b Yardley	0	(188–5)
McCool	not out		104	
Tallon	c Evans	b Edrich	35	(255–7)
Lindwall		b Bedser	9	(272–8)
Dooland	c Hammond	b Edrich	19	(355–9)
Toshack	c Hutton	b Edrich	6	(365)
Extras: 2				

Edrich 3–50; Bedser 3–99

AUSTRALIA: 536

Barnes	c Evans	b Yardley	32	(68–1)
Morris		b Bedser	155	(333–5)
Bradman*	c &	b Yardley	49	(159–2)
Hassett		b Wright	9	(177–3)
Miller	c Hammond	b Yardley	34	(242–4)
McCool	c Evans	b Bedser	43	(341–7)
Johnson	run out		0	(335–6)
Tallon	c &	b Wright	92	(495–8)
Lindwall	c Washbrook	b Bedser	100	(536)
Dooland	c Compton	b Wright	1	(511–9)
Toshack	not out		2	
Extras: 19				

Yardley 3–67; Wright 3–131; Bedser 3–176

ENGLAND: 351

Hutton	c McCool	b Lindwall	2	(8–1)
Washbrook	c Tallon	b Dooland	62	(179–5)
Edrich	lbw	b Lindwall	89	(155–2)
Compton	lbw	b Toshack	11	(167–3)
Hammond*	c &	b Dooland	9	(176–4)
Ikin	c Miller	b Dooland	48	(298–7)
Yardley		b McCool	61	(292–6)
Evans		b McCool	17	(324–9)
Voce	lbw	b Dooland	0	(298–8)
Bedser	not out		27	
Wright		b Johnson	10	(351)
Extras: 15				

Dooland 4–69

ENGLAND: 310 for 7

Hutton	c Bradman	b Toshack	40	(138–1)
Washbrook		b Dooland	112	(197–4)
Edrich	lbw	b McCool	13	(163–2)
Compton	run out		14	(186–3)
Hammond*		b Lindwall	26	(249–6)
Ikin	c Hassett	b Miller	5	(221–5)
Yardley	not out		53	
Bedser	lbw	b Miller	25	(294–7)
Evans	not out		0	
Extras: 22				

Cyril Washbrook's four-hour century enabled England to achieve a respectable draw after the tourists were set the unrealistic target of 551.

MATCH DRAWN. Australia still lead the series 2–0.

4TH TEST: at Adelaide; January 31, February 1, 3, 4, 5, and 6 1947; England won the toss

ENGLAND: 460

Hutton	lbw	b McCool	94	(196–3)
Washbrook	c Tallon	b Dooland	65	(137–1)
Edrich	c &	b Dooland	17	(173–2)
Hammond*		b Toshack	18	(202–4)
Compton	c &	b Lindwall	147	(455–7)
Hardstaff Jun.		b Miller	67	(320–5)
Ikin	c Toshack	b Dooland	21	(381–6)
Yardley	not out		18	
Bedser		b Lindwall	2	(460–8)
Evans		b Lindwall	0	(460–9)
Wright		b Lindwall	0	(460)
Extras: 11				

Lindwall 4–52; Dooland 3–133

ENGLAND: 340 for 8 declared

Hutton		b Johnson	76	(137–2)
Washbrook	c Tallon	b Lindwall	39	(100–1)
Edrich	c Bradman	b Toshack	46	(178–3)
Hammond*	c Lindwall	b Toshack	22	(188–4)
Compton	not out		103	
Hardstaff Jun.		b Toshack	9	(207–5)
Ikin	lbw	b Toshack	1	(215–6)
Yardley	c Tallon	b Lindwall	18	(250–7)
Bedser	c Tallon	b Miller	3	(255–8)
Evans	not out		10	
Extras: 13				

Toshack 4–76

AUSTRALIA: 487

Harvey		b Bedser	12	(18–1)
Morris	c Evans	b Bedser	122	(222–4)
Bradman*		b Bedser	0	(18–2)
Hassett	c Hammond	b Wright	78	(207–3)
Miller	not out		141	
Johnson	lbw	b Wright	52	(372–5)
McCool	c Bedser	b Yardley	2	(389–6)
Tallon		b Wright	3	(396–7)
Lindwall	c Evans	b Yardley	20	(423–8)
Dooland	c Bedser	b Yardley	29	(486–9)
Toshack	run out		0	(487)
Extras: 28				

Bedser 3–97; Yardley 3–101; Wright 3–152

AUSTRALIA 215 for 1

Harvey		b Yardley	31	(116–1)
Morris	not out		124	
Bradman*	not out		56	
Extras: 4				

Denis Compton, an icon at Arsenal Football Club, hit a century in each innings and still Australia came close to another victory.

MATCH DRAWN. Australia still lead the series 2–0.

5TH TEST: at Sydney; February 28, March 1, 3, 4, and 5 1947; England won the toss

ENGLAND: 280

Hutton	retired hurt		122	
Washbrook		b Lindwall	0	(1–1)
Edrich	c Tallon	b Lindwall	60	(151–2)
Fishlock		b McCool	14	(188–3)
Compton	hit wicket	b Lindwall	17	(215–4)
Yardley*	c Miller	b Lindwall	2	(225–5)
Ikin		b Lindwall	0	(225–6)
Evans		b Lindwall	29	(269–8)
Smith		b Lindwall	2	(244–7)
Bedser	not out		10	
Wright	c Tallon	b Miller	7	(280–9)
Extras: 17				
Lindwall 7–63				

ENGLAND: 186

Fishlock	lbw	b Lindwall	0	(0–1)
Washbrook		b McCool	24	(42–2)
Edrich	st Tallon	b McCool	24	(65–3)
Compton	c Miller	b Toshack	76	(184–8)
Ikin	st Tallon	b McCool	0	(65–4)
Yardley*		b McCool	11	(85–5)
Evans		b Miller	20	(120–6)
Smith	c Tallon	b Lindwall	24	(157–7)
Bedser	st Tallon	b McCool	4	(186–9)
Wright	not out		1	
Hutton	Absent hurt			
Extras: 2				
McCool 5–44				

AUSTRALIA: 253

Barnes	c Evans	b Bedser	71	(126–1)
Morris	lbw	b Bedser	57	(146–2)
Bradman*		b Wright	12	(146–3)
Hassett	c Ikin	b Wright	24	(218–5)
Miller	c Ikin	b Wright	23	(187–4)
Hamence	not out		30	
McCool	c Yardley	b Wright	3	(230–6)
Tallon	c Compton	b Wright	0	(230–7)
Lindwall	c Smith	b Wright	0	(233–8)
Tribe	c Fishlock	b Wright	9	(245–9)
Toshack	run out		5	(253)
Extras: 19				
Wright 7–105				

AUSTRALIA: 214 for 5

Barnes	c Evans	b Bedser	30	(51–2)
Morris	run out		17	(45–1)
Bradman*	c Compton	b Bedser	63	(149–3)
Hassett	c Ikin	b Wright	47	(173–4)
Miller	not out		34	
Hamence	c Edrich	b Wright	1	(180–5)
McCool	not out		13	
Extras: 9				

Australia recovered from 51 for 2 to chase down the target of 214, scoring at 4 runs per over. England's second innings was undermined by the absence of Len Hutton.

AUSTRALIA won by 5 wickets to win the series 3–0.

1ST TEST: at Nottingham; June 10, 11, 12, 14, and 15 1948; England won the toss

ENGLAND: 165

Hutton		b Miller	3	(9–1)
Washbrook	c Brown	b Lindwall	6	(15–2)
Edrich		b Johnston	18	(46–3)
Compton		b Miller	19	(48–5)
Hardstaff Jun.	c Miller	b Johnston	0	(46–4)
Barnett		b Johnston	8	(60–6)
Yardley*	lbw	b Toshack	3	(74–8)
Evans	c Morris	b Johnston	12	(74–7)
Laker	c Tallon	b Miller	63	(165)
Bedser	c Brown	b Johnston	22	(163–9)
Young	not out		1	
Extras: 10				

Johnston 5–36; Miller 3–38

ENGLAND: 441

Hutton		b Miller	74	(150–3)
Washbrook	c Tallon	b Miller	1	(5–1)
Edrich	c Tallon	b Johnson	13	(39–2)
Compton	hit wicket	b Miller	184	(405–7)
Hardstaff Jun.	c Hassett	b Toshack	43	(243–4)
Barnett	c Miller	b Johnston	6	(264–5)
Yardley*	c &	b Johnston	22	(321–6)
Evans	c Tallon	b Johnston	50	(423–9)
Laker		b Miller	4	(413–8)
Bedser	not out		3	
Young		b Johnston	9	(441)
Extras: 32				

Miller 4–125; Johnston 4–147

AUSTRALIA: 509

Barnes	c Evans	b Laker	62	(121–2)
Morris		b Laker	31	(73–1)
Bradman*	c Hutton	b Bedser	138	(305–5)
Miller	c Edrich	b Laker	0	(121–3)
Brown	lbw	b Yardley	17	(185–4)
Hassett		b Bedser	137	(472–8)
Johnson		b Laker	21	(338–6)
Tallon	c &	b Young	10	(365–7)
Lindwall	c Evans	b Yardley	42	(476–9)
Johnston	not out		17	
Toshack	lbw	b Bedser	19	(509)
Extras: 15				

Laker 4–138; Bedser 3–113

AUSTRALIA: 98–2

Barnes	not out		64
Morris		b Bedser	9	(38–1)
Bradman*	c Hutton	b Bedser	0	(48–2)
Hassett	not out		21
Extras: 4			

A poor first innings was England's undoing as Johnston took 5 for 36 off 25 8-ball overs. Compton's huge second-innings knock proved to be in vain.

AUSTRALIA won by 8 wickets to lead the series 1–0

2ND TEST: at Lord's; June 24, 25, 26, 28, and 29 1948; Australia won the toss

AUSTRALIA: 350

Barnes	c Hutton	b Coxon	0	(3–1)
Morris	c Hutton	b Coxon	105	(166–3)
Bradman*	c Hutton	b Bedser	38	(87–2)
Hassett		b Yardley	47	(216–5)
Miller	lbw	b Bedser	4	(173–4)
Brown	lbw	b Yardley	24	(225–6)
Johnson	c Evans	b Edrich	4	(246–7)
Tallon	c Yardley	b Bedser	53	(320–9)
Lindwall		b Bedser	15	(275–8)
Johnston	st Evans	b Wright	29	(350)
Toshack	not out		20	
Extras: 11				

Bedser 4–100

AUSTRALIA: 460 for 7 declared

Barnes	c Washbrook	b Yardley	141	(296–2)
Morris		b Wright	62	(122–1)
Bradman*	c Edrich	b Bedser	89	(329–4)
Hassett		b Yardley	0	(296–3)
Miller	c Bedser	b Laker	74	(445–6)
Brown	c Evans	b Coxon	32	(416–5)
Lindwall	st Evans	b Laker	25	(460–7)
Johnson	not out		9	
Extras: 28				

ENGLAND: 215

Hutton		b Johnson	20	(32–2)
Washbrook	c Tallon	b Lindwall	8	(17–1)
Edrich		b Lindwall	5	(46–3)
Compton	c Miller	b Johnston	53	(133–5)
Dollery		b Lindwall	0	(46–4)
Yardley*		b Lindwall	44	(134–6)
Coxon	c &	b Johnson	19	(186–8)
Evans	c Miller	b Johnston	9	(145–7)
Laker	c Tallon	b Johnson	28	(197–9)
Bedser		b Lindwall	9	(215)
Wright	not out		13	
Extras: 7				

Lindwall 5–70; Johnson 3–72

ENGLAND: 186

Hutton	c Johnson	b Lindwall	13	(42–1)
Washbrook	c Tallon	b Toshack	37	(65–3)
Edrich	c Johnson	b Toshack	2	(52–2)
Compton	c Miller	b Johnston	29	(106–4)
Dollery		b Lindwall	37	(141–7)
Yardley*		b Toshack	11	(133–5)
Coxon	lbw	b Toshack	0	(133–6)
Evans	not out		24	
Laker		b Lindwall	0	(141–8)
Bedser	c Hassett	b Johnston	9	(158–9)
Wright	c Lindwall	b Toshack	4	(186)
Extras: 20				

Toshack 5–40; Lindwall 3–61

Both Australian openers, Barnes and Morris, helped themselves to centuries as 'the invincibles' inflicted another humiliating defeat.

AUSTRALIA won by 409 runs to lead the series 2–0.

3RD TEST: at Manchester; July 8, 9, 10, 12, and 13 1948; England won the toss

ENGLAND: 363

Washbrook		b Johnston	11	(22–1)
Emmett	c Barnes	b Lindwall	10	(28–2)
Edrich	c Tallon	b Lindwall	32	(119–5)
Compton	not out		145	
Crapp	lbw	b Lindwall	37	(96–3)
Dollery		b Johnston	1	(97–4)
Yardley*	c Johnson	b Toshack	22	(141–6)
Evans	c Johnston	b Lindwall	34	(216–7)
Bedser	run out		37	(337–8)
Pollard		b Toshack	3	(352–9)
Young	c Bradman	b Johnston	4	(363)
Extras: 27				

Lindwall 4–99; Johnston 3–67

ENGLAND: 174 for 3 declared

Washbrook	not out		85
Emmett	c Tallon	b Lindwall	0 (1–1)
Edrich	run out		53 (125–2)
Compton	c Miller	b Toshack	0 (129–3)
Crapp	not out		19
Extras: 17			

AUSTRALIA: 221

Morris	c Compton	b Bedser	51	(139–5)
Johnson	c Evans	b Bedser	1	(3–1)
Bradman*	lbw	b Pollard	7	(13–2)
Hassett	c Washbrook	b Young	38	(82–3)
Miller	lbw	b Pollard	31	(135–4)
Barnes	retired hurt		1	
Loxton		b Pollard	36	(208–7)
Tallon	c Evans	b Edrich	18	(172–6)
Lindwall	c Washbrook	b Bedser	23	(221–9)
Johnston	c Crapp	b Bedser	3	(219–8)
Toshack	not out		0	
Extras: 12				

Bedser 4–81; Pollard 3–53

AUSTRALIA: 92 for 1

Morris	not out		54
Johnson	c Crapp	b Young	6 (10–1)
Bradman*	not out		30
Extras: 2			

Another big century from Compton put England in the ascendancy, but Bradman was happy to play out a draw as he accumulated an unbeaten 30 over two hours.

MATCH DRAWN. Australia still lead the series 2–0.

4TH TEST: at Leeds; July 22, 23, 24, 26, and 27 1948; England won the toss

ENGLAND: 496

Hutton		b Lindwall	81	(168–1)
Washbrook	c Lindwall	b Johnston	143	(268–2)
Edrich	c Morris	b Johnson	111	(426–4)
Bedser	c &	b Johnson	79	(423–3)
Compton	c Saggers	b Lindwall	23	(473–6)
Crapp		b Toshack	5	(447–5)
Yardley*		b Miller	25	(496)
Cranston		b Loxton	10	(486–7)
Evans	c Hassett	b Loxton	3	(490–8)
Laker	c Saggers	b Loxton	4	(496–9)
Pollard	not out		0	
Extras: 12				

Loxton 3–55

ENGLAND: 365 for 8 declared

Hutton	c Bradman	b Johnson	57	(129–2)
Washbrook	c Harvey	b Johnston	65	(129–1)
Edrich	lbw	b Lindwall	54	(232–3)
Compton	c Miller	b Johnston	66	(293–7)
Crapp		b Lindwall	18	(260–4)
Yardley*	c Harvey	b Johnston	7	(277–5)
Cranston	c Saggers	b Johnston	0	(278–6)
Evans	not out		47	
Bedser	c Hassett	b Miller	17	(330–8)
Laker	not out		15	
Extras: 19				

Johnston 4–95

AUSTRALIA: 458

Morris	c Cranston	b Bedser	6	(13–1)
Hassett	c Crapp	b Pollard	13	(65–2)
Bradman*		b Pollard	33	(68–3)
Miller	c Edrich	b Yardley	58	(189–4)
Harvey		b Laker	112	(294–5)
Loxton		b Yardley	93	(344–7)
Johnson	c Cranston	b Laker	10	(329–6)
Lindwall	c Crapp	b Bedser	77	(458)
Saggers	st Evans	b Laker	5	(355–8)
Johnston	c Edrich	b Bedser	13	(403–9)
Toshack	not out		12	
Extras: 26				

Bedser 3–92; Laker 3–113

AUSTRALIA: 404 for 3

Morris	c Pollard	b Yardley	182	(358–2)
Hassett	c &	b Compton	17	(57–1)
Bradman*	not out		173	
Miller	lbw	b Cranston	12	(396–3)
Harvey	not out		4	
Extras: 16				

England were strolling at 423 for 2 in the first innings, only to lose after Australia produced a record-breaking run chase, courtesy of tons from Morris and Bradman.

AUSTRALIA won by 7 wickets to lead the series 3–0.

5TH TEST: at the Oval; August 14, 16, 17, and 18 1948; England won the toss

ENGLAND: 52

Hutton	c Tallon	b Lindwall	30	(52)
Dewes		b Miller	1	(2–1)
Edrich	c Hassett	b Johnston	3	(10–2)
Compton	c Morris	b Lindwall	4	(17–3)
Crapp	c Tallon	b Miller	0	(23–4)
Yardley*		b Lindwall	7	(35–5)
Watkins	lbw	b Johnston	0	(42–6)
Evans		b Lindwall	1	(45–7)
Bedser		b Lindwall	0	(45–8)
Young		b Lindwall	0	(47–9)
Hollies	not out		0	
Extras: 6				

Lindwall 6–20

ENGLAND: 188

Hutton	c Tallon	b Miller	64	(153–4)
Dewes		b Lindwall	10	(20–1)
Edrich		b Lindwall	28	(64–2)
Compton	c Lindwall	b Johnston	39	(125–3)
Crapp		b Miller	9	(164–5)
Yardley*	c Miller	b Johnston	9	(188–9)
Watkins	c Hassett	b Ring	2	(167–6)
Evans		b Lindwall	8	(178–7)
Bedser		b Johnston	0	(181–8)
Young	not out		3	
Hollies	c Morris	b Johnston	0	(188)
Extras: 16				

Johnston 4–40; Lindwall 3–50

AUSTRALIA: 389

Barnes	c Evans	b Hollies	61	(117–1)
Morris	run out		196	(359–8)
Bradman*		b Hollies	0	(117–2)
Hassett	lbw	b Young	37	(226–3)
Miller	st Evans	b Hollies	5	(243–4)
Harvey	c Young	b Hollies	17	(265–5)
Loxton	c Evans	b Edrich	15	(304–6)
Lindwall	c Edrich	b Young	9	(332–7)
Tallon	c Crapp	b Hollies	31	(389–9)
Ring	c Crapp	b Bedser	9	(389)
Johnston	not out		0	
Extras: 9				

Hollies 5–131

Arthur Morris tormented England again, while Bradman, needing only 4 runs to finish his career with an average of 100, was dismissed for a duck by a Hollies googly.

AUSTRALIA won by an innings and 149 runs to win the series 4–0

1ST TEST: at Brisbane; December 1, 2, 4, and 5 1950; Australia won the toss

AUSTRALIA: 228

Moroney	c Hutton	b Bailey	0	(0–1)
Morris	lbw	b Bedser	25	(69–2)
Harvey	c Evans	b Bedser	74	(118–4)
Miller	c McIntyre	b Wright	15	(116–3)
Hassett*		b Bedser	8	(129–5)
Loxton	c Evans	b Brown	24	(156–6)
Lindwall	c Bedser	b Bailey	41	(226–9)
Tallon	c Simpson	b Brown	5	(172–7)
Johnson	c Simpson	b Bailey	23	(219–8)
Johnston	c Hutton	b Bedser	1	(228)
Iverson	not out		1	

Extras: 11

Bedser 4–45; Bailey 3–28

AUSTRALIA: 32 for 7 declared

Moroney	lbw	b Bailey	0	(0–1)
Morris	c Bailey	b Bedser	0	(0–2)
Johnson	lbw	b Bailey	8	(19–5)
Loxton	c Bailey	b Bedser	0	(0–3)
Hassett*	lbw	b Bailey	3	(12–4)
Harvey	c Simpson	b Bedser	12	(32–7)
Miller	c Simpson	b Bailey	8	(31–6)
Lindwall	not out		0	

Extras: 1

Bailey 4–22; Bedser 3–9

ENGLAND: 68 for 7 declared

Simpson		b Johnston	12	(49–2)
Washbrook	c Hassett	b Johnston	19	(28–1)
Evans	c Iverson	b Johnston	16	(52–3)
Compton	c Lindwall	b Johnston	3	(52–4)
Dewes	c Loxton	b Miller	1	(56–5)
Hutton	not out		8	
McIntyre		b Johnston	1	(57–6)
Brown*	c Tallon	b Miller	4	(67–7)
Bailey	not out		1	

Extras: 3

Johnston 5–35

ENGLAND: 122

Simpson		b Lindwall	0	(0–1)
Washbrook	c Loxton	b Lindwall	6	(16–2)
Dewes		b Miller	9	(22–3)
Bailey	c Johnston	b Iverson	7	(23–4)
Bedser	c Harvey	b Iverson	0	(23–5)
Evans	c Loxton	b Johnston	5	(46–7)
McIntyre	run out		7	(30–6)
Hutton	not out		62	
Compton	c Loxton	b Johnston	0	(46–8)
Brown*	c Loxton	b Iverson	17	(77–9)
Wright	c Lindwall	b Iverson	2	(122)

Extras: 7

Iverson 4–43

Bailey and Bedser shared 14 wickets as the Aussies were reduced to 32 for 7 in the second innings. England however fell badly short of the victory target of 193.

AUSTRALIA won by 70 runs to lead the series 1–0

2ND TEST: at Melbourne; December 22, 23, 26, and 27 1950; Australia won the toss

AUSTRALIA: 194

Archer	c Bedser	b Bailey	26	(89–3)
Morris	c Hutton	b Bedser	2	(6–1)
Harvey	c Evans	b Bedser	42	(67–2)
Miller	lbw	b Brown	18	(93–4)
Hassett*		b Bailey	52	(177–6)
Loxton	c Evans	b Close	32	(177–5)
Lindwall	lbw	b Bailey	8	(192–7)
Tallon	not out		7	
Johnson	c Parkhouse	b Bedser	0	(193–8)
Johnston	c Hutton	b Bedser	0	(193–9)
Iverson		b Bailey	1	(194)
Extras: 6				

Bedser 4–37; Bailey 4–40

AUSTRALIA: 181

Archer	c Bailey	b Bedser	46	(99–2)
Morris	lbw	b Wright	18	(43–1)
Harvey	run out		31	(100–3)
Miller		b Bailey	14	(126–4)
Hassett*	c Bailey	b Brown	19	(156–8)
Loxton	c Evans	b Brown	2	(131–5)
Lindwall	c Evans	b Brown	7	(151–6)
Tallon	lbw	b Brown	0	(151–7)
Johnson	c Close	b Bedser	23	(181)
Johnston		b Bailey	6	(181–9)
Iverson	not out		0	
Extras: 15				

Brown 4–26

ENGLAND: 197

Simpson	c Johnson	b Miller	4	(11–1)
Washbrook	lbw	b Lindwall	21	(37–3)
Dewes	c Miller	b Johnston	8	(33–2)
Hutton	c Tallon	b Iverson	12	(54–4)
Parkhouse	c Hassett	b Miller	9	(61–6)
Close	c Loxton	b Iverson	0	(54–5)
Brown*	c Johnson	b Iverson	62	(153–8)
Bailey		b Lindwall	12	(126–7)
Evans	c Johnson	b Iverson	49	(194–9)
Bedser	not out		4	
Wright	lbw	b Johnston	2	(197)
Extras: 14				

Iverson 4–37

ENGLAND: 150

Simpson		b Lindwall	23	(52–3)
Washbrook		b Iverson	8	(21–1)
Bailey		b Johnson	0	(22–2)
Hutton	c Lindwall	b Johnston	40	(92–5)
Dewes	c Harvey	b Iverson	5	(82–4)
Parkhouse	lbw	b Johnston	28	(134–9)
Close	lbw	b Johnston	1	(95–6)
Brown*		b Lindwall	8	(122–7)
Evans		b Lindwall	2	(124–8)
Bedser	not out		14	
Wright	lbw	b Johnston	2	(150)
Extras: 19				

Johnston 4–26; Lindwall 3–29

Melbourne's knack of providing nailbiting tests was in evidence here as the away team fell narrowly short of the required total of 179 in an evenly-contested skirmish.

AUSTRALIA won by 28 runs to lead the series 2–0

3RD TEST: at Sydney; January 5, 6, 8, and 9 1951; England won the toss

ENGLAND: 290

Batsman			Runs	Fall
Hutton	lbw	b Miller	62	(128–2)
Washbrook	c Miller	b Johnson	18	(34–1)
Simpson	c Loxton	b Miller	49	(137–4)
Compton		b Miller	0	(128–3)
Parkhouse	c Morris	b Johnson	25	(187–5)
Brown*		b Lindwall	79	(258–6)
Bailey	c Tallon	b Johnson	15	(286–9)
Evans	not out		23	
Bedser		b Lindwall	3	(267–7)
Warr		b Miller	4	(281–8)
Wright	run out		0	(290)

Extras: 12

Miller 4–37; Johnson 3–94

ENGLAND: 123

Batsman			Runs	Fall
Hutton	c Tallon	b Iverson	9	(32–1)
Washbrook		b Iverson	34	(45–3)
Simpson	c Tallon	b Iverson	0	(40–2)
Compton	c Johnson	b Johnston	23	(91–5)
Parkhouse	run out		15	(74–4)
Brown*		b Iverson	18	(119–7)
Evans		b Johnson	14	(119–6)
Bailey	not out		0	
Bedser		b Iverson	4	(123–8)
Warr		b Iverson	0	(123–9)
Wright	Absent Hurt			

Extras: 6

Iverson 6–27

AUSTRALIA: 426

Batsman			Runs	Fall
Archer	c Evans	b Bedser	48	(122–2)
Morris		b Bedser	0	(1–1)
Hassett*	c Bedser	b Brown	70	(122–3)
Harvey		b Bedser	39	(190–4)
Miller	not out		145	
Loxton	c Bedser	b Brown	17	(223–5)
Tallon	lbw	b Bedser	18	(252–6)
Johnson		b Brown	77	(402–7)
Lindwall	lbw	b Brown	1	(406–8)
Johnston	run out		0	(418–9)
Iverson	run out		1	(426)

Extras: 10

Bedser 4–107; Brown 4–153

Keith Miller produced an outstanding display with bat and ball as woeful England were once more conquered with an innings to spare.

AUSTRALIA won by an innings and 13 runs to lead the series 3–0

4TH TEST: at Adelaide; February 2, 3, 5, 6, 7, and 8 1951; Australia won the toss

AUSTRALIA: 371

Archer	c Compton	b Bedser	0	(0–1)
Morris		b Tattersall	206	(371)
Hassett*	c Evans	b Wright	43	(95–2)
Harvey		b Bedser	43	(205–3)
Miller	c Brown	b Wright	44	(281–4)
Burke		b Tattersall	12	(310–5)
Johnson	c Evans	b Bedser	16	(357–6)
Lindwall	lbw	b Wright	1	(363–7)
Tallon		b Tattersall	1	(366–8)
Johnston	c Hutton	b Wright	0	(367–9)
Iverson	not out		0	
Extras: 5				

Wright 4–99; Bedser 3–74; Tattersall 3–95

AUSTRALIA: 403 for 8 declared

Archer	c Bedser	b Tattersall	32	(79–2)
Morris	run out		16	(26–1)
Hassett*	lbw	b Wright	31	(95–3)
Harvey		b Brown	68	(194–4)
Miller		b Wright	99	(281–5)
Burke	not out		101	
Johnson	c Evans	b Warr	3	(297–6)
Lindwall	run out		31	(367–7)
Tallon	c Hutton	b Compton	5	(378–8)
Johnston	not out		9	
Extras: 8				

ENGLAND: 272

Hutton	not out		156	
Washbrook	c Iverson	b Lindwall	2	(7–1)
Simpson		b Johnston	29	(80–2)
Compton	c Tallon	b Lindwall	5	(96–3)
Sheppard		b Iverson	9	(132–4)
Brown*		b Miller	16	(161–5)
Evans	c Burke	b Johnston	13	(195–6)
Bedser	lbw	b Iverson	7	(206–7)
Tattersall	c Harvey	b Iverson	0	(214–8)
Warr		b Johnston	0	(219–9)
Wright	lbw	b Lindwall	14	(272)
Extras: 21				

Lindwall 3–51; Johnston 3–58; Iverson 3–68

ENGLAND: 228

Hutton	c sub	b Johnston	45	(74–1)
Washbrook	lbw	b Johnston	31	(90–2)
Simpson	c Burke	b Johnston	61	(181–4)
Compton	c sub	b Johnston	0	(90–3)
Sheppard	lbw	b Miller	41	(228–7)
Evans	c Johnson	b Miller	21	(221–5)
Bedser	c Morris	b Miller	0	(221–6)
Tattersall	c Morris	b Johnson	6	(228–8)
Warr		b Johnson	0	(228–9)
Wright	not out		0	
Brown*	Absent Hurt			
Extras: 23				

Johnston 4–73 Miller 3–27

Not even the stout resistance of Len Hutton could prevent another annihilation as Morris rescued Australia's first innings with a double century.

AUSTRALIA won by 274 runs to lead the series 4–0.

5TH TEST: at Melbourne; February 23, 24, 26, 27, and 28 1951; Australia won the toss

AUSTRALIA: 217

Burke	c Tattersall	b Bedser	11	(23–1)
Morris	lbw	b Brown	50	(111–2)
Hassett*	c Hutton	b Brown	92	(184–7)
Harvey	c Evans	b Brown	1	(115–3)
Miller	c &	b Brown	7	(123–4)
Hole		b Bedser	18	(156–5)
Johnson	lbw	b Bedser	1	(166–6)
Lindwall	c Compton	b Bedser	21	(216–9)
Tallon	c Hutton	b Bedser	1	(187–8)
Johnston	not out		12	
Iverson	c Washbrook	b Brown	0	(217)
Extras: 3				

Bedser 5–46; Brown 5–49

AUSTRALIA: 197

Burke	c Hutton	b Bedser	1	(6–2)
Morris	lbw	b Bedser	4	(5–1)
Hassett*		b Wright	48	(142–5)
Harvey	lbw	b Wright	52	(87–3)
Miller	c &	b Brown	0	(89–4)
Hole		b Bailey	63	(196–8)
Johnson	c Brown	b Wright	0	(142–6)
Lindwall		b Bedser	14	(192–7)
Tallon	not out		2	
Johnston		b Bedser	1	(197–9)
Iverson	c Compton	b Bedser	0	(197)
Extras: 12				

Bedser 5–59; Wright 3–56

ENGLAND: 320

Hutton		b Hole	79	(171–2)
Washbrook	c Tallon	b Miller	27	(40–1)
Simpson	not out		156	
Compton	c Miller	b Lindwall	11	(204–3)
Sheppard	c Tallon	b Miller	1	(205–4)
Brown*		b Lindwall	6	(212–5)
Evans		b Miller	1	(213–6)
Bedser		b Lindwall	11	(228–7)
Bailey	c Johnson	b Iverson	5	(236–8)
Wright	lbw	b Iverson	3	(246–9)
Tattersall		b Miller	10	(320)
Extras: 10				

Miller 4–76; Lindwall 3–77

ENGLAND: 95 for 2

Hutton	not out		60	
Washbrook	c Lindwall	b Johnston	7	(32–1)
Simpson	run out		15	(62–2)
Compton	not out		11	
Extras: 2				

Alec Bedser took ten wickets and Reg Simpson recorded his highest test score as England finally registered their first Ashes test victory for more than a decade.

ENGLAND won by 8 wickets, but AUSTRALIA win the series 4–1.

1ST TEST: at Nottingham; June 11, 12, 13, 15, and 16 1953;
Australia won the toss

AUSTRALIA: 249

Hole		b Bedser	0	(2-1)
Morris	lbw	b Bedser	67	(124-2)
Hassett*		b Bedser	115	(244-6)
Harvey	c Compton	b Bedser	0	(128-3)
Miller	c Bailey	b Wardle	55	(237-4)
Benaud	c Evans	b Bailey	3	(244-5)
Davidson		b Bedser	4	(249)
Tallon		b Bedser	0	(246-7)
Lindwall	c Evans	b Bailey	0	(247-8)
Hill		b Bedser	0	(248-9)
Johnston	not out		0	
Extras: 5				
Bedser 7-55				

AUSTRALIA: 123

Hole		b Bedser	5	(28-1)
Morris		b Tattersall	60	(81-6)
Hassett*	c Hutton	b Bedser	5	(44-2)
Harvey	c Graveney	b Bedser	2	(50-3)
Miller	c Kenyon	b Bedser	5	(64-4)
Benaud		b Bedser	0	(68-5)
Davidson	c Graveney	b Tattersall	6	(92-7)
Tallon	c Simpson	b Tattersall	15	(106-8)
Lindwall	c Tattersall	b Bedser	12	(115-9)
Hill	c Tattersall	b Bedser	4	(123)
Johnston	not out		4	
Extras: 5				
Bedser 7-44; Tattersall 3-22				

ENGLAND: 144

Hutton*	c Benaud	b Davidson	43	(82-5)
Kenyon	c Hill	b Lindwall	8	(17-1)
Simpson	lbw	b Lindwall	0	(17-2)
Compton	c Morris	b Lindwall	0	(17-3)
Graveney	c Benaud	b Hill	22	(76-4)
May	c Tallon	b Hill	9	(92-6)
Bailey	lbw	b Hill	13	(121-8)
Evans	c Tallon	b Davidson	8	(107-7)
Wardle	not out		29	
Bedser	lbw	b Lindwall	2	(136-9)
Tattersall		b Lindwall	2	(144)
Extras: 8				
Lindwall 5-57; Hill 3-35				

ENGLAND: 120 for 1

Hutton*	not out		60	
Kenyon	c Hassett	b Hill	16	(26-1)
Simpson	not out		28	
Extras: 16				

Bedser plundered fourteen wickets at a cost of 99 but England, poised for victory, couldn't get over the finishing line because of the weather's intervention.

MATCH DRAWN. The series remained level at 0-0.

2ND TEST: at Lord's; June 25, 26, 27, 29, and 30 1953; Australia won the toss

AUSTRALIA: 346

Hassett*	c Bailey	b Bedser	104	(291–7)
Morris	st Evans	b Bedser	30	(65–1)
Harvey	lbw	b Bedser	59	(190–2)
Miller		b Wardle	25	(225–3)
Hole	c Compton	b Wardle	13	(240–5)
Benaud	lbw	b Wardle	0	(229–4)
Davidson	c Statham	b Bedser	76	(346)
Ring	lbw	b Wardle	18	(280–6)
Lindwall		b Statham	9	(330–8)
Langley	c Watson	b Bedser	1	(331–9)
Johnston	not out		3	
Extras: 8				

Bedser 5–105; Wardle 4–77

AUSTRALIA: 368

Hassett*	c Evans	b Statham	3	(3–1)
Morris	c Statham	b Compton	89	(168–2)
Miller		b Wardle	109	(235–4)
Harvey		b Bedser	21	(227–3)
Hole	lbw	b Brown	47	(305–7)
Benaud	c Graveney	b Bedser	5	(248–5)
Davidson	c &	b Brown	15	(296–6)
Ring	lbw	b Brown	7	(308–8)
Lindwall		b Bedser	50	(368)
Langley		b Brown	9	(362–9)
Johnston	not out		0	
Extras: 13				

Brown 4–82; Bedser 3–77

ENGLAND: 372

Hutton*	c Hole	b Johnston	145	(279–3)
Kenyon	c Davidson	b Lindwall	3	(9–1)
Graveney		b Lindwall	78	(177–2)
Compton	c Hole	b Benaud	57	(301–5)
Watson	st Langley	b Johnston	4	(291–4)
Bailey	c &	b Miller	2	(332–8)
Brown	c Langley	b Lindwall	22	(328–6)
Evans		b Lindwall	0	(328–7)
Wardle		b Davidson	23	(372)
Bedser		b Lindwall	1	(341–9)
Statham	not out		17	
Extras: 20				

Lindwall 5–66

ENGLAND: 282 for 7

Hutton*	c Hole	b Lindwall	5	(10–2)
Kenyon	c Hassett	b Lindwall	2	(6–1)
Graveney	c Langley	b Johnston	2	(12–3)
Compton	lbw	b Johnston	33	(73–4)
Watson	c Hole	b Ring	109	(236–5)
Bailey	c Benaud	b Ring	71	(246–6)
Brown	c Hole	b Benaud	28	(282–7)
Evans	not out		11	
Wardle	not out		0	
Extras: 21				

Both captains scored tons as a fascinating encounter ended with England 61 runs short of victory and Australia a mere three wickets away from triumph.

MATCH DRAWN. The series remained level at 0–0.

3RD TEST: at Manchester; July 9, 10, 11, 13, and 14 1953; Australia won the toss

AUSTRALIA: 318

Hassett*		b Bailey	26	(48–2)
Morris		b Bedser	1	(15–1)
Miller		b Bedser	17	(48–3)
Harvey	c Evans	b Bedser	122	(256–5)
Hole	c Evans	b Bedser	66	(221–4)
de Courcy	lbw	b Wardle	41	(302–9)
Davidson	st Evans	b Laker	15	(285–6)
Archer	c Compton	b Bedser	5	(290–7)
Lindwall	c Edrich	b Wardle	1	(291–8)
Hill	not out		8	
Langley	c Edrich	b Wardle	8	(318)
Extras: 8				

Bedser 5–115; Wardle 3–70

AUSTRALIA: 35 for 8

Hassett*	c Bailey	b Bedser	8	(12–2)
Morris	c Hutton	b Laker	0	(8–1)
Miller	st Evans	b Laker	6	(18–3)
Hole	c Evans	b Bedser	2	(18–4)
de Courcy	st Evans	b Wardle	8	(31–5)
Davidson	not out		4	
Harvey		b Wardle	0	(31–6)
Archer	lbw	b Wardle	0	(31–7)
Lindwall		b Wardle	4	(35–8)
Hill	not out		0	
Extras: 3				

Wardle 4–7

ENGLAND: 276

Hutton*	lbw	b Lindwall	66	(126–3)
Edrich	c Hole	b Hill	6	(19–1)
Graveney	c de Courcy	b Miller	5	(32–2)
Compton	c Langley	b Archer	45	(126–4)
Wardle		b Lindwall	5	(149–6)
Watson		b Davidson	16	(149–5)
Simpson	c Langley	b Davidson	31	(209–7)
Bailey	c Hole	b Hill	27	(231–8)
Evans	not out		44	
Laker	lbw	b Hill	5	(243–9)
Bedser		b Morris	10	(276)
Extras: 16				

Hill 3–97

The tourists, staring defeat in the face, were rescued by the weather again after they collapsed to 35 for 8 in their second innings, with no-one reaching double figures!

MATCH DRAWN. The series remained level at 0–0.

4TH TEST: at Leeds; July 23, 24, 25, 27, and 28 1953;
Australia won the toss

ENGLAND: 167

Hutton*		b Lindwall	0	(0–1)
Edrich	lbw	b Miller	10	(33–2)
Graveney	c Benaud	b Miller	55	(98–4)
Compton	c Davidson	b Lindwall	0	(36–3)
Watson		b Lindwall	24	(108–5)
Simpson	c Langley	b Lindwall	15	(167–9)
Bailey	run out		7	(110–6)
Evans	lbw	b Lindwall	25	(133–7)
Laker	c Lindwall	b Archer	10	(149–8)
Lock		b Davidson	9	(167)
Bedser	not out		0	
Extras: 12				

Lindwall 5–54

ENGLAND: 275

Hutton*	c Langley	b Archer	25	(57–1)
Edrich	c de Courcy	b Lindwall	64	(139–3)
Graveney		b Lindwall	3	(62–2)
Compton	lbw	b Lindwall	61	(244–8)
Watson	c Davidson	b Miller	15	(167–4)
Simpson	c de Courcy	b Miller	0	(171–5)
Bailey	c Hole	b Davidson	38	(239–7)
Evans	c Lindwall	b Miller	1	(182–6)
Laker	c Benaud	b Davidson	48	(275)
Lock	c Morris	b Miller	8	(258–9)
Bedser	not out		3	
Extras: 9				

Miller 4–63; Lindwall 3–104

AUSTRALIA: 266

Hassett*	c Lock	b Bedser	37	(70–2)
Morris	c Lock	b Bedser	10	(27–1)
Harvey	lbw	b Bailey	71	(168–4)
Miller	c Edrich	b Bailey	5	(84–3)
Hole	c Lock	b Bedser	53	(203–7)
de Courcy	lbw	b Lock	10	(183–5)
Benaud		b Bailey	7	(203–6)
Davidson	c Evans	b Bedser	2	(208–8)
Archer	not out		31	
Lindwall		b Bedser	9	(218–9)
Langley	c Hutton	b Bedser	17	(266)
Extras: 14				

Bedser 6–95; Bailey 3–71

AUSTRALIA: 147 for 4

Hassett*		b Lock	4	(27–1)
Morris	st Evans	b Laker	38	(54–2)
Hole	c Graveney	b Bailey	33	(117–4)
Harvey	lbw	b Bedser	34	(111–3)
Davidson	not out		17	
de Courcy	not out		13	
Extras: 8				

It was the away team's turn to fall agonisingly short of a win when they were just thirty runs shy at the test conclusion. The series remained deadlocked at nil-nil.

MATCH DRAWN: The series remained level at 0–0.

5TH TEST: at the Oval; August 15, 17, 18, and 19 1953; Australia won the toss

AUSTRALIA: 275

Hassett*	c Evans	b Bedser	53	(107–3)
Morris	lbw	b Bedser	16	(38–1)
Miller	lbw	b Bailey	1	(41–2)
Harvey	c Hutton	b Trueman	36	(107–4)
Hole	c Evans	b Trueman	37	(160–6)
de Courcy	c Evans	b Trueman	5	(118–5)
Archer	c &	b Bedser	10	(160–7)
Davidson	c Edrich	b Laker	22	(207–8)
Lindwall	c Evans	b Trueman	62	(275)
Langley	c Edrich	b Lock	18	(245–9)
Johnston	not out		9	
Extras: 6				

Trueman 4–86; Bedser 3–88

AUSTRALIA: 162

Hassett*	lbw	b Laker	10	(23–1)
Morris	lbw	b Lock	26	(61–5)
Hole	lbw	b Laker	17	(59–2)
Harvey		b Lock	1	(60–3)
Miller	c Trueman	b Laker	0	(61–4)
de Courcy	run out		4	(85–6)
Archer	c Edrich	b Lock	49	(140–8)
Davidson		b Lock	21	(135–7)
Lindwall	c Compton	b Laker	12	(162)
Langley	c Trueman	b Lock	2	(144–9)
Johnston	not out		6	
Extras: 14				

Lock 5–45; Laker 4–75

ENGLAND: 306

Hutton*		b Johnston	82	(154–3)
Edrich	lbw	b Lindwall	21	(37–1)
May	c Archer	b Johnston	39	(137–2)
Compton	c Langley	b Lindwall	16	(167–4)
Graveney	c Miller	b Lindwall	4	(170–5)
Bailey		b Archer	64	(306)
Evans	run out		28	(210–6)
Laker	c Langley	b Miller	1	(225–7)
Lock	c Davidson	b Lindwall	4	(237–8)
Trueman		b Johnston	10	(262–9)
Bedser	not out		22	
Extras: 15				

Lindwall 4–70; Johnston 3–94

ENGLAND: 132 for 2

Hutton*	run out		17	(24–1)
Edrich	not out		55	
May	c Davidson	b Miller	37	(88–2)
Compton	not out		22	
Extras: 1				

Tony Lock's five-wicket effort in the second innings helped set up an historic win as England finally regained the Ashes for the first time in two barren decades.

ENGLAND won by 8 wickets and win the series 1–0.

1ST TEST: at Brisbane; November 26, 27, 29, 30, and December 1 1954; England won the toss

AUSTRALIA: 601 for 8 declared

Favell	c Cowdrey	b Statham	23	(51–1)
Morris	c Cowdrey	b Bailey	153	(325–3)
Miller		b Bailey	49	(123–2)
Harvey	c Bailey	b Bedser	162	(463–5)
Hole	run out		57	(456–4)
Benaud	c May	b Tyson	34	(545–7)
Archer	c Bedser	b Statham	0	(464–6)
Lindwall	not out		64	
Langley		b Bailey	16	(572–8)
Johnson*	not out	24		
Extras: 19				

Bailey 3–140

ENGLAND: 190

Hutton*	c Langley	b Lindwall	4	(4–1)
Simpson		b Miller	2	(10–2)
Edrich	c Langley	b Archer	15	(25–4)
May		b Lindwall	1	(11–3)
Cowdrey	c Hole	b Johnston	40	(107–5)
Bailey		b Johnston	88	(190)
Tyson		b Johnson	7	(132–6)
Bedser		b Johnson	5	(141–7)
Andrew		b Lindwall	6	(156–8)
Statham		b Johnson	11	(181–9)
Compton	not out		2	
Extras: 9				

Lindwall 3–27; Johnson 3–46

ENGLAND: 257

Hutton*	lbw	b Miller	13	(23–2)
Simpson	run out		9	(22–1)
Edrich		b Johnston	88	(163–4)
May	lbw	b Lindwall	44	(147–3)
Cowdrey		b Benaud	10	(181–5)
Bailey	c Langley	b Lindwall	23	(220–6)
Tyson	not out		37	
Bedser	c Archer	b Johnson	5	(231–7)
Andrew		b Johnson	5	(242–8)
Compton	c Langley	b Benaud	0	(243–9)
Statham	c Harvey	b Benaud	14	(257)
Extras: 9				

Benaud 3–43

Colin Cowdrey's debut saw England elect to field first, only for her bowlers to be savaged by the Australian batsmen en route to another comfortable innings victory.

AUSTRALIA won by an innings and 154 runs to lead the series 1–0.

2ND TEST: at Sydney; December 17, 18, 20, 21, and 22 1954; Australia won the toss

ENGLAND: 154

Hutton*	c Davidson	b Johnston	30	(58–3)
Bailey		b Lindwall	0	(14–1)
May	c Johnston	b Archer	5	(19–2)
Graveney	c Favell	b Johnston	21	(63–4)
Cowdrey	c Langley	b Davidson	23	(99–8)
Edrich	c Benaud	b Archer	10	(84–5)
Tyson		b Lindwall	0	(85–6)
Evans	c Langley	b Archer	3	(88–7)
Wardle	c Burke	b Johnston	35	(154)
Appleyard	c Hole	b Davidson	8	(111–9)
Statham	not out		14	
Extras: 5				

Archer 3–12; Johnston 3–56

ENGLAND: 296

Hutton*	c Benaud	b Johnston	28	(55–2)
Bailey	c Langley	b Archer	6	(18–1)
May		b Lindwall	104	(222–5)
Graveney	c Langley	b Johnston	0	(55–3)
Cowdrey	c Archer	b Benaud	54	(171–4)
Edrich		b Archer	29	(232–6)
Tyson		b Lindwall	9	(239–7)
Evans	c Lindwall	b Archer	4	(249–8)
Wardle	lbw	b Lindwall	8	(250–9)
Appleyard	not out		19	
Statham	c Langley	b Johnston	25	(296)
Extras: 10				

Archer 3–53; Lindwall 3–69; Johnston 3–70

AUSTRALIA: 228

Favell	c Graveney	b Bailey	26	(65–2)
Morris*	c Hutton	b Bailey	12	(18–1)
Burke	c Graveney	b Bailey	44	(100–3)
Harvey	c Cowdrey	b Tyson	12	(104–4)
Hole		b Tyson	12	(122–5)
Benaud	lbw	b Statham	20	(141–6)
Archer	c Hutton	b Tyson	49	(213–8)
Davidson		b Statham	20	(193–7)
Lindwall	c Evans	b Tyson	19	(224–9)
Langley		b Bailey	5	(228)
Johnston	not out		0	
Extras: 9				

Tyson 4–45; Bailey 4–59

AUSTRALIA: 184

Favell	c Edrich	b Tyson	16	(34–2)
Morris*	lbw	b Statham	10	(27–1)
Burke		b Tyson	14	(77–3)
Harvey	not out		92	
Hole		b Tyson	0	(77–4)
Benaud	c Tyson	b Appleyard	12	(102–5)
Archer		b Tyson	6	(122–6)
Davidson	c Evans	b Statham	5	(127–7)
Lindwall		b Tyson	8	(136–8)
Langley		b Statham	0	(145–9)
Johnston	c Evans	b Tyson	11	(184)
Extras: 10				

Tyson 6–85; Statham 3–45

Peter May's century (the only ton in the match) and Frank Tyson's ten-wicket haul contributed largely to a narrow win, as England restored parity to the series.

ENGLAND won by 38 runs to level the series at 1–1.

3RD TEST: at Melbourne; December 31 1954, January 1, 3, 4, and 5 1955; England won the toss

ENGLAND: 191

Hutton*	c Hole	b Miller	12	(29–3)
Edrich	c Lindwall	b Miller	4	(14–1)
May	c Benaud	b Lindwall	0	(21–2)
Cowdrey		b Johnson	102	(181–8)
Compton	c Harvey	b Miller	4	(41–4)
Bailey	c Maddocks	b Johnston	30	(115–5)
Evans	lbw	b Archer	20	(169–6)
Wardle		b Archer	0	(181–7)
Tyson		b Archer	6	(191)
Statham		b Archer	3	(190–9)
Appleyard	not out		1	

Extras: 9

Archer 4–33; Miller 3–14

ENGLAND: 279

Hutton*	lbw	b Archer	42	(96–2)
Edrich		b Johnston	13	(40–1)
May		b Johnston	91	(173–4)
Cowdrey		b Benaud	7	(128–3)
Compton	c Maddocks	b Archer	23	(185–5)
Bailey	not out		24	
Evans	c Maddocks	b Miller	22	(211–6)
Wardle		b Johnson	38	(257–7)
Tyson	c Harvey	b Johnston	6	(273–8)
Statham	c Favell	b Johnston	0	(273–9)
Appleyard		b Johnston	6	(279)

Extras: 7

Johnston 5–85

AUSTRALIA: 231

Favell	lbw	b Statham	25	(43–3)
Morris	lbw	b Tyson	3	(15–1)
Miller	c Evans	b Statham	7	(38–2)
Harvey		b Appleyard	31	(92–5)
Hole		b Tyson	11	(65–4)
Benaud	c sub	b Appleyard	15	(115–6)
Archer		b Wardle	23	(134–7)
Maddocks	c Evans	b Statham	47	(205–9)
Lindwall		b Statham	13	(151–8)
Johnson*	not out		33	
Johnston		b Statham	11	(231)

Extras: 12

Statham 5–60

AUSTRALIA: 111

Favell		b Appleyard	30	(57–2)
Morris	c Cowdrey	b Tyson	4	(23–1)
Benaud		b Tyson	22	(86–4)
Harvey	c Evans	b Tyson	11	(77–3)
Miller	c Edrich	b Tyson	6	(87–5)
Hole	c Evans	b Statham	5	(97–6)
Archer		b Statham	15	(110–9)
Maddocks		b Tyson	0	(98–7)
Lindwall	lbw	b Tyson	0	(98–8)
Johnson*	not out		4	
Johnston	c Evans	b Tyson	0	(111)

Extras: 14

Tyson 7–27

The pace duo of Statham and Tyson destroyed Australia's batting as England took the lead in the series. Earlier, Colin Cowdrey had recorded his first test century.

ENGLAND won by 128 runs to lead the series 2–1.

4TH TEST: at Adelaide; January 28, 29, 31, February 1, and 2 1955; Australia won the toss

AUSTRALIA: 323

McDonald	c May	b Appleyard	48	(86–2)
Morris	c Evans	b Tyson	25	(59–1)
Burke	c May	b Tyson	18	(115–3)
Harvey	c Edrich	b Bailey	25	(129–4)
Miller	c Bailey	b Appleyard	44	(182–6)
Benaud	c May	b Appleyard	14	(175–5)
Maddocks	run out		69	(323)
Archer	c May	b Tyson	21	(212–7)
Davidson	c Evans	b Bailey	5	(229–8)
Johnson*	c Statham	b Bailey	41	(321–9)
Johnston	not out		0	
Extras: 12				

Bailey 3–39; Appleyard 3–58; Tyson 3–85

AUSTRALIA: 111

McDonald		b Statham	29	(69–4)
Morris	c &	b Appleyard	16	(24–1)
Burke		b Appleyard	5	(40–2)
Harvey		b Appleyard	7	(54–3)
Miller		b Statham	14	(76–5)
Maddocks	lbw	b Statham	2	(79–7)
Benaud	lbw	b Tyson	1	(77–6)
Archer	c Evans	b Tyson	3	(83–8)
Davidson	lbw	b Wardle	23	(111)
Johnston	c Appleyard	b Tyson	3	(101–9)
Johnson*	not out		3	
Extras: 5				

Appleyard 3–13; Statham 3–38; Tyson 3–47

ENGLAND: 341

Hutton*	c Davidson	b Johnston	80	(162–3)
Edrich		b Johnson	21	(60–1)
May	c Archer	b Benaud	1	(63–2)
Cowdrey	c Maddocks	b Davidson	79	(232–5)
Compton	lbw	b Miller	44	(232–4)
Bailey	c Davidson	b Johnston	38	(336–9)
Evans	c Maddocks	b Benaud	37	(283–6)
Wardle	c &	b Johnson	23	(321–7)
Tyson	c Burke	b Benaud	1	(323–8)
Appleyard	not out		10	
Statham	c Maddocks	b Benaud	0	(341)
Extras: 7				

Benaud 4–120

ENGLAND: 97 for 5

Hutton*	c Davidson	b Miller	5	(10–2)
Edrich		b Miller	0	(3–1)
May	c Miller	b Johnston	26	(49–4)
Cowdrey	c Archer	b Miller	4	(18–3)
Compton	not out		34	
Bailey	lbw	b Johnston	15	(90–5)
Evans	not out		6	
Extras: 7				

Miller 3–40

The home team's fragile batting was exposed again in the second innings as England ensured a series victory in Australia for the first time since 'Bodyline'.

ENGLAND won by 5 wickets to lead the series 3–1.

5TH TEST: at Sydney; February 25, 26, 28, March 1, 2, and 3 1955; Australia won the toss

ENGLAND: 371 for 7 declared

Hutton*	c Burge	b Lindwall	6	(6–1)
Graveney	c &	b Johnson	111	(188–2)
May	c Davidson	b Benaud	79	(196–4)
Cowdrey	c Maddocks	b Johnson	0	(188–3)
Compton	c &	b Johnson	84	(330–5)
Bailey		b Lindwall	72	(371–7)
Evans	c McDonald	b Lindwall	10	(359–6)
Wardle	not out		5	
Extras: 4				

Johnson 3–68; Lindwall 3–77

AUSTRALIA: 221

Watson		b Wardle	18	(52–1)
McDonald	c May	b Appleyard	72	(138–5)
Favell		b Tyson	1	(53–2)
Harvey	c &	b Tyson	13	(85–3)
Miller	run out		19	(129–4)
Burge	c Appleyard	b Wardle	17	(157–7)
Benaud		b Wardle	7	(147–6)
Maddocks	c Appleyard	b Wardle	32	(202–8)
Davidson	c Evans	b Wardle	18	(217–9)
Johnson*	run out		11	(221)
Lindwall	not out		2	
Extras: 11				

Wardle 5–79

AUSTRALIA: 118 for 6

Watson	c Graveney	b Statham	3	(14–1)
McDonald	c Evans	b Graveney	37	(67–4)
Favell	c Graveney	b Wardle	9	(27–2)
Harvey	c &	b Wardle	1	(29–3)
Miller		b Wardle	28	(87–5)
Burge	not out		18	
Benaud		b Hutton	22	(118–6)
Extras: 0				

Wardle 3–51

Tom Graveney's ton and Johnny Wardle's 8 wickets would surely have created another win if the first three days had not been lost due to inclement weather.

MATCH DRAWN. ENGLAND win the series 3–1.

1ST TEST: at Nottingham; June 7, 8, 9, 11, and 12 1956; England won the toss

ENGLAND: 217 for8 declared

Richardson	c Langley	b Miller	81	(180–3)
Cowdrey	c Miller	b Davidson	25	(53–1)
Graveney	c Archer	b Johnson	8	(72–2)
May*	c Langley	b Miller	73	(201–5)
Watson	lbw	b Archer	0	(181–4)
Bailey	c Miller	b Archer	14	(213–7)
Evans	c Langley	b Miller	0	(203–6)
Laker	not out		9	
Lock	lbw	b Miller	0	(214–8)
Appleyard	not out		1	
Extras: 6				

Miller 4–69

ENGLAND: 188 for 3 declared

Richardson	c Langley	b Archer	73	(163–2)
Cowdrey	c Langley	b Miller	81	(151–1)
Watson	c Langley	b Miller	8	(178–3)
Graveney	not out		10	
Evans	not out		8	
Extras: 8				

AUSTRALIA: 148

McDonald	lbw	b Lock	1	(10–1)
Burke	c Lock	b Laker	11	(12–2)
Harvey	lbw	b Lock	64	(148–7)
Burge	c sub	b Lock	7	(33–3)
Miller	lbw	b Laker	0	(36–4)
Archer	c Lock	b Appleyard	33	(90–5)
Benaud		b Appleyard	17	(110–6)
Johnson*	c Bailey	b Laker	12	(148–8)
Lindwall	c Bailey	b Laker	0	(148–9)
Langley	not out		0	
Davidson	Absent hurt			
Extras: 3				

Laker 4–58; Lock 3–61

AUSTRALIA: 120 for 3

McDonald	c Lock	b Laker	6	(13–1)
Burke	not out		58	
Harvey		b Lock	3	(18–2)
Miller	lbw	b Laker	4	(41–3)
Burge	not out		35	
Extras: 14				

The weather again wrecked a probable England triumph after the debutant Peter Richardson had notched two impressive half centuries.

MATCH DRAWN. The series remained level at 0–0.

2ND TEST: at Lord's; June 21, 22, 23, 25, and 26 1956; Australia won the toss

AUSTRALIA: 285

McDonald	c Trueman	b Bailey	78	(137–1)
Burke	st Evans	b Laker	65	(151–3)
Harvey	c Evans	b Bailey	0	(137–2)
Burge		b Statham	21	(185–4)
Miller		b Trueman	28	(196–5)
Mackay	c Bailey	b Laker	38	(265–8)
Archer		b Wardle	28	(249–6)
Benaud		b Statham	5	(255–7)
Johnson*	c Evans	b Trueman	6	(285–9)
Langley	c Bailey	b Laker	14	(285)
Crawford	not out		0	
Extras: 2				
Laker 3–47				

AUSTRALIA: 257

McDonald	c Cowdrey	b Bailey	26	(36–1)
Burke	c Graveney	b Trueman	16	(69–3)
Harvey	c Bailey	b Trueman	10	(47–2)
Burge		b Trueman	14	(70–4)
Mackay	c Evans	b Statham	31	(229–7)
Archer	c Evans	b Bailey	1	(79–5)
Miller	c Evans	b Trueman	30	(112–6)
Benaud	c Evans	b Trueman	97	(243–8)
Johnson*	lbw	b Bailey	17	(257–9)
Langley	not out		7	
Crawford	lbw	b Bailey	0	(257)
Extras: 8				
Trueman 5–90; Bailey 4–64				

ENGLAND: 171

Richardson	c Langley	b Miller	9	(22–1)
Cowdrey	c Benaud	b Mackay	23	(60–3)
Graveney		b Miller	5	(32–2)
May*		b Benaud	63	(128–5)
Watson	c Benaud	b Miller	6	(87–4)
Bailey		b Miller	32	(171)
Evans	st Langley	b Benaud	0	(128–6)
Laker		b Archer	12	(161–7)
Wardle	c Langley	b Archer	0	(161–8)
Trueman	c Langley	b Miller	7	(170–9)
Statham	not out		0	
Extras: 14				
Miller 5–72				

ENGLAND: 186

Richardson	c Langley	b Archer	21	(35–1)
Cowdrey	lbw	b Benaud	27	(91–4)
Graveney	c Langley	b Miller	18	(59–2)
Watson		b Miller	18	(89–3)
May*	c Langley	b Miller	53	(180–7)
Bailey	c Harvey	b Archer	18	(142–5)
Evans	c Langley	b Miller	20	(175–6)
Laker	c Langley	b Archer	4	(184–8)
Wardle		b Miller	0	(184–9)
Trueman		b Archer	2	(186)
Statham	not out		0	
Extras: 5				
Miller 5–80; Archer 4–71				

Nobody reached three figures in this contest as Australia had Keith Miller's outstanding bowling performance to thank for their triumph.

AUSTRALIA won by 185 runs to lead the series 1–0.

3RD TEST: at Leeds; July 12, 13, 14, 16, and 17 1956; England won the toss

ENGLAND: 325

Richardson	c Maddocks	b Archer	5	(17–3)
Cowdrey	c Maddocks	b Archer	0	(2–1)
Oakman		b Archer	4	(8–2)
May*	c Lindwall	b Johnson	101	(204–4)
Washbrook	lbw	b Benaud	98	(226–5)
Lock	c Miller	b Benaud	21	(243–6)
Insole	c Mackay	b Benaud	5	(248–7)
Bailey	not out		33	
Evans		b Lindwall	40	(301–8)
Laker		b Lindwall	5	(321–9)
Trueman	c &	b Lindwall	0	(325)
Extras: 13				

Lindwall 3–67; Archer 3–68; Benaud 3–89

AUSTRALIA: 143

McDonald	c Evans	b Trueman	2	(2–1)
Burke	lbw	b Lock	41	(59–4)
Harvey	c Trueman	b Lock	11	(40–2)
Burge	lbw	b Laker	2	(59–3)
Mackay	c Bailey	b Laker	2	(63–5)
Miller		b Laker	41	(43–9)
Archer		b Laker	4	(69–6)
Benaud	c Oakman	b Laker	30	(142–7)
Maddocks	c Trueman	b Lock	0	(143–8)
Johnson*	c Richardson	b Lock	0	(143)
Lindwall	not out		0	
Extras: 10				

Laker 5–58; Lock 4–41

AUSTRALIA: 140

McDonald		b Trueman	6	(10–1)
Burke		b Laker	16	(45–2)
Harvey	c &	b Lock	69	(138–7)
Miller	c Trueman	b Laker	26	(108–3)
Burge	lbw	b Laker	5	(120–4)
Benaud		b Laker	1	(128–5)
Johnson*	c Oakman	b Laker	3	(136–6)
Mackay		b Laker	2	(140)
Archer	c Washbrook	b Lock	1	(140–8)
Maddocks	lbw	b Lock	0	(140–9)
Lindwall	not out		0	
Extras: 11				

Laker 6–55; Lock 3–40

Not for the last time this summer, the spin duo of Jim Laker and Tony Lock destroyed Australia, after Peter May had registered another century against the tourists.

ENGLAND won by an innings and 42 runs to level the series at 1–1.

4TH TEST: at Manchester; July 26, 27, 28, 30, and 31 1956; England won the toss

ENGLAND: 459

Richardson	c Maddocks	b Benaud	104	(195–2)
Cowdrey	c Maddocks	b Lindwall	80	(174–1)
Sheppard		b Archer	113	(458–9)
May*	c Archer	b Benaud	43	(288–3)
Bailey		b Johnson	20	(321–4)
Washbrook	lbw	b Johnson	6	(327–5)
Oakman	c Archer	b Johnson	10	(339–6)
Evans	st Maddocks	b Johnson	47	(401–7)
Laker	run out		3	(417–8)
Lock	not out		25	
Statham	c Maddocks	b Lindwall	0	(459)
Extras: 8				

Johnson 4–151

AUSTRALIA: 84

McDonald	c Lock	b Laker	32	(48–1)
Burke	c Cowdrey	b Lock	22	(62–3)
Harvey		b Laker	0	(48–2)
Craig	lbw	b Laker	8	(62–4)
Miller	c Oakman	b Laker	6	(73–6)
Mackay	c Oakman	b Laker	0	(62–5)
Archer	st Evans	b Laker	6	(78–8)
Benaud	c Statham	b Laker	0	(73–7)
Lindwall	not out		6	
Maddocks		b Laker	4	(84–9)
Johnson*		b Laker	0	(84)
Extras: 0				

Laker 9–37

AUSTRALIA: 205

McDonald	c Oakman	b Laker	89	(181–7)
Burke	c Lock	b Laker	33	(55–2)
Harvey	c Cowdrey	b Laker	0	(28–1)
Craig	lbw	b Laker	38	(114–3)
Mackay	c Oakman	b Laker	0	(124–4)
Miller		b Laker	0	(130–5)
Archer	c Oakman	b Laker	0	(130–6)
Benaud		b Laker	18	(198–8)
Lindwall	c Lock	b Laker	8	(203–9)
Johnson*	not out		1	
Maddocks	lbw	b Laker	2	(205)
Extras: 16				

Laker 10–53

The Reverend David Sheppard scored a ton, but the divine inspiration came from Jim Laker who bowled his way into history with the unsurpassable 19 for 90!

ENGLAND won by an innings and 170 runs to lead the series 2–1.

5TH TEST: at the Oval; August 23, 24, 25, 27, and 28 1956; England won the toss

ENGLAND: 247

Richardson	c Langley	b Miller	37	(66–3)
Cowdrey	c Langley	b Lindwall	0	(1–1)
Sheppard	c Archer	b Miller	24	(53–2)
May*	not out		83	
Compton	c Davidson	b Archer	94	(222–4)
Lock	c Langley	b Archer	0	(222–5)
Washbrook	lbw	b Archer	0	(222–6)
Evans	lbw	b Miller	0	(223–7)
Laker	c Archer	b Miller	4	(231–8)
Tyson	c Davidson	b Archer	3	(243–9)
Statham		b Archer	0	(247)
Extras: 2				

Archer 5–53; Miller 4–91

ENGLAND: 182 for 3 declared

Richardson	c Langley	b Lindwall	34	(100–2)
Cowdrey	c Benaud	b Davidson	8	(17–1)
Sheppard	c Archer	b Miller	62	(108–3)
May*	not out		37	
Compton	not out		35	
Extras: 6				

AUSTRALIA: 202

McDonald	c Lock	b Tyson	3	(3–1)
Burke		b Laker	8	(17–2)
Harvey	c May	b Lock	39	(90–6)
Craig	c Statham	b Lock	2	(20–3)
Johnson*		b Laker	12	(35–4)
Davidson	c May	b Laker	8	(47–5)
Miller	c Washbrook	b Statham	61	(202–9)
Archer	c Tyson	b Laker	9	(111–7)
Benaud		b Statham	32	(154–8)
Lindwall	not out		22	
Langley	lbw	b Statham	0	(202)
Extras: 6				

Laker 4–80; Statham 3–33

AUSTRALIA: 27 for 5

McDonald	lbw	b Statham	0	(0–1)
Burke	lbw	b Laker	1	(5–3)
Harvey	c May	b Lock	1	(1–2)
Craig	c Lock	b Laker	7	(10–4)
Miller	not out		7	
Johnson*	c Lock	b Laker	10	(27–5)
Benaud	not out		0	
Extras: 1				

Laker 3–8

The weather helped Australia again, with no play on Day Four. In the tourists' run chase, Laker bowled 18 overs for 8 runs and Lock conceded 17 runs from 18 overs.

MATCH DRAWN. ENGLAND win the series 2–1.

1ST TEST: at Brisbane; December 5, 6, 8, 9, and 10 1958; England won the toss

ENGLAND: 134

Richardson	c Mackay	b Davidson	11	(16–2)
Milton		b Meckiff	5	(16–1)
Graveney	c Grout	b Davidson	19	(62–3)
May*	c Grout	b Meckiff	26	(75–4)
Cowdrey	c Kline	b Meckiff	13	(79–5)
Bailey	st Grout	b Benaud	27	(134)
Evans	c Burge	b Davidson	4	(83–6)
Lock	c Davidson	b Benaud	5	(92–7)
Laker	c Burke	b Benaud	13	(112–8)
Statham	c Grout	b Mackay	2	(116–9)
Loader	not out		6	
Extras: 3				

Meckiff 3–33; Davidson 3–36; Benaud 3–46

ENGLAND: 198

Richardson	c &	b Benaud	8	(28–1)
Milton	c Grout	b Davidson	17	(34–2)
Bailey		b Mackay	68	(198–9)
Graveney	run out		36	(96–3)
May*	lbw	b Benaud	4	(102–4)
Cowdrey	c Kline	b Meckiff	28	(153–5)
Evans	lbw	b Davidson	4	(161–6)
Lock		b Meckiff	1	(169–7)
Laker		b Benaud	15	(190–8)
Statham	c McDonald	b Benaud	3	(198)
Loader	not out		0	
Extras: 14				

Benaud 4–66

AUSTRALIA: 186

McDonald	c Graveney	b Bailey	42	(65–2)
Burke	c Evans	b Loader	20	(55–1)
Harvey	lbw	b Loader	14	(88–3)
O'Neill	c Graveney	b Bailey	34	(136–6)
Burge	c Cowdrey	b Bailey	2	(94–4)
Mackay	c Evans	b Laker	16	(122–5)
Benaud*	lbw	b Loader	16	(162–7)
Davidson	lbw	b Laker	25	(186)
Grout		b Statham	2	(165–8)
Meckiff		b Loader	5	(178–9)
Kline	not out		4	
Extras: 6				

Loader 4–56; Bailey 3–35

AUSTRALIA: 147 for 2

McDonald	c Statham	b Laker	15	(20–1)
Burke	not out		28	
Harvey	c Milton	b Lock	23	(58–2)
O'Neill	not out		71	
Extras: 10				

Trevor 'the barnacle' Bailey batted 7 and a half hours for his 68 but Australia cruised to victory, helped by seven wickets from their new skipper, Richie Benaud.

AUSTRALIA won by 8 wickets to lead the series 1–0.

2ND TEST: at Melbourne; December 31 1958, January 1, 2, 3, and 5 1959; England won the toss

ENGLAND: 259

Richardson	c Grout	b Davidson	3	(7–1)
Bailey	c Benaud	b Meckiff	48	(92–4)
Watson		b Davidson	0	(7–2)
Graveney	lbw	b Davidson	0	(7–3)
May*		b Meckiff	113	(210–5)
Cowdrey	c Grout	b Davidson	44	(218–7)
Evans	c Davidson	b Meckiff	4	(218–6)
Lock	st Grout	b Benaud	5	(233–8)
Laker	not out		22	
Statham		b Davidson	13	(253–9)
Loader		b Davidson	1	(259)
Extras: 6				

Davidson 6–64; Meckiff 3–69

ENGLAND: 87

Richardson	c Harvey	b Meckiff	2	(3–1)
Bailey	c Burke	b Meckiff	14	(27–4)
Watson		b Davidson	7	(14–2)
Graveney	c Davidson	b Meckiff	3	(21–3)
May*	c Davidson	b Meckiff	17	(71–7)
Cowdrey	c Grout	b Meckiff	12	(44–5)
Evans	run out		11	(57–6)
Lock	c &	b Davidson	6	(75–8)
Laker	c Harvey	b Davidson	3	(80–9)
Statham	not out		8	
Loader		b Meckiff	0	(87)
Extras: 4				

Meckiff 6–38; Davidson 3–41

AUSTRALIA: 308

McDonald	c Graveney	b Statham	47	(137–2)
Burke		b Statham	3	(11–1)
Harvey		b Loader	167	(257–4)
O'Neill	c Evans	b Statham	37	(255–3)
Mackay	c Evans	b Statham	18	(295–7)
Simpson	lbw	b Loader	0	(261–5)
Benaud*	lbw	b Statham	0	(262–6)
Davidson		b Statham	24	(300–8)
Grout	c May	b Loader	8	(308)
Meckiff		b Statham	0	(300–9)
Kline	not out		1	
Extras: 3				

Statham 7–57; Loader 3–97

AUSTRALIA: 42 for 2

McDonald	lbw	b Statham	5	(6–1)
Burke	not out		18	
Grout	st Evans	b Laker	12	(26–2)
Harvey	not out		7	
Extras: 0				

Davidson and Meckiff shared 18 wickets as England were skittled out for only 87 in the second innings. Earlier, Neil Harvey launched the home victory with a big ton.

AUSTRALIA won by 8 wickets to lead the series 2–0.

3RD TEST: at Sydney; January 9, 10, 12, 13, 14, and 15 1959; England won the toss

ENGLAND: 219

Bailey	lbw	b Meckiff	8	(19–1)
Milton	c Meckiff	b Davidson	8	(23–2)
Graveney	c Harvey	b Benaud	33	(97–4)
May*	c Mackay	b Slater	42	(91–3)
Cowdrey	c Harvey	b Benaud	34	(155–6)
Dexter	lbw	b Slater	1	(98–5)
Swetman	c Mackay	b Benaud	41	(200–8)
Lock	lbw	b Mackay	21	(194–7)
Trueman	c Burke	b Benaud	18	(219)
Laker	c Harvey	b Benaud	2	(202–9)
Statham	not out		0	
Extras: 11				

Benaud 5–83

ENGLAND: 287 for 7 declared

Bailey	c sub	b Benaud	25	(37–2)
Milton	c Davidson	b Benaud	8	(30–1)
Graveney	lbw	b Davidson	22	(64–3)
May*		b Burke	92	(246–4)
Cowdrey	not out		100	
Dexter	c Grout	b Benaud	11	(262–5)
Swetman	lbw	b Burke	5	(269–6)
Trueman	st Grout	b Benaud	0	(270–7)
Lock	not out		11	
Extras: 13				

Benaud 4–94

AUSTRALIA: 357

McDonald	c Graveney	b Lock	40	(87–3)
Burke	c Lock	b Laker	12	(26–1)
Harvey		b Laker	7	(52–2)
O'Neill	c Swetman	b Laker	77	(199–5)
Favell	c Cowdrey	b Lock	54	(197–4)
Mackay		b Trueman	57	(323–7)
Benaud*		b Laker	6	(208–6)
Davidson	lbw	b Lock	71	(353–8)
Grout	c Statham	b Laker	14	(355–9)
Slater	not out		1	
Meckiff		b Lock	2	(357)
Extras: 16				

Laker 5–107; Lock 4–130

AUSTRALIA: 54 for 2

McDonald		b Laker	16	(33–2)
Burke		b Laker	7	(22–1)
Harvey	not out		18	
O'Neill	not out		7	
Extras: 6				

Colin Cowdrey's unbeaten century prompted a tempting declaration from England, but Australia had no desire to risk their pursuit of 150 in the limited time left.

MATCH DRAWN. Australia still lead the series 2–0.

4TH TEST: at Adelaide; January 30, 31, February 2, 3, 4, and 5 1959; England won the toss

AUSTRALIA: 476

McDonald		b Trueman	170	(473–9)
Burke	c Cowdrey	b Bailey	66	(171–1)
Harvey	run out		41	(276–2)
O'Neill		b Statham	56	(369–5)
Favell		b Statham	4	(286–3)
Mackay	c Evans	b Statham	4	(294–4)
Benaud*		b Trueman	46	(388–6)
Davidson	c Bailey	b Tyson	43	(455–8)
Grout	lbw	b Trueman	9	(407–7)
Lindwall		b Trueman	19	(476)
Rorke	not out		2	
Extras: 16				

Trueman 4–90; Statham 3–83

AUSTRALIA: 36 for 0

Favell	not out	15
Burke	not out	16
Extras: 5		

ENGLAND: 240

Richardson	lbw	b Lindwall	4	(7–1)
Bailey		b Davidson	4	(11–2)
May*		b Benaud	37	(74–3)
Cowdrey		b Rorke	84	(170–4)
Graveney	c Benaud	b Rorke	41	(173–5)
Watson		b Rorke	25	(240)
Trueman	c Grout	b Benaud	0	(180–6)
Lock	c Grout	b Benaud	2	(184–7)
Tyson	c &	b Benaud	0	(184–8)
Evans	c Burke	b Benaud	4	(188–9)
Statham	not out		36	
Extras: 3				

Benaud 5–91; Rorke 3–23

ENGLAND: 270

Richardson	lbw	b Benaud	43	(110–2)
Watson	c Favell	b Benaud	40	(89–1)
May*	lbw	b Rorke	59	(177–4)
Cowdrey		b Lindwall	8	(125–3)
Graveney	not out		53	
Bailey	c Grout	b Lindwall	6	(198–5)
Trueman	c Grout	b Davidson	0	(199–6)
Lock		b Rorke	9	(222–7)
Tyson	c Grout	b Benaud	33	(268–8)
Statham	c O'Neill	b Benaud	2	(270–9)
Evans	c Benaud	b Davidson	0	(270)
Extras: 17				

Benaud 4–82

Colin McDonald made light work of the tourists' bowling attack and Benaud helped himself to 9 wickets. England were again emphatically beaten and lost the Ashes.

AUSTRALIA won by 10 wickets to lead the series 3–0.

5TH TEST: at Melbourne; February 13, 14, 16, 17, and 18 1959; Australia won the toss

ENGLAND: 205

Richardson	c &	b Benaud	68	(128–7)
Bailey	c Davidson	b Lindwall	0	(0–1)
May*	c Benaud	b Meckiff	11	(13–2)
Cowdrey	c Lindwall	b Davidson	22	(61–3)
Graveney	c McDonald	b Benaud	19	(109–4)
Dexter	c Lindwall	b Meckiff	0	(112–5)
Swetman	c Grout	b Davidson	1	(124–6)
Mortimore	not out		44	
Trueman	c &	b Benaud	21	(191–8)
Tyson	c Grout	b Benaud	9	(203–9)
Laker	c Harvey	b Davidson	2	(205)
Extras: 8				

Benaud 4–43; Davidson 3–38

ENGLAND: 214

Richardson	lbw	b Benaud	23	(105–4)
Bailey		b Lindwall	0	(0–1)
May*	c Harvey	b Lindwall	4	(12–2)
Cowdrey	run out		46	(78–3)
Graveney	c Harvey	b Davidson	54	(158–7)
Dexter	c Grout	b Davidson	6	(131–5)
Swetman	lbw	b Lindwall	9	(142–6)
Mortimore		b Rorke	11	(172–8)
Trueman		b Rorke	36	(214)
Tyson	c Grout	b Rorke	6	(182–9)
Laker	not out		5	
Extras: 14				

Lindwall 3–37; Rorke 3–41

AUSTRALIA: 351

McDonald	c Cowdrey	b Laker	133	(209–6)
Burke	c Trueman	b Tyson	16	(41–1)
Harvey	c Swetman	b Trueman	13	(83–2)
O'Neill	c Cowdrey	b Trueman	0	(83–3)
Mackay	c Graveney	b Laker	23	(154–4)
Davidson		b Mortimore	17	(207–5)
Benaud*	c Swetman	b Laker	64	(351)
Grout	c Trueman	b Laker	74	(324–7)
Lindwall	c Cowdrey	b Trueman	0	(327–8)
Meckiff	c &	b Trueman	2	(329–9)
Rorke	not out		0	
Extras: 9				

Trueman 4–92; Laker 4–93

AUSTRALIA: 69 for 1

McDonald	not out		51	
Burke	lbw	b Tyson	13	(66–1)
Harvey	not out		1	
Extras: 4				

It took the home team less than 13 overs to polish off the required runs as McDonald followed his career best at Adelaide with two more impressive efforts.

AUSTRALIA won by 9 wickets and win the series 4–0.

1ST TEST: at Birmingham; June 8, 9, 10, 12, and 13 1961; England won the toss

ENGLAND: 195

Pullar		b Davidson	17	(36–1)
Subba Row	c Simpson	b Mackay	59	(122–6)
Dexter	c Davidson	b Mackay	10	(53–2)
Cowdrey*		b Misson	13	(88–3)
Barrington	c Misson	b Mackay	21	(121–4)
Smith	c Lawry	b Mackay	0	(121–5)
Illingworth	c Grout	b Benaud	15	(156–8)
Murray	c Davidson	b Benaud	16	(153–7)
Allen	run out		11	(181–9)
Trueman	c Burge	b Benaud	20	(195)
Statham	not out		7	
Extras: 6				

Mackay 4–57; Benaud 3–15

ENGLAND: 401 for 4

Pullar	c Grout	b Misson	28	(93–1)
Subba Row		b Misson	112	(202–2)
Dexter	st Grout	b Simpson	180	(400–4)
Cowdrey*		b Mackay	14	(239–3)
Barrington	not out		48	
Smith	not out		1	
Extras: 18				

AUSTRALIA: 516 for 9 declared

Lawry	c Murray	b Illingworth	57	(106–2)
McDonald	c Illingworth	b Statham	22	(47–1)
Harvey	lbw	b Allen	114	(299–4)
O'Neill		b Statham	82	(252–3)
Burge	lbw	b Allen	25	(322–5)
Simpson	c &	b Trueman	76	(469–7)
Davidson	c &	b Illingworth	22	(381–6)
Mackay	c Barrington	b Statham	64	(501–8)
Benaud*	not out		36	
Grout	c Dexter	b Trueman	5	(516–9)
Extras: 13				

Statham 3–147

Debutant Bill Lawry was one of five Aussie batsmen to score at least 50, but the home team salvaged a draw courtesy of Ted Dexter's 180 which included 31 fours.

MATCH DRAWN. The series remained level at 0–0.

2ND TEST: at Lord's; June 22, 23, 24, and 26 1961; England won the toss

ENGLAND: 206

Pullar		b Davidson	11	(26–1)
Subba Row	lbw	b Mackay	48	(87–2)
Dexter	c McKenzie	b Misson	27	(87–3)
Cowdrey*	c Grout	b McKenzie	16	(127–6)
May	c Grout	b Davidson	17	(111–4)
Barrington	c Mackay	b Davidson	4	(115–5)
Illingworth		b Misson	13	(164–8)
Murray	lbw	b Mackay	18	(156–7)
Lock	c Grout	b Davidson	5	(167–9)
Trueman		b Davidson	25	(206)
Statham	not out		11	
Extras: 11				

Davidson 5–42

ENGLAND: 202

Pullar	c Grout	b Misson	42	(67–3)
Subba Row	c Grout	b Davidson	8	(33–1)
Dexter		b McKenzie	17	(63–2)
Cowdrey*	c Mackay	b Misson	7	(80–4)
May	c Grout	b McKenzie	22	(127–5)
Barrington	lbw	b Davidson	66	(191–7)
Illingworth	c Harvey	b Simpson	0	(144–6)
Murray	c Grout	b McKenzie	25	(199–8)
Lock		b McKenzie	1	(202)
Trueman	c Grout	b McKenzie	0	(199–9)
Statham	not out		2	
Extras: 12				

McKenzie 5–37

AUSTRALIA: 340

Lawry	c Murray	b Dexter	130	(238–7)
McDonald		b Statham	4	(5–1)
Simpson	c Illingworth	b Trueman	0	(6–2)
Harvey*	c Barrington	b Trueman	27	(81–3)
O'Neill		b Dexter	1	(88–4)
Burge	c Murray	b Statham	46	(183–5)
Davidson	lbw	b Trueman	6	(194–6)
Mackay	c Barrington	b Illingworth	54	(340)
Grout	lbw	b Dexter	0	(238–8)
McKenzie		b Trueman	34	(291–9)
Misson	not out		25	
Extras: 13				

Trueman 4–118; Dexter 3–56

AUSTRALIA: 71 for 5

Lawry	c Murray	b Statham	1	(15–2)
McDonald	c Illingworth	b Trueman	14	(15–1)
Harvey*	c Murray	b Trueman	4	(19–3)
O'Neill		b Statham	0	(19–4)
Burge	not out		37	
Simpson	c Illingworth	b Statham	15	(58–5)
Davidson	not out		0	
Extras: 0				

Statham 3–31

Lawry's century put the tourists in the ascendancy, but not for the last time, Australia made heavy work of pursuing a small victory target.

AUSTRALIA won by 5 wickets to lead the series 1–0.

3RD TEST: at Leeds; July 6, 7, and 8 1961;
Australia won the toss

AUSTRALIA: 237

McDonald	st Murray	b Lock	54	(113–2)
Lawry	lbw	b Lock	28	(65–1)
Harvey	c Lock	b Trueman	73	(192–4)
O'Neill	c Cowdrey	b Trueman	27	(187–3)
Burge	c Cowdrey	b Jackson	5	(196–5)
Mackay	lbw	b Jackson	6	(203–7)
Simpson	lbw	b Trueman	2	(203–6)
Davidson	not out		22	
Benaud*		b Trueman	0	(204–8)
Grout	c Murray	b Trueman	3	(208–9)
McKenzie		b Allen	8	(237)
Extras: 9				
Trueman 5–58				

AUSTRALIA: 120

McDonald		b Jackson	1	(4–1)
Lawry	c Murray	b Allen	28	(49–2)
Harvey	c Dexter	b Trueman	53	(99–3)
O'Neill	c Cowdrey	b Trueman	19	(102–5)
Burge	lbw	b Allen	0	(102–4)
Simpson		b Trueman	3	(105–6)
Davidson	c Cowdrey	b Trueman	7	(120)
Benaud*		b Trueman	0	(109–7)
Mackay	c Murray	b Trueman	0	(109–8)
Grout	c &	b Jackson	7	(120–9)
McKenzie	not out		0	
Extras: 2				
Trueman 6–30				

ENGLAND: 299

Pullar		b Benaud	53	(145–2)
Subba Row	lbw	b Davidson	35	(59–1)
Cowdrey	c Grout	b McKenzie	93	(223–4)
May*	c &	b Davidson	26	(190–3)
Dexter		b Davidson	28	(248–6)
Barrington	c Simpson	b Davidson	6	(239–5)
Murray		b McKenzie	6	(291–9)
Trueman	c Burge	b Davidson	4	(252–7)
Lock	lbw	b McKenzie	30	(286–8)
Allen	not out		5	
Jackson	run out		8	(299)
Extras: 5				
Davidson 5–63; McKenzie 3–64				

ENGLAND: 62 for 2

Pullar	not out		26	
Subba Row		b Davidson	6	(14–1)
Cowdrey	c Grout	b Benaud	22	(45–2)
May*	not out		8	
Extras: 0				

Neil Harvey recorded half centuries in each innings but his team were destroyed by fiery Fred Trueman who enjoyed match figures of 11 for 88 on his own home turf.

ENGLAND won by 8 wickets to level the series at 1–1.

4TH TEST: at Manchester; July 27, 28, 29, 31, and 1 August 1961; Australia won the toss

AUSTRALIA: 190

Lawry	lbw	b Statham	74	(150–5)
Simpson	c Murray	b Statham	4	(8–1)
Harvey	c Subba Row	b Statham	19	(51–2)
O'Neill	hit wicket	b Trueman	11	(89–3)
Burge		b Flavell	15	(106–4)
Booth	c Close	b Statham	46	(185–7)
Mackay	c Murray	b Statham	11	(174–6)
Davidson	c Barrington	b Dexter	0	(185–8)
Benaud*		b Dexter	2	(190)
Grout	c Murray	b Dexter	2	(189–9)
McKenzie	not out		1	
Extras: 5				

Statham 5–53; Dexter 3–16

AUSTRALIA: 432

Lawry	c Trueman	b Allen	102	(210–3)
Simpson	c Murray	b Flavell	51	(113–1)
Harvey	c Murray	b Dexter	35	(175–2)
O'Neill	c Murray	b Statham	67	(290–5)
Burge	c Murray	b Dexter	23	(274–4)
Booth	lbw	b Dexter	9	(296–6)
Mackay	c Close	b Allen	18	(332–7)
Davidson	not out		77	
Benaud*	lbw	b Allen	1	(334–8)
Grout	c Statham	b Allen	0	(334–9)
McKenzie		b Flavell	32	(432)
Extras: 17				

Allen 4–58; Dexter 3–61

ENGLAND: 367

Pullar		b Davidson	63	(154–3)
Subba Row	c Simpson	b Davidson	2	(3–1)
Dexter	c Davidson	b McKenzie	16	(43–2)
May*	c Simpson	b Davidson	95	(212–4)
Close	lbw	b McKenzie	33	(212–5)
Barrington	c O'Neill	b Simpson	78	(358–7)
Murray	c Grout	b Mackay	24	(272–6)
Allen	c Booth	b Simpson	42	(362–8)
Trueman	c Harvey	b Simpson	3	(367–9)
Statham	c Mackay	b Simpson	4	(367)
Flavell	not out		0	
Extras: 7				

Simpson 4–23; Davidson 3–70

ENGLAND: 201

Pullar	c O'Neill	b Davidson	26	(40–1)
Subba Row		b Benaud	49	(163–5)
Dexter	c Grout	b Benaud	76	(150–2)
May*		b Benaud	0	(150–3)
Close	c O'Neill	b Benaud	8	(158–4)
Barrington	lbw	b Mackay	5	(171–7)
Murray	c Simpson	b Benaud	4	(171–6)
Allen	c Simpson	b Benaud	10	(189–8)
Trueman	c Benaud	b Simpson	8	(193–9)
Statham		b Davidson	8	(201)
Flavell	not out		0	
Extras: 7				

Benaud 6–70

England seemed poised for victory at 150 for 1 in the second innings but Benaud's six wicket haul prompted the hosts to lose their last 9 wickets for 51 runs.

AUSTRALIA won by 54 runs to lead the series 2–1.

5TH TEST: at the Oval; August 17, 18, 19, 21, and 22 1961; England won the toss

ENGLAND: 256

Pullar		b Davidson	8	(18–1)
Subba Row	lbw	b Gaunt	12	(20–2)
Cowdrey	c Grout	b Davidson	0	(20–3)
May*	c Lawry	b Benaud	71	(147–5)
Dexter	c Grout	b Gaunt	24	(67–4)
Barrington	c Grout	b Gaunt	53	(193–6)
Murray	c O'Neill	b Mackay	27	(202–8)
Lock	c Grout	b Mackay	3	(199–7)
Allen	not out		22	
Statham		b Davidson	18	(238–9)
Flavell	c Simpson	b Davidson	14	(256)
Extras: 4				

Davidson 4–83; Gaunt 3–53

ENGLAND: 370 for 8

Pullar	c Grout	b Mackay	13	(33–1)
Subba Row	c &	b Benaud	137	(283–6)
Dexter	c Gaunt	b Mackay	0	(33–2)
May*	c O'Neill	b Mackay	33	(83–3)
Cowdrey	c Benaud	b Mackay	3	(90–4)
Barrington	c O'Neill	b Benaud	83	(262–5)
Murray	c Grout	b Benaud	40	(355–8)
Lock	c Benaud	b Mackay	0	(283–7)
Allen	not out		42	
Statham	not out		9	
Extras: 10				

Mackay 5–121; Benaud 3–113

AUSTRALIA: 494

Lawry	c Murray	b Statham	0	(0–1)
Simpson		b Allen	40	(88–3)
Harvey	lbw	b Flavell	13	(15–2)
O'Neill	c sub	b Allen	117	(211–4)
Burge		b Allen	181	(472–9)
Booth	c Subba Row	b Lock	71	(396–5)
Mackay	c Murray	b Flavell	5	(401–6)
Davidson	lbw	b Statham	17	(441–7)
Benaud*		b Allen	6	(455–8)
Grout	not out		30	
Gaunt		b Statham	3	(494)
Extras: 11				

Allen 4–133; Statham 3–75

England's chances of at least levelling the series were scuppered by Peter Burge whose seven-hour innings was his test career best.

MATCH DRAWN. AUSTRALIA win the series 2–1.

AUSTRALIA: 404

Lawry	c Smith	b Trueman	5	(5–1)
Simpson	c Trueman	b Dexter	50	(92–3)
O'Neill	c Statham	b Trueman	15	(46–2)
Harvey		b Statham	39	(140–5)
Burge	c Dexter	b Trueman	6	(101–4)
Booth	c Dexter	b Titmus	112	(297–7)
Davidson	c Trueman	b Barrington	23	(194–6)
Mackay	not out		86	
Benaud*	c Smith	b Knight	51	(388–8)
McKenzie	c &	b Knight	4	(392–9)
Jarman	c Barrington	b Knight	2	(404)
Extras: 7				

Knight 3–65; Trueman 3–76

AUSTRALIA: 362 for 4 declared

Lawry	c Sheppard	b Titmus	98	(216–2)
Simpson	c Smith	b Dexter	71	(136–1)
O'Neill	lbw	b Statham	56	(241–3)
Harvey	c Statham	b Dexter	57	(325–4)
Burge	not out		47	
Booth	not out		19	
Extras: 14				

ENGLAND: 389

Pullar	c &	b Benaud	33	(62–1)
Sheppard	c McKenzie	b Benaud	31	(65–2)
Dexter*		b Benaud	70	(169–4)
Cowdrey	c Lawry	b Simpson	21	(145–3)
Barrington	c Burge	b Benaud	78	(297–6)
Smith	c Jarman	b McKenzie	21	(220–5)
Parfitt	c Davidson	b Benaud	80	(362–9)
Titmus	c Simpson	b Benaud	21	(361–7)
Knight	c Davidson	b McKenzie	0	(362–8)
Trueman	c Jarman	b McKenzie	19	(389)
Statham	not out		8	
Extras: 7				

Benaud 6–115; McKenzie 3–78

ENGLAND: 278 for 6

Pullar	c &	b Davidson	56	(114–1)
Sheppard	c Benaud	b Davidson	53	(135–2)
Dexter*		b McKenzie	99	(257–4)
Cowdrey	c &	b Benaud	9	(191–3)
Barrington	c McKenzie	b Davidson	23	(257–5)
Parfitt	c Jarman	b McKenzie	4	(261–6)
Titmus	not out		3	
Knight	not out		4	
Extras: 27				

Davidson 3–43

Brian Booth was the only person to reach three figures in this high-scoring contest while Bobby Simpson and Ted Dexter each registered a pair of half-centuries.

MATCH DRAWN. The series remained level at 0–0.

2ND TEST: at Melbourne; December 29, 31 1962, January 1, 2, and 3 1963; Australia won the toss

AUSTRALIA: 316

Lawry		b Trueman	52	(112–4)
Simpson	c Smith	b Coldwell	38	(62–1)
O'Neill	c Graveney	b Statham	19	(111–2)
Harvey		b Coldwell	0	(112–3)
Burge	lbw	b Titmus	23	(155–5)
Booth	c Barrington	b Titmus	27	(164–6)
Davidson	c Smith	b Trueman	40	(237–7)
Mackay	lbw	b Titmus	49	(294–9)
Benaud*	c Barrington	b Titmus	36	(289–8)
McKenzie		b Trueman	16	(316)
Jarman	not out		10	
Extras: 6				

Titmus 4–43; Trueman 3–83

AUSTRALIA: 248

Simpson		b Trueman	14	(30–1)
Lawry		b Dexter	57	(161–5)
O'Neill	c Cowdrey	b Trueman	0	(30–2)
Harvey	run out		10	(46–3)
Burge		b Statham	14	(69–4)
Booth	c Trueman	b Statham	103	(248)
Davidson	c Smith	b Titmus	17	(193–6)
Mackay	lbw	b Trueman	9	(212–7)
Benaud*	c Cowdrey	b Trueman	4	(228–8)
McKenzie		b Trueman	0	(228–9)
Jarman	not out		11	
Extras: 9				

Trueman 5–62

ENGLAND: 331

Sheppard	lbw	b Davidson	0	(0–1)
Pullar		b Davidson	11	(19–2)
Dexter*	c Simpson	b Benaud	93	(194–3)
Cowdrey	c Burge	b McKenzie	113	(254–4)
Barrington	lbw	b McKenzie	35	(255–5)
Graveney	run out		41	(315–7)
Titmus	c Jarman	b Davidson	15	(292–6)
Smith	not out		6	
Trueman	c O'Neill	b Davidson	6	(324–8)
Statham		b Davidson	1	(327–9)
Coldwell	c Benaud	b Davidson	1	(331)
Extras: 9				

Davidson 6–75

ENGLAND: 237 for 3

Sheppard	run out		113	(233–3)
Pullar	c Jarman	b McKenzie	5	(5–1)
Dexter*	run out		52	(129–2)
Cowdrey	not out		58	
Barrington	not out		0	
Extras: 9				

The Reverend David Sheppard shared in two century stands which helped England over the finishing line in an otherwise evenly-contested test match.

ENGLAND won by 7 wickets to lead the series 1–0.

3RD TEST: at Sydney; January 11, 12, 14, and 15 1963; England won the toss

ENGLAND: 279

Pullar	c Benaud	b Simpson	53	(132–3)
Sheppard	c McKenzie	b Davidson	3	(4–1)
Dexter*	c Lawry	b Benaud	32	(65–2)
Cowdrey	c Jarman	b Simpson	85	(201–4)
Barrington	lbw	b Davidson	35	(221–6)
Parfitt	c Lawry	b Simpson	0	(203–5)
Titmus		b Davidson	32	(279)
Murray	lbw	b Davidson	0	(221–7)
Trueman		b Simpson	32	(272–8)
Statham	c Benaud	b Simpson	0	(272–9)
Coldwell	not out		2	
Extras: 5				

Simpson 5–57; Davidson 4–54

ENGLAND: 104

Pullar		b Davidson	0	(0–1)
Sheppard	c Simpson	b Davidson	12	(25–3)
Dexter*	c Simpson	b Davidson	11	(20–2)
Cowdrey	c Simpson	b Benaud	8	(37–4)
Barrington		b McKenzie	21	(53–5)
Parfitt	c O'Neill	b McKenzie	28	(90–7)
Titmus	c Booth	b O'Neill	6	(71–6)
Murray	not out		3	
Trueman	c Jarman	b McKenzie	9	(100–8)
Statham		b Davidson	2	(104–9)
Coldwell	c Shepherd	b Davidson	0	(104)
Extras: 4				

Davidson 5–25; McKenzie 3–26

AUSTRALIA: 319

Lawry	c Murray	b Coldwell	8	(14–1)
Simpson		b Titmus	91	(177–3)
Harvey	c Barrington	b Titmus	64	(174–2)
Booth	c Trueman	b Titmus	16	(212–5)
O'Neill		b Titmus	3	(187–4)
Shepherd	not out		71	
Jarman	run out		0	(216–6)
Davidson	c Trueman	b Titmus	15	(242–7)
Benaud*	c &	b Titmus	15	(274–8)
McKenzie	lbw	b Titmus	4	(280–9)
Guest		b Statham	11	(319)
Extras: 21				

Titmus 7–79

AUSTRALIA: 67 for 2

Lawry		b Trueman	8	(28–1)
Simpson	not out		34	
Harvey	lbw	b Trueman	15	(54–2)
Booth	not out		5	
Extras: 5				

Left-arm paceman Alan Davidson plundered nine wickets as Australia levelled the series. Nobody managed to pass one hundred in this encounter.

AUSTRALIA won by 8 wickets to level the series at 1–1.

4TH TEST: at Adelaide; January 25, 26, 28, 29, and 30 1963; Australia won the toss

AUSTRALIA: 393

Lawry		b Illingworth	10	(16–2)
Simpson	c Smith	b Statham	0	(2–1)
Harvey	c Statham	b Dexter	154	(302–5)
Booth	c Cowdrey	b Titmus	34	(101–3)
O'Neill	c Cowdrey	b Dexter	100	(295–4)
Davidson		b Statham	46	(383–9)
Shepherd	c Trueman	b Statham	10	(331–6)
Mackay	c Smith	b Trueman	1	(336–7)
Benaud*		b Dexter	16	(366–8)
McKenzie	c Sheppard	b Titmus	15	(393)
Grout	not out		1	
Extras: 6				

Statham 3–66; Dexter 3–94

AUSTRALIA: 293

Lawry	c Graveney	b Trueman	16	(27–1)
Simpson	c Smith	b Dexter	71	(170–3)
Harvey	c Barrington	b Statham	6	(37–2)
Booth	c Smith	b Dexter	77	(175–4)
O'Neill	c Cowdrey	b Trueman	23	(228–7)
Shepherd	c Titmus	b Dexter	13	(199–5)
Mackay	c Graveney	b Trueman	3	(205–6)
Benaud*	c Barrington	b Trueman	48	(293)
McKenzie	c Smith	b Statham	13	(254–8)
Davidson		b Statham	2	(258–9)
Grout	not out		16	
Extras: 5				

Trueman 4–60; Dexter 3–65; Statham 3–71

ENGLAND: 331

Pullar		b McKenzie	9	(17–1)
Sheppard	st Grout	b Benaud	30	(84–2)
Barrington		b Simpson	63	(117–3)
Cowdrey	c Grout	b McKenzie	13	(119–4)
Dexter*	c Grout	b McKenzie	61	(226–6)
Graveney	c Booth	b McKenzie	22	(165–5)
Titmus	not out		59	
Illingworth	c Grout	b McKenzie	12	(246–7)
Smith	c Lawry	b Mackay	13	(275–8)
Trueman	c Benaud	b Mackay	38	(327–9)
Statham		b Mackay	1	(331)
Extras: 10				

McKenzie 5–89; Mackay 3–80

ENGLAND: 223 for 4

Pullar	c Simpson	b McKenzie	3	(4–2)
Sheppard	c Grout	b Mackay	1	(2–1)
Barrington	not out		132	
Cowdrey	run out		32	(98–3)
Dexter*	c Simpson	b Benaud	10	(122–4)
Graveney	not out		36	
Extras: 9				

England were reeling at 4 for 2 in the seond innings but then achieved an honourable draw, courtesy of Ken Barrington's unbeaten four-hour stint at the crease.

MATCH DRAWN. The series remained level at 1–1.

5TH TEST: at Sydney; February 15, 16, 18, 19, and 20 1963; England won the toss

ENGLAND: 321

Sheppard	c &	b Hawke	19	(39–2)
Cowdrey	c Harvey	b Davidson	2	(5–1)
Barrington	c Harvey	b Benaud	101	(189–5)
Dexter*	c Simpson	b O'Neill	47	(129–3)
Graveney	c Harvey	b McKenzie	14	(177–4)
Illingworth	c Grout	b Davidson	27	(224–6)
Titmus	c Grout	b Hawke	34	(286–8)
Trueman	c Harvey	b Benaud	30	(276–7)
Smith		b Simpson	6	(293–9)
Allen	c Benaud	b Davidson	14	(321)
Statham	not out		17	
Extras: 10				

Davidson 3–43

ENGLAND: 268 for 8 declared

Sheppard	c Harvey	b Benaud	68	(137–2)
Illingworth	c Hawke	b Benaud	18	(40–1)
Barrington	c Grout	b McKenzie	94	(249–6)
Dexter*	st Grout	b Benaud	6	(145–3)
Cowdrey	c Benaud	b Davidson	53	(239–4)
Graveney	c &	b Davidson	3	(247–5)
Titmus	not out		12	
Trueman	c Harvey	b McKenzie	8	(257–7)
Smith	c Simpson	b Davidson	1	(268–8)
Extras: 5				

Benaud 3–71; Davidson 3–80

AUSTRALIA: 349

Lawry	c Smith	b Trueman	11	(28–1)
Simpson	c Trueman	b Titmus	32	(71–3)
Booth		b Titmus	11	(50–2)
O'Neill	c Graveney	b Allen	73	(180–4)
Burge	lbw	b Titmus	103	(299–7)
Harvey	c sub	b Statham	22	(231–5)
Davidson	c Allen	b Dexter	15	(271–6)
Benaud*	c Graveney	b Allen	57	(347–9)
McKenzie	c &	b Titmus	0	(303–8)
Hawke	c Graveney	b Titmus	14	(349)
Grout	not out		0	
Extras: 11				

Titmus 5–103

AUSTRALIA: 152 for 4

Lawry	not out		45	
Simpson		b Trueman	0	(0–1)
Harvey		b Allen	28	(39–2)
O'Neill	c Smith	b Allen	17	(70–3)
Booth		b Allen	0	(70–4)
Burge	not out		52	
Extras: 10				

Allen 3–26

Australia held on to the Ashes after Bill Lawry batted four hours for his 45. England had glimpsed victory when they had reduced the hosts to 70 for 4.

MATCH DRAWN. The series finished 1–1.

ENGLAND: 216 for 8 declared

Boycott	c Simpson	b Corling	48	(90–3)
Titmus	c Redpath	b Hawke	16	(38–1)
Dexter*	c Grout	b Hawke	9	(70–2)
Cowdrey		b Hawke	32	(141–5)
Barrington	c Lawry	b Veivers	22	(135–4)
Sharpe	not out		35	
Parks	c Booth	b Veivers	15	(164–6)
Trueman	c Simpson	b Veivers	0	(165–7)
Allen	c Grout	b McKenze	21	(212–8)
Coldwell	not out		0	
Extras: 18				

Veivers 3–39; Hawke 3–68

ENGLAND: 193 for 9 declared

Dexter*	c O'Neill	b McKenzie	68	(90–1)
Titmus	lbw	b McKenzie	17	(95–2)
Cowdrey		b McKenzie	33	(180–6)
Barrington	lbw	b Corling	33	(147–3)
Parks	c Hawke	b Veivers	19	(174–4)
Sharpe	c &	b Veivers	1	(179–5)
Trueman	c Grout	b McKenzie	4	(187–8)
Allen	lbw	b McKenzie	3	(186–7)
Flavell	c Booth	b Corling	7	(193–9)
Coldwell	not out		0	
Extras: 8				

McKenzie 5–53

AUSTRALIA: 168

Lawry	c Barrington	b Coldwell	11	(37–2)
Redpath		b Trueman	6	(8–1)
O'Neill		b Allen	26	(57–3)
Burge	lbw	b Trueman	31	(91–5)
Booth	run out		0	(61–4)
Simpson*	c Barrington	b Titmus	50	(141–8)
Veivers	c Trueman	b Flavell	8	(118–6)
McKenzie	c Parks	b Coldwell	4	(137–7)
Hawke	not out		10	
Grout	c Parks	b Coldwell	13	(165–9)
Corling		b Trueman	3	(168)
Extras: 6				

Coldwell 3–48; Trueman 3–58

AUSTRALIA: 40 for 2

Lawry	run out		3	(3–1)
Redpath	c Parks	b Flavell	2	(25–2)
O'Neill	Retired hurt		24	
Burge	not out		4	
Booth	not out		6	
Extras: 1				

Geoff Boycott was unable to bat in the second innings of his debut due to a fielding injury. This low-scoring test was ruined by the English weather.

MATCH DRAWN. The series remained level at 0–0.

AUSTRALIA: 176

Lawry		b Trueman	4	(8–1)
Redpath	c Parfitt	b Coldwell	30	(84–5)
O'Neill	c Titmus	b Dexter	26	(46–2)
Burge	lbw	b Dexter	1	(58–3)
Booth	lbw	b Trueman	14	(84–4)
Simpson*	c Parfitt	b Trueman	0	(88–6)
Veivers		b Gifford	54	(167–9)
McKenzie		b Trueman	10	(132–7)
Grout	c Dexter	b Gifford	14	(163–8)
Hawke	not out		5	
Corling		b Trueman	0	(176)
Extras: 18				

Trueman 5–48

AUSTRALIA: 168 for 4

Lawry	c Dexter	b Gifford	20	(35–1)
Redpath	lbw	b Titmus	36	(143–3)
O'Neill	c Parfitt	b Trueman	22	(76–2)
Burge	c Parfitt	b Titmus	59	(148–4)
Booth	not out		2	
Simpson*	not out		15	
Extras: 14				

ENGLAND: 246

Dexter*		b McKenzie	2	(2–1)
Edrich	c Redpath	b McKenzie	120	(229–8)
Cowdrey	c Burge	b Hawke	10	(33–2)
Barrington	lbw	b McKenzie	5	(42–3)
Parfitt	lbw	b Corling	20	(83–4)
Sharpe	lbw	b Hawke	35	(138–5)
Parks	c Simpson	b Hawke	12	(170–6)
Titmus		b Corling	15	(227–7)
Trueman		b Corling	8	(235–9)
Gifford	c Hawke	b Corling	5	(246)
Coldwell	not out		6	
Extras: 8				

Corling 4–60; Hawke 3–41; McKenzie 3–69

The home team were unable to profit from John Edrich's century as rainfall rescued Australia from the possibility of defeat.

MATCH DRAWN. The series remained level at 0–0.

3RD TEST: at Leeds; July 2, 3, 4, and 6 1964; England won the toss

ENGLAND: 268

Boycott	c Simpson	b Corling	38	(74–2)
Edrich	c Veivers	b McKenzie	3	(17–1)
Dexter*	c Grout	b McKenzie	66	(129–3)
Barrington		b McKenzie	29	(138–4)
Parfitt		b Hawke	32	(215–6)
Taylor	c Grout	b Hawke	9	(163–5)
Parks	c Redpath	b Hawke	68	(260–8)
Titmus	c Burge	b McKenzie	3	(232–7)
Trueman	c Cowper	b Hawke	4	(263–9)
Gifford	not out		1	
Flavell	c Redpath	b Hawke	5	(268)
Extras: 10				

Hawke 5–75; McKenzie 4–74

ENGLAND: 229

Boycott	c Simpson	b Corling	4	(13–1)
Edrich	c Grout	b McKenzie	32	(88–2)
Parfitt	c Redpath	b Hawke	6	(199–8)
Barrington	lbw	b Veivers	85	(156–4)
Dexter*	c Redpath	b Veivers	17	(145–3)
Parks	c Booth	b McKenzie	23	(184–6)
Gifford		b McKenzie	1	(169–5)
Taylor		b Veivers	15	(192–7)
Titmus	c Cowper	b Corling	14	(212–9)
Trueman	not out		12	
Flavell	c Simpson	b Corling	5	(229)
Extras: 15				

Corling 3–52; McKenzie 3–53; Veivers 3–70

AUSTRALIA: 389

Lawry	run out		78	(124–2)
Simpson*		b Gifford	24	(50–1)
Redpath		b Gifford	20	(129–3)
Burge	c sub	b Trueman	160	(389)
Booth	st Parks	b Titmus	4	(154–4)
Cowper		b Trueman	2	(157–5)
Veivers	c Parks	b Titmus	8	(178–6)
McKenzie		b Titmus	0	(178–7)
Hawke	c Parfitt	b Trueman	37	(283–8)
Grout	lbw	b Titmus	37	(372–9)
Corling	not out		2	
Extras: 17				

Titmus 4–69; Trueman 3–98

AUSTRALIA: 111 for 3

Lawry	c Gifford	b Trueman	1	(3–1)
Simpson*	c Barrington	b Titmus	30	(45–2)
Redpath	not out		58	
Burge		b Titmus	8	(64–3)
Booth	not out		12	
Extras: 2				

Another big ton from Peter Burge laid the foundations for a comfortable triumph. England now had to win the last two tests to reclaim the little urn.

AUSTRALIA won by 7 wickets to lead the series 1–0.

4TH TEST: at Manchester; July 23, 24, 25, 27, and 28 1964; Australia won the toss

AUSTRALIA: 656 for 8 declared

Lawry	run out		106	(201–1)
Simpson*	c Parks	b Price	311	(646–6)
Redpath	lbw	b Cartwright	19	(233–2)
O'Neill		b Price	47	(318–3)
Burge	c Price	b Cartwright	34	(382–4)
Booth	c &	b Price	98	(601–5)
Veivers	c Edrich	b Rumsey	22	(656–8)
Grout	c Dexter	b Rumsey	0	(652–7)
McKenzie	not out		0	
Extras: 19				
Price 3–183				

AUSTRALIA: 4 for 0

Simpson*	not out	4
Lawry	not out	0
Extras: 0		

ENGLAND: 611

Boycott		b McKenzie	58	(126–2)
Edrich	c Redpath	b McKenzie	6	(15–1)
Dexter*		b Veivers	174	(372–3)
Barrington	lbw	b McKenzie	256	(594–7)
Parfitt	c Grout	b McKenzie	12	(417–4)
Parks	c Hawke	b Veivers	60	(560–5)
Titmus	c Simpson	b McKenzie	9	(589–6)
Mortimore	c Burge	b McKenzie	12	(602–8)
Cartwright		b McKenzie	4	(607–9)
Price		b Veivers	1	(611)
Rumsey	not out		3	
Extras: 16				
McKenzie 7–153; Veivers 3–155				

Tom Cartwright was forced to bowl 77 overs on his debut as Bobby Simpson batted for almost 13 hours. Ken Barrington replied with 11 hours at the crease.

MATCH DRAWN. Australia still lead the series 1–0.

5TH TEST: at the Oval; August 13, 14, 15, 17, and 18 1964; England won the toss

ENGLAND: 182

Boycott		b Hawke	30	(61–2)
Barber		b Hawke	24	(44–1)
Dexter*	c Booth	b Hawke	23	(82–3)
Cowdrey	c Grout	b McKenzie	20	(111–4)
Barrington	c Simpson	b Hawke	47	(173–8)
Parfitt		b McKenzie	3	(117–5)
Parks	c Simpson	b Corling	10	(141–6)
Titmus	c Grout	b Hawke	8	(160–7)
Trueman	c Redpath	b Hawke	14	(182)
Cartwright	c Grout	b McKenzie	0	(174–9)
Price	not out		0	
Extras: 3				

Hawke 6–47; McKenzie 3–87

ENGLAND: 381 for 4

Boycott	c Redpath	b Simpson	113	(200–3)
Barber	lbw	b McKenzie	29	(80–1)
Dexter*	c Simpson	b McKenzie	25	(120–2)
Titmus		b McKenzie	56	(255–4)
Cowdrey	not out		93	
Barrington	not out		54	
Extras: 11				

McKenzie 3–112

AUSTRALIA: 379

Simpson*	c Dexter	b Cartwright	24	(45–1)
Lawry	c Trueman	b Dexter	94	(202–4)
O'Neill	c Parfitt	b Cartwright	11	(57–2)
Burge	lbw	b Titmus	25	(96–3)
Booth	c Trueman	b Price	74	(245–5)
Redpath		b Trueman	45	(343–7)
Grout		b Cartwright	20	(279–6)
Veivers	not out		67	
McKenzie	c Cowdrey	b Trueman	0	(343–8)
Hawke	c Cowdrey	b Trueman	14	(367–9)
Corling	c Parfitt	b Trueman	0	(379)
Extras: 5				

Trueman 4–87; Cartwright 3–110

Boycott's debut test century saved England from defeat, but the tourists were not complaining. They had won their second successive Ashes series in England.

MATCH DRAWN. AUSTRALIA win the series 1–0.

1ST TEST: at Brisbane; December 10, 11, 13, 14, and 15 1965; Australia won the toss

AUSTRALIA: 443 for 6 declared

Lawry	c Parks	b Higgs	166	(312–5)
Redpath		b Brown	17	(51–1)
Cowper	c Barrington	b Brown	22	(90–2)
Burge		b Brown	0	(90–3)
Booth*	c &	b Titmus	16	(125–4)
Walters	c Parks	b Higgs	155	(431–6)
Veivers	not out		56	
Hawke	not out		6	
Extras: 5				

Brown 3–71

ENGLAND: 280

Barber	c Walters	b Hawke	5	(5–1)
Boycott		b Philpott	45	(86–3)
Edrich	c Lawry	b Philpott	32	(75–2)
Barrington		b Hawke	53	(221–6)
Smith*		b Allan	16	(115–4)
Parks	c Redpath	b Philpott	52	(191–5)
Titmus	st Grout	b Philpott	60	(280)
Allen	c Cowper	b Walters	3	(232–7)
Brown		b Philpott	3	(253–8)
Higgs	lbw	b Allan	4	(272–9)
Russell	not out		0	
Extras: 7				

Philpott 5–90

ENGLAND: 186 for 3

Barber	c Veivers	b Walters	34	(46–1)
Boycott	not out		63	
Edrich	c Veivers	b Philpott	37	(114–2)
Barrington	c Booth	b Cowper	38	(168–3)
Smith*	not out		10	
Extras: 4				

Doug Walters hit the ground running on his test debut as he and Bill Lawry brushed England's bowling aside. The tourists had to follow on, but achieved a draw.

MATCH DRAWN. The series remained level at 0–0.

2ND TEST: at Melbourne; December 30, 31 1965, January 1, 3, and 4 1966; Australia won the toss

AUSTRALIA: 358

Simpson*	c Edrich	b Allen	59	(93–1)
Lawry	c Cowdrey	b Allen	88	(203–3)
Burge		b Jones	5	(109–2)
Cowper	c Titmus	b Jones	99	(297–5)
Booth	lbw	b Jones	23	(262–4)
Walters	c Parks	b Knight	22	(318–6)
Veivers	run out		19	(342–8)
Philpott		b Knight	10	(330–7)
Grout	c Barber	b Knight	11	(352–9)
McKenzie	not out		12	
Connolly	c Parks	b Knight	0	(358)
Extras: 10				

Knight 4–84; Jones 3–92

AUSTRALIA: 426

Simpson*	c Barrington	b Knight	67	(120–1)
Lawry	c Smith	b Barber	78	(163–3)
Cowper	lbw	b Jones	5	(141–2)
Burge	c Edrich	b Boycott	120	(374–5)
Booth		b Allen	10	(176–4)
Walters	c &	b Barrington	115	(426)
Veivers	st Parks	b Boycott	3	(382–6)
Philpott		b Knight	2	(385–7)
Grout	c Allen	b Barrington	16	(417–8)
McKenzie	run out		2	(426–9)
Connolly	not out		0	
Extras: 8				

ENGLAND: 558

Boycott	c McKenzie	b Walters	51	(98–1)
Barber	c Grout	b McKenzie	48	(110–2)
Edrich	c &	b Veivers	109	(333–4)
Barrington	c Burge	b Veivers	63	(228–3)
Cowdrey	c Connolly	b Cowper	104	(409–5)
Smith*	c Grout	b McKenzie	41	(443–6)
Parks	c Cowper	b McKenzie	71	(540–8)
Knight	c Simpson	b McKenzie	1	(447–7)
Titmus	not out		56	
Allen	c Grout	b Connolly	2	(551–9)
Jones		b McKenzie	1	(558)
Extras: 11				

McKenzie 5–134

ENGLAND: 5 for 0

Boycott	not out		5
Barber	not out		0
Extras: 0			

Centuries from Burge and again from Walters salvaged a draw after tons from Cowdrey and Edrich had given the away team a healthy advantage.

MATCH DRAWN. The series remained level at 0–0.

3RD TEST: at Sydney; January 7, 8, 10, and 11 1966; England won the toss

ENGLAND: 488

Boycott	c &	b Philpott	84	(234–1)
Barber		b Hawke	185	(303–2)
Edrich	c &	b Philpott	103	(433–9)
Barrington	c McKenzie	b Hawke	1	(309–3)
Cowdrey	c Grout	b Hawke	0	(309–4)
Smith*	c Grout	b Hawke	6	(317–5)
Brown	c Grout	b Hawke	1	(328–6)
Parks	c Grout	b Hawke	13	(358–7)
Titmus	c Grout	b Walters	14	(395–8)
Allen	not out		50	
Jones		b Hawke	16	(488)
Extras: 15				

Hawke 7–105

AUSTRALIA: 221

Lawry	c Parks	b Jones	0	(0–1)
Thomas	c Titmus	b Brown	51	(81–2)
Cowper	st Parks	b Allen	60	(155–5)
Burge	c Parks	b Brown	6	(91–3)
Booth*	c Cowdrey	b Jones	8	(105–4)
Sincock	c Parks	b Brown	29	(174–6)
Walters	st Parks	b Allen	23	(203–9)
Hawke	c Barber	b Brown	0	(174–7)
Grout		b Brown	0	(174–8)
McKenzie	c Cowdrey	b Barber	24	(221)
Philpott	not out		5	
Extras: 15				

Brown 5–63

AUSTRALIA: 174

Lawry	c Cowdrey	b Brown	33	(86–5)
Thomas	c Cowdrey	b Titmus	25	(46–1)
Cowper	c Boycott	b Titmus	0	(50–2)
Burge	run out		1	(51–3)
Booth*		b Allen	27	(86–4)
Walters	not out		35	
Sincock	c Smith	b Allen	27	(119–6)
Philpott	lbw	b Allen	5	(131–7)
Hawke	c Smith	b Titmus	2	(135–8)
Grout	c Smith	b Allen	3	(140–9)
McKenzie	c Barber	b Titmus	12	(174)
Extras: 4				

Titmus 4–40; Allen 4–47

Barber and Boycott amassed over 200 for the first wicket and although 4 colleagues were then caught behind off Hawke, England won with an innings to spare.

ENGLAND won by an innings and 93 runs to lead the series 1–0.

4TH TEST: at Adelaide; January 28, 29, 31, and February 1 1966; England won the toss

ENGLAND: 241

Boycott	c Chappell	b Hawke	22	(25–2)
Barber		b McKenzie	0	(7–1)
Edrich	c Simpson	b McKenzie	5	(33–3)
Barrington	lbw	b Walters	60	(150–5)
Cowdrey	run out		38	(105–4)
Smith*		b Veivers	29	(178–6)
Parks	c Stackpole	b McKenzie	49	(210–7)
Titmus	lbw	b McKenzie	33	(241)
Allen	c Simpson	b McKenzie	2	(212–8)
Brown	c Thomas	b McKenzie	1	(222–9)
Jones	not out		0	
Extras: 2				

McKenzie 6–48

ENGLAND: 266

Boycott	lbw	b McKenzie	12	(23–1)
Barber	c Grout	b Hawke	19	(31–2)
Edrich	c Simpson	b Hawke	1	(32–3)
Barrington	c Chappell	b Hawke	102	(253–8)
Cowdrey	c Grout	b Stackpole	35	(114–4)
Smith*	c McKenzie	b Stackpole	5	(123–5)
Parks	run out		16	(163–6)
Titmus	c Grout	b Hawke	53	(244–7)
Allen	not out		5	
Brown	c &	b Hawke	0	(257–9)
Jones	c Lawry	b Veivers	8	(266)
Extras: 10				

Hawke 5–54

AUSTRALIA: 516

Simpson*	c Titmus	b Jones	225	(480–7)
Lawry		b Titmus	119	(244–1)
Thomas		b Jones	52	(331–2)
Veivers	c Parks	b Jones	1	(333–3)
Burge	c Parks	b Jones	27	(379–4)
Walters	c Parks	b Brown	0	(383–5)
Chappell	c Edrich	b Jones	17	(415–6)
Stackpole	c Parks	b Jones	43	(501–8)
Hawke	not out		20	
Grout		b Titmus	4	(506–9)
McKenzie	lbw	b Titmus	1	(516)
Extras: 7				

Jones 6–118; Titmus 3–116

Simpson and Lawry passed England's first innings total before their stand was stopped. Their centuries laid the foundations for a convincing innings triumph.

AUSTRALIA won by an innings and 9 runs to level the series at 1–1.

5TH TEST: at Melbourne; February 11, 12, 14, 15, and 16 1966; England won the toss

ENGLAND: 485 for 9 declared

Boycott	c Stackpole	b McKenzie	17	(41–2)
Barber	run out		17	(36–1)
Edrich	c McKenzie	b Walters	85	(254–4)
Barrington	c Grout	b Walters	115	(219–3)
Cowdrey	c Grout	b Walters	79	(392–6)
Smith*	c Grout	b Walters	0	(254–5)
Parks	run out		89	(419–7)
Titmus	not out		42	
Knight	c Grout	b Hawke	13	(449–8)
Brown	c &	b Chappell	12	(474–9)
Jones	not out		4	
Extras: 12				

Walters 4–53

ENGLAND: 69 for 3

Boycott	lbw	b McKenzie	1	(6–1)
Barber		b McKenzie	20	(21–2)
Edrich		b McKenzie	3	(34–3)
Barrington	not out		32	
Cowdrey	not out		11	
Extras: 2				

McKenzie 3–17

AUSTRALIA: 543 for 8 declared

Lawry	c Edrich	b Jones	108	(248–3)
Simpson*		b Brown	4	(15–1)
Thomas	c Titmus	b Jones	19	(36–2)
Cowper		b Knight	307	(543–8)
Walters	c &	b Barber	60	(420–4)
Chappell	c Parks	b Jones	19	(481–5)
Stackpole		b Knight	9	(532–6)
Veivers		b Titmus	4	(543–7)
Hawke	not out		0	
Extras: 13				

Jones 3–145

The in-form Ken Barrington gave England the best possible start, but Bob Cowper's twelve-hour career best triple hundred kept the Ashes Down Under.

MATCH DRAWN. The series finished 1–1.

1ST TEST: at Manchester; June 6, 7, 8, 10, and 11 1968; Australia won the toss

AUSTRALIA: 357

Lawry*	c Boycott	b Barber	81	(174–4)
Redpath	lbw	b Snow	8	(29–1)
Cowper		b Snow	0	(29–2)
Walters	lbw	b Barber	81	(173–3)
Sheahan	c D'Oliveira	b Snow	88	(341–6)
Chappell	run out		73	(326–5)
Jarman	c &	b Higgs	12	(357–9)
Hawke	c Knott	b Snow	5	(351–7)
McKenzie	c Cowdrey	b D'Oliveira	0	(353–8)
Gleeson	c Knott	b Higgs	0	(357)
Connolly	not out		0	

Extras: 9

Snow 4–97

AUSTRALIA: 220

Lawry*	c Pocock	b D'Oliveira	16	(24–2)
Redpath	lbw	b Snow	8	(24–1)
Cowper	c &	b Pocock	37	(106–3)
Walters	lbw	b Pocock	86	(211–6)
Sheahan	c Graveney	b Pocock	8	(122–4)
Chappell	c Knott	b Pocock	9	(140–5)
Jarman		b Pocock	41	(214–8)
Hawke	c Edrich	b Pocock	0	(211–7)
McKenzie	c Snow	b Barber	0	(214–9)
Gleeson	run out		2	(220)
Connolly	not out		2	

Extras: 11

Pocock 6–79

ENGLAND: 165

Edrich	run out		49	(86–1)
Boycott	c Jarman	b Cowper	35	(87–2)
Cowdrey*	c Lawry	b McKenzie	4	(97–5)
Graveney	c McKenzie	b Cowper	2	(89–3)
Amiss	c Cowper	b McKenzie	0	(90–4)
Barber	c Sheahan	b McKenzie	20	(137–8)
D'Oliveira		b Connolly	9	(120–6)
Knott	c McKenzie	b Cowper	5	(137–7)
Snow	not out		18	
Higgs	lbw	b Cowper	2	(144–9)
Pocock	c Redpath	b Gleeson	6	(165)

Extras: 15

Cowper 4–48; McKenzie 3–33

ENGLAND: 253

Edrich	c Jarman	b Cowper	38	(91–3)
Boycott	c Redpath	b McKenzie	11	(13–1)
Cowdrey*	c Jarman	b McKenzie	11	(25–2)
Graveney	c Jarman	b Gleeson	33	(105–5)
Amiss		b Cowper	0	(91–4)
Barber	c Cowper	b Hawke	46	(185–6)
D'Oliveira	not out		87	
Knott	lbw	b Connolly	4	(214–7)
Snow	c Lawry	b Connolly	2	(218–8)
Higgs	c Jarman	b Gleeson	0	(219–9)
Pocock	lbw	b Gleeson	10	(253)

Extras: 11

Gleeson 3–44

A brace of eighties from Doug Walters paved the way for victory as poor Basil D'Oliveira ran out of batting partners in England's second innings.

AUSTRALIA won by 159 runs to lead the series 1–0.

2ND TEST: at Lord's; June 20, 21, 22, 24, and 25 1968; England won the toss

ENGLAND: 351 for 7 declared

Edrich	c Cowper	b McKenzie	7	(10–1)
Boycott	c Sheahan	b McKenzie	49	(147–3)
Milburn	c Walters	b Gleeson	83	(142–2)
Cowdrey*	c Cowper	b McKenzie	45	(244–4)
Barrington	c Jarman	b Connolly	75	(351–7)
Graveney	c Jarman	b Connolly	14	(271–5)
Knight	not out		27	
Knott	run out		33	(330–6)
Snow	not out		0	
Extras: 18				

McKenzie 3–111

AUSTRALIA: 78

Lawry*	c Knott	b Brown	0	(1–1)
Redpath	c Cowper	b Brown	4	(12–2)
Cowper	c Graveney	b Snow	8	(23–3)
Walters	c Knight	b Brown	26	(52–5)
Sheahan	c Knott	b Knight	6	(46–4)
Chappell	lbw	b Knight	7	(58–6)
Hawke	c Cowdrey	b Knight	2	(78–9)
McKenzie		b Brown	5	(63–7)
Gleeson	c Cowdrey	b Brown	14	(78–8)
Jarman	retired hurt		0	
Connolly	not out		0	
Extras: 6				

Brown 5–42; Knight 3–16

AUSTRALIA: 127 for 4

Lawry*	c Brown	b Snow	28	(66–1)
Redpath		b Underwood	53	(93–2)
Cowper	c Underwood	b Barrington	32	(115–4)
Walters		b Underwood	0	(97–3)
Sheahan	not out		0	
Chappell	not out		12	
Extras: 2				

England's first innings lasted three days, courtesy of the weather, which was just as well for the Aussies after they were turned over for a dismal 78 in reply.

MATCH DRAWN. Australia still lead the series 1–0.

3RD TEST: at Birmingham; July 11, 12, 13, 15, and 16 1968;
England won the toss

ENGLAND: 409

Edrich	c Taber	b Freeman	88	(188–2)
Boycott	lbw	b Gleeson	36	(80–1)
Cowdrey*		b Freeman	104	(282–4)
Barrington	lbw	b Freeman	0	(189–3)
Graveney		b Connolly	96	(374–7)
Knight	c Chappell	b Connolly	6	(293–5)
Knott		b McKenzie	4	(323–6)
Illingworth	lbw	b Gleeson	27	(376–9)
Brown		b Connolly	0	(374–8)
Snow	c Connolly	b Freeman	19	(409)
Underwood	not out		14	
Extras: 15				

Freeman 4–78; Connolly 3–84

ENGLAND: 142 for 3 declared

Edrich	c Cowper	b Freeman	64	(131–2)
Boycott	c Taber	b Connolly	31	(57–1)
Graveney	not out		39	
Knight		b Connolly	1	(134–3)
Knott	not out		4	
Extras: 3				

AUSTRALIA: 222

Lawry*	retired hurt		6	
Redpath		b Brown	0	(10–1)
Cowper		b Snow	57	(121–2)
Chappell		b Knight	71	(165–3)
Walters	c &	b Underwood	46	(213–6)
Sheahan		b Underwood	4	(176–4)
Taber	c Barrington	b Illingworth	16	(213–5)
Freeman		b Illingworth	6	(219–7)
McKenzie	not out		0	
Gleeson	c Illingworth	b Underwood	3	(222–8)
Connolly		b Illingworth	0	(222–9)
Extras: 13				

Illingworth 3–37; Underwood 3–48

AUSTRALIA: 68 for 1

Redpath	lbw	b Snow	22	(44–1)
Cowper	not out		25	
Chappell	not out		18	
Extras: 3				

Cowdrey celebrated becoming the first player to reach 100 tests by scoring 100 runs! Edrich's pair of half-centuries were ultimately spoiled by more weather resistance.

MATCH DRAWN. Australia still lead the series 1–0.

4TH TEST: at Leeds; July 25, 26, 27, 29, and 30 1968; Australia won the toss

AUSTRALIA: 315

Inverarity		b Snow	8	(10–1)
Cowper		b Snow	27	(104–2)
Redpath		b Illingworth	92	(152–3)
Walters	c Barrington	b Underwood	42	(188–4)
Chappell		b Brown	65	(309–8)
Sheahan	c Knott	b Snow	38	(248–5)
Jarman*	c Dexter	b Brown	10	(267–6)
Freeman		b Underwood	21	(307–7)
McKenzie	lbw	b Underwood	5	(315–9)
Gleeson	not out		2	
Connolly	c Graveney	b Underwood	0	(315)
Extras: 5				

Underwood 4–41; Snow 3–98

AUSTRALIA: 312

Inverarity	lbw	b Illingworth	34	(81–2)
Cowper	st Knott	b Illingworth	5	(28–1)
Redpath	c Edrich	b Snow	48	(119–3)
Walters	c Graveney	b Snow	56	(198–4)
Chappell	c Barrington	b Underwood	81	(281–6)
Sheahan	st Knott	b Illingworth	31	(273–5)
Jarman*	st Knott	b Illingworth	4	(283–7)
Freeman		b Illingworth	10	(296–8)
McKenzie	c Snow	b Illingworth	10	(311–9)
Gleeson	c Knott	b Underwood	7	(312)
Connolly	not out		0	
Extras: 26				

Illingworth 6–87

ENGLAND: 302

Edrich	c Jarman	b McKenzie	62	(136–2)
Prideaux	c Freeman	b Gleeson	64	(123–1)
Dexter		b McKenzie	10	(141–3)
Graveney*	c Cowper	b Connolly	37	(209–4)
Barrington		b Connolly	49	(235–6)
Fletcher	c Jarman	b Connolly	0	(215–5)
Knott	lbw	b Freeman	4	(237–7)
Illingworth	c Gleeson	b Connolly	6	(241–8)
Snow		b Connolly	0	(241–9)
Brown		b Cowper	14	(302)
Underwood	not out		45	
Extras: 11				

Connolly 5–72

ENGLAND: 230 for 4

Edrich	c Jarman	b Connolly	65	(134–3)
Prideaux		b McKenzie	2	(4–1)
Dexter		b Connolly	38	(81–2)
Graveney*	c &	b Cowper	41	(168–4)
Barrington	not out		46	
Fletcher	not out		23	
Extras: 15				

Tom Graveney and Barry Jarman deputised as captains while Ian Chappell's two half-centuries ensured that the Ashes would stay in the southern hemisphere.

MATCH DRAWN. Australia still lead the series 1–0.

5TH TEST: at the Oval; August 22, 23, 24, 26, and 27 1968; England won the toss

ENGLAND: 494

Edrich		b Chappell	164	(359–5)
Milburn		b Connolly	8	(28–1)
Dexter		b Gleeson	21	(84–2)
Cowdrey*	lbw	b Mallett	16	(113–3)
Graveney	c Redpath	b McKenzie	63	(238–4)
D'Oliveira	c Inverarity	b Mallett	158	(489–9)
Knott	c Jarman	b Mallett	28	(421–6)
Illingworth	lbw	b Connolly	8	(458–7)
Snow	run out		4	(468–8)
Underwood	not out		9	
Brown	c Sheahan	b Gleeson	2	(494)
Extras: 13				
Mallett 3–87				

ENGLAND: 181

Edrich	c Lawry	b Mallett	17	(53–2)
Milburn	c Lawry	b Connolly	18	(23–1)
Dexter		b Connolly	28	(67–3)
Cowdrey*		b Mallett	35	(126–6)
Graveney	run out		12	(90–4)
D'Oliveira	c Gleeson	b Connolly	9	(114–5)
Knott	run out		34	(179–9)
Illingworth		b Gleeson	10	(149–7)
Snow	c Sheahan	b Gleeson	13	(179–8)
Underwood	not out		1	
Brown		b Connolly	1	(181)
Extras: 3				
Connolly 4–65				

AUSTRALIA: 324

Lawry*	c Knott	b Snow	135	(269–8)
Inverarity	c Milburn	b Snow	1	(7–1)
Redpath	c Cowdrey	b Snow	67	(136–2)
Chappell	c Knott	b Brown	10	(151–3)
Walters	c Knott	b Brown	5	(161–4)
Sheahan		b Illingworth	14	(185–5)
Jarman	st Knott	b Illingworth	0	(188–6)
McKenzie		b Brown	12	(237–7)
Mallett	not out		43	
Gleeson	c Dexter	b Underwood	19	(302–9)
Connolly		b Underwood	3	(324)
Extras: 15				
Brown 3–63; Snow 3–67				

AUSTRALIA: 125

Lawry*	c Milburn	b Brown	4	(4–1)
Inverarity	lbw	b Underwood	56	(125)
Redpath	lbw	b Underwood	8	(13–2)
Chappell	lbw	b Underwood	2	(19–3)
Walters	c Knott	b Underwood	1	(29–4)
Sheahan	c Snow	b Illingworth	24	(65–5)
Jarman		b D'Oliveira	21	(110–6)
Mallett	c Brown	b Underwood	0	(110–7)
McKenzie	c Brown	b Underwood	0	(110–8)
Gleeson		b Underwood	5	(120–9)
Connolly	not out		0	
Extras: 4				
Underwood 7–50				

Australia were destroyed in the final couple of hours as deadly Derek Underwood took advantage of the uncovered pitch. England were worthy of the drawn series.

ENGLAND won by 226 runs. The series finished 1–1.

1ST TEST: at Brisbane; November 27, 28, 29, December 1, and 2 1970; Australia won the toss

AUSTRALIA: 433

Lawry*	c Knott	b Snow	4	(12–1)
Stackpole	c Knott	b Snow	207	(372–3)
Chappell	run out		59	(163–2)
Walters		b Underwood	112	(421–6)
Redpath	c Illingworth	b Underwood	22	(418–4)
Sheahan	c Knott	b Underwood	0	(418–5)
Marsh		b Snow	9	(433–8)
Jenner	c Cowdrey	b Snow	0	(422–7)
McKenzie	not out		3	
Gleeson	c Cowdrey	b Snow	0	(433–9)
Thomson		b Snow	0	(433)
Extras: 17				

Snow 6–114; Underwood 3–101

AUSTRALIA: 214

Lawry*	c Snow	b Fletcher	84	(152–5)
Stackpole	c Knott	b Shuttleworth	8	(30–1)
Chappell	st Knott	b Illingworth	10	(47–2)
Walters	c Luckhurst	b Snow	7	(64–3)
Redpath	c &	b Underwood	28	(137–4)
Sheahan	c Shuttleworth	b Snow	36	(201–8)
Marsh		b Shuttleworth	14	(193–6)
Jenner	c Boycott	b Shuttleworth	2	(199–7)
McKenzie		b Shuttleworth	1	(214)
Gleeson		b Shuttleworth	6	(208–9)
Thomson	not out		4	
Extras: 14				

Shuttleworth 5–47

ENGLAND: 464

Boycott	c Marsh	b Gleeson	37	(92–1)
Luckhurst	run out		74	(136–2)
Knott	c Lawry	b Walters	73	(245–3)
Edrich	c Chappell	b Jenner	79	(284–4)
Cowdrey	c Chappell	b Gleeson	28	(336–5)
Fletcher	c Marsh	b McKenzie	34	(346–6)
D'Oliveira	c Sheahan	b McKenzie	57	(449–8)
Illingworth*	c Marsh	b Thomson	8	(371–7)
Snow	c Marsh	b Walters	34	(456–9)
Underwood	not out		2	
Shuttleworth	c Lawry	b Walters	7	(464)
Extras: 31				

Walters 3–12

ENGLAND: 39 for 1

Boycott	c &	b Jenner	16	(39–1)
Luckhurst	not out		20	
Extras: 3				

Luckhurst and Shuttleworth made impressive debuts, but this high-scoring draw was dominated by a double hundred from Keith Stackpole, his highest test score.

MATCH DRAWN. The series remained level at 0–0.

2ND TEST: at Perth; December 11, 12, 13, 15, and 16 1970; Australia won the toss

ENGLAND: 397

Boycott	c McKenzie	b Gleeson	70	(171–1)
Luckhurst		b McKenzie	131	(243–2)
Edrich	run out		47	(291–4)
Knott	c Stackpole	b Thomson	24	(281–3)
Fletcher		b Walters	22	(310–5)
Cowdrey	c &	b Chappell. G	40	(389–7)
D'Oliveira	c Stackpole	b Thomson	8	(327–6)
Illingworth*		b McKenzie	34	(389–8)
Snow	not out		4	
Shuttleworth		b McKenzie	2	(393–9)
Lever		b McKenzie	2	(397)
Extras: 13				

McKenzie 4–66

ENGLAND: 287 for 6 declared

Boycott	st Marsh	b Gleeson	50	(98–2)
Luckhurst	c Stackpole	b Walters	19	(60–1)
Edrich	not out		115	
Fletcher	lbw	b Gleeson	0	(98–3)
Cowdrey	c Marsh	b Thomson	1	(101–4)
D'Oliveira		b Gleeson	31	(152–5)
Illingworth*	c Marsh	b Stackpole	29	(209–6)
Knott	not out		30	
Extras: 12				

Gleeson 3–68

AUSTRALIA: 440

Lawry*	c Illingworth	b Snow	0	(8–2)
Stackpole	c Lever	b Snow	5	(5–1)
Chappell. I	c Knott	b Snow	50	(105–4)
Walters	c Knott	b Lever	7	(17–3)
Redpath	c &	b Illingworth	171	(393–7)
Sheahan	run out		2	(107–5)
Chappell. G	c Luckhurst	b Shuttleworth	108	(326–6)
Marsh	c D'Oliveira	b Shuttleworth	44	(426–9)
McKenzie	c Lever	b D'Oliveira	7	(408–8)
Gleeson	c Knott	b Snow	15	(440)
Thomson	not out		12	
Extras: 19				

Snow 4–143

AUSTRALIA: 100 for 3

Lawry*	not out		38	
Stackpole	c sub	b Snow	0	(0–1)
Chappell. I	c sub	b Snow	17	(20–2)
Walters		b Lever	8	(40–3)
Redpath	not out		26	
Extras: 11				

Another high-scoring occasion featured two tons on either team, notably one for Greg Chappell on his debut and Ian Redpath's biggest test score.

MATCH DRAWN. The series remained level at 0–0.

3RD TEST: at Melbourne; December 31 1970, January 1 and 2 1971; England won the toss

AUSTRALIA:

Lawry*
Stackpole
Chappell. I
Walters
Redpath
Chappell. G
Marsh
Mallett
McKenzie
Gleeson
Connolly

ENGLAND:

Boycott
Luckhurst
Edrich
Cowdrey
D'Oliveira
Illingworth*
Knott
Snow
Shuttleworth
Lever
Underwood

The world's first-ever one day international was hastily arranged to compensate for the total washout of this test match.

MATCH ABANDONED on the third day without a ball being bowled. The series remained level at 0–0.

4TH TEST: at Sydney; January 9, 10, 11, 13, and 14 1971; England won the toss

ENGLAND: 332

Boycott	c Gleeson	b Connolly	77	(116–1)
Luckhurst	lbw	b Gleeson	38	(130–2)
Edrich	c Gleeson	b Chappell. G	55	(205–4)
Fletcher	c Walters	b Mallett	23	(201–3)
D'Oliveira	c Connolly	b Mallett	0	(208–5)
Illingworth*		b Gleeson	25	(262–7)
Knott	st Marsh	b Mallett	6	(219–6)
Snow	c Lawry	b Gleeson	37	(291–8)
Lever	c Connolly	b Mallett	36	(332)
Underwood	c Chappell. G	b Gleeson	0	(291–9)
Willis	not out		15	
Extras: 20				

Mallett 4–40; Gleeson 4–83

ENGLAND: 319 for 5 declared

Boycott	not out		142	
Luckhurst	c Chappell. I	b McKenzie	5	(7–1)
Edrich	run out		12	(35–2)
Fletcher	c Stackpole	b Mallett	8	(48–3)
D'Oliveira	c Chappell. I	b Chappell. G	56	(181–4)
Illingworth*	st Marsh	b Mallett	53	(276–5)
Knott	not out		21	
Extras: 22				

AUSTRALIA: 236

Lawry*	c Edrich	b Lever	9	(38–2)
Chappell. I	c Underwood	b Snow	12	(14–1)
Redpath	c Fletcher	b D'Oliveira	64	(189–5)
Walters	c Luckhurst	b Illingworth	55	(137–3)
Chappell. G	c &	b Underwood	15	(160–4)
Stackpole	c Boycott	b Underwood	33	(199–6)
Marsh	c D'Oliveira	b Underwood	8	(208–7)
Mallett		b Underwood	4	(208–8)
McKenzie	not out		11	
Gleeson	c Fletcher	b D'Oliveira	0	(219–9)
Connolly		b Lever	14	(236)
Extras: 11				

Underwood 4–66

AUSTRALIA: 116

Lawry*	not out		60	
Chappell. I	c D'Oliveira	b Snow	0	(1–1)
Redpath	c Edrich	b Snow	6	(11–2)
Walters	c Knott	b Lever	3	(14–3)
Chappell. G		b Snow	2	(21–4)
Stackpole	c Lever	b Snow	30	(66–5)
Marsh	c Willis	b Snow	0	(66–6)
Mallett	c Knott	b Willis	6	(86–7)
McKenzie	retired hurt		6	
Gleeson		b Snow	0	(116–8)
Connolly	c Knott	b Snow	0	(116–9)
Extras: 3				

Snow 7–40

Geoff Boycott laid the foundations for this convincing win, as John Snow's uncompromising pace wrecked havoc upon Australia's second innings.

ENGLAND won by 299 runs to lead the series 1–0.

5TH TEST: at Melbourne; January 21, 22, 23, 25, and 26 1971; Australia won the toss

AUSTRALIA: 493 for 9 declared

Stackpole	c Lever	b D'Oliveira	30	(64–1)
Lawry*	c Snow	b Willis	56	(310–4)
Chappell. I	c Luckhurst	b Snow	111	(166–2)
Redpath		b Snow	72	(269–3)
Walters		b Underwood	55	(374–6)
Chappell. G	c Edrich	b Willis	3	(314–5)
Marsh	not out		92	
O'Keeffe	c Luckhurst	b Illingworth	27	(471–7)
Gleeson	c Cowdrey	b Willis	5	(477–8)
Duncan	c Edrich	b Illingworth	3	(480–9)
Thomson	not out		0	
Extras: 39				

Willis 3–73

AUSTRALIA: 169 for 4 declared

Stackpole	c Knott	b Willis	18	(51–1)
Lawry*	c sub	b Snow	42	(84–2)
Chappell. I		b Underwood	30	(132–4)
Redpath	c Knott	b Snow	5	(91–3)
Walters	not out		39	
Chappell. G	not out		20	
Extras: 15				

ENGLAND: 392

Boycott	c Redpath	b Thomson	12	(40–1)
Luckhurst		b Walters	109	(228–4)
Edrich	c Marsh	b Thomson	9	(64–2)
Cowdrey	c &	b Gleeson	13	(88–3)
D'Oliveira	c Marsh	b Thomson	117	(340–6)
Illingworth*	c Redpath	b Gleeson	41	(306–5)
Knott	lbw	b Stackpole	19	(362–8)
Snow		b Chappell. I	1	(354–7)
Lever	run out		19	(392)
Underwood	c &	b Gleeson	5	(379–9)
Willis	not out		5	
Extras: 42				

Gleeson 3–60; Thomson 3–110

ENGLAND: 161 for 0

Boycott	not out		76
Edrich	not out		74
Extras: 11			

The bat dominated the ball again as England ran out of time to polish off the target of 271. Geoff Boycott and John Edrich were well en route to this demanding total.

MATCH DRAWN. England still lead the series 1–0.

6TH TEST: at Adelaide; January 29, 30, February 1, 2, and 3 1971; England won the toss

ENGLAND: 470

Boycott	run out		58	(107–1)
Edrich	c Stackpole	b Lillee	130	(276–2)
Fletcher		b Thomson	80	(289–4)
Knott	c Redpath	b Lillee	7	(289–3)
D'Oliveira	c Marsh	b Chappell. G	47	(385–5)
Hampshire	c Lillee	b Chappell. G	55	(402–6)
Illingworth*		b Lillee	24	(458–7)
Snow		b Lillee	38	(465–8)
Lever		b Thomson	5	(465–9)
Underwood	not out		1	
Willis	c Walters	b Lillee	4	(470)
Extras: 21				

Lillee 5–84

ENGLAND: 233 for 4 declared

Boycott	not out		119	
Edrich		b Thomson	40	(103–1)
Fletcher		b Gleeson	5	(128–2)
D'Oliveira	c Walters	b Thomson	5	(143–3)
Hampshire	lbw	b Thomson	3	(151–4)
Illingworth*	not out		48	
Extras: 13				

Thomson 3–79

AUSTRALIA: 235

Stackpole		b Underwood	87	(117–2)
Lawry*	c Knott	b Snow	10	(61–1)
Chappell. I	c Knott	b Lever	28	(131–3)
Redpath	c Lever	b Illingworth	9	(163–6)
Walters	c Knott	b Lever	8	(141–4)
Chappell. G	c Edrich	b Lever	0	(145–5)
Marsh	c Knott	b Willis	28	(180–7)
Mallett	c Illingworth	b Snow	28	(219–8)
Gleeson	c Boycott	b Willis	16	(221–9)
Lillee	c Boycott	b Lever	10	(235)
Thomson	not out		6	
Extras: 5				

Lever 4–49

AUSTRALIA: 328 for 3

Stackpole		b Snow	136	(267–2)
Lawry*	c Knott	b Willis	21	(65–1)
Chappell. I	c Willis	b Underwood	104	(271–3)
Redpath	not out		21	
Walters	not out		36	
Extras: 10				

Dennis Lillee began his test career with a 5-wicket haul but his team had to settle for a draw after a morale-boosting pursuit of 469 in the final innings.

MATCH DRAWN. England still lead the series 1–0.

7TH TEST: at Sydney; February 12, 13, 14, 16, and 17 1971; Australia won the toss

ENGLAND: 184

Edrich	c Chappell. G	b Dell	30	(60–2)
Luckhurst	c Redpath	b Walters	0	(5–1)
Fletcher	c Stackpole	b O'Keeffe	33	(68–3)
Hampshire	c Marsh	b Lillee	10	(98–5)
D'Oliveira		b Dell	1	(69–4)
Illingworth*		b Jenner	42	(165–8)
Knott	c Stackpole	b O'Keeffe	27	(145–6)
Snow		b Jenner	7	(156–7)
Lever	c Jenner	b O'Keeffe	4	(165–9)
Underwood	not out		8	
Willis		b Jenner	11	(184)
Extras: 11				

Jenner 3–42; O'Keeffe 3–48

ENGLAND: 302

Edrich	c Chappell. I	b O'Keeffe	57	(158–3)
Luckhurst	c Lillee	b O'Keeffe	59	(94–1)
Fletcher	c Stackpole	b Eastwood	20	(130–2)
Hampshire	c Chappell. I	b O'Keeffe	24	(165–4)
D'Oliveira	c Chappell. I	b Lillee	47	(251–6)
Illingworth*	lbw	b Lillee	29	(234–5)
Knott		b Dell	15	(276–7)
Snow	c Stackpole	b Dell	20	(302)
Lever	c Redpath	b Jenner	17	(298–8)
Underwood	c Marsh	b Dell	0	(299–9)
Willis	not out		2	
Extras: 12				

Dell 3–65; O'Keeffe 3–96

AUSTRALIA: 264

Eastwood	c Knott	b Lever	5	(11–1)
Stackpole		b Snow	6	(13–2)
Marsh	c Willis	b Lever	4	(32–3)
Chappell. I*		b Willis	25	(66–4)
Redpath	c &	b Underwood	59	(162–6)
Walters	st Knott	b Underwood	42	(147–5)
Chappell. G		b Willis	65	(239–9)
O'Keeffe	c Knott	b Illingworth	3	(178–7)
Jenner		b Lever	30	(264)
Lillee	c Knott	b Willis	6	(235–8)
Dell	not out		3	
Extras: 16				

Lever 3–43; Willis 3–58

AUSTRALIA: 160

Eastwood		b Snow	0	(0–1)
Stackpole		b Illingworth	67	(96–5)
Chappell. I*	c Knott	b Lever	6	(22–2)
Redpath	c Hampshire	b Illingworth	14	(71–3)
Walters	c D'Oliveira	b Willis	1	(82–4)
Chappell. G	st Knott	b Illingworth	30	(142–7)
Marsh		b Underwood	16	(131–6)
O'Keeffe	c sub	b D'Oliveira	12	(154–8)
Jenner	c Fletcher	b Underwood	4	(160)
Lillee	c Hampshire	b D'Oliveira	0	(154–9)
Dell	not out		3	
Extras: 7				

Illingworth 3–39

Australia had to win to retain the Ashes but fell short in this cliffhanger, after sitting ominously at 71 for 2 in the run chase. England had won back the Ashes.

ENGLAND won by 62 runs to win the series 2–0.

ENGLAND: 249

Boycott	c Stackpole	b Gleeson	8	(127–5)
Edrich	run out		49	(99–3)
Luckhurst		b Colley	14	(50–1)
Smith	lbw	b Lillee	10	(86–2)
D'Oliveira		b Chappell. G	23	(118–4)
Greig	lbw	b Colley	57	(190–6)
Knott	c Marsh	b Lillee	18	(200–7)
Illingworth*	not out		26	
Snow		b Colley	3	(209–8)
Gifford	run out		15	(243–9)
Arnold	c Francis	b Gleeson	1	(249)
Extras: 25				
Colley 3–83				

ENGLAND: 234

Boycott	lbw	b Gleeson	47	(60–1)
Edrich	c Marsh	b Watson	26	(81–3)
Luckhurst	c Marsh	b Colley	0	(65–2)
Smith	c Marsh	b Lillee	34	(182–5)
D'Oliveira	c Watson	b Lillee	37	(140–4)
Greig		b Chappell. G	62	(234)
Knott	c Marsh	b Lillee	1	(192–6)
Illingworth*	c Chappell. I	b Lillee	14	(234–7)
Snow	lbw	b Lillee	0	(234–8)
Gifford	c Marsh	b Lillee	0	(234–9)
Arnold	not out		0	
Extras: 13				
Lillee 6–66				

AUSTRALIA: 142

Stackpole	lbw	b Arnold	53	(91–3)
Francis	lbw	b D'Oliveira	27	(68–1)
Chappell. I*	c Smith	b Greig	0	(69–2)
Chappell. G	c Greig	b Snow	24	(119–5)
Watson	c Knott	b Arnold	2	(99–4)
Walters	c Illingworth	b Snow	17	(142)
Inverarity	c Knott	b Arnold	4	(124–6)
Marsh	c Edrich	b Arnold	8	(134–7)
Colley		b Snow	1	(137–8)
Gleeson		b Snow	0	(137–9)
Lillee	not out		1	
Extras: 5				
Snow 4–41; Arnold 4–62				

AUSTRALIA: 252

Stackpole		b Greig	67	(136–7)
Francis	lbw	b Snow	6	(9–1)
Chappell. I*	c Knott	b Snow	7	(31–2)
Chappell. G	c D'Oliveira	b Arnold	23	(77–3)
Watson	c &	b Snow	0	(78–4)
Walters		b Greig	20	(115–5)
Inverarity	c Luckhurst	b D'Oliveira	3	(120–6)
Marsh	c Knott	b Greig	91	(251–9)
Colley	c Greig	b Snow	4	(147–8)
Gleeson		b Greig	30	(252)
Lillee	not out		0	
Extras: 1				
Greig 4–53; Snow 4–87				

Tony Greig hit two half-centuries and took five wickets on his debut. John Snow also helped himself to eight wickets to ensure victory for the host nation.

ENGLAND won by 89 runs to lead the series 1–0.

ENGLAND: 272

Boycott		b Massie	11	(22–1)
Edrich	lbw	b Lillee	10	(28–3)
Luckhurst		b Lillee	1	(23–2)
Smith		b Massie	34	(97–5)
D'Oliveira	lbw	b Massie	32	(84–4)
Greig	c Marsh	b Massie	54	(200–7)
Knott	c Colley	b Massie	43	(193–6)
Illingworth*	lbw	b Massie	30	(260–8)
Snow		b Massie	37	(265–9)
Gifford	c Marsh	b Massie	3	(272)
Price	not out		4	
Extras: 13				
Massie 8–84				

ENGLAND: 116

Boycott		b Lillee	6	(12–1)
Edrich	c Marsh	b Massie	6	(18–3)
Luckhurst	c Marsh	b Lillee	4	(16–2)
Smith	c Edwards	b Massie	30	(81–9)
D'Oliveira	c Chappell. G	b Massie	3	(25–4)
Greig	c Chappell. I	b Massie	3	(31–5)
Knott	c Chappell. G	b Massie	12	(52–6)
Illingworth*	c Stackpole	b Massie	12	(74–7)
Snow	c Marsh	b Massie	0	(74–8)
Gifford	not out		16	
Price	c Chappell. G	b Massie	19	(116)
Extras: 5				
Massie 8–53				

AUSTRALIA: 308

Stackpole	c Gifford	b Price	5	(7–2)
Francis		b Snow	0	(1–1)
Chappell. I*	c Smith	b Snow	56	(82–3)
Chappell. G		b D'Oliveira	131	(250–7)
Walters	c Illingworth	b Snow	1	(84–4)
Edwards	c Smith	b Illingworth	28	(190–5)
Gleeson	c Knott	b Greig	1	(212–6)
Marsh	c Greig	b Snow	50	(290–8)
Colley	c Greig	b Price	25	(308)
Massie	c Knott	b Snow	0	(290–9)
Lillee	not out		2	
Extras: 9				
Snow 5–57				

AUSTRALIA: 81 for 2

Stackpole	not out		57	
Francis	c Knott	b Price	9	(20–1)
Chappell. I*	c Luckhurst	b D'Oliveira	6	(51–2)
Chappell. G	not out		7	
Extras: 2				

Bob Massie bowled himself into the record books with an astonishing 16 wickets on his debut. Luckhurst was the only England batsman that he failed to dismiss.

AUSTRALIA won by 8 wickets to level the series at 1–1.

3RD TEST: at Nottingham; July 13, 14, 15, 17, and 18 1972; England won the toss

AUSTRALIA: 315

Stackpole	c Parfitt	b Greig	114	(227–6)
Francis	c Smith	b Lever	10	(16–1)
Chappell. I*	c Knott	b Snow	34	(98–2)
Chappell. G	c Parfitt	b Snow	26	(157–3)
Walters	c Parfitt	b Snow	2	(165–4)
Edwards	c Knott	b Snow	13	(189–5)
Marsh	c D'Oliveira	b Gifford	41	(289–7)
Colley	c Greig	b D'Oliveira	54	(315–9)
Massie	c Parfitt	b Snow	0	(298–8)
Gleeson	not out		6	
Lillee	c Knott	b Greig	0	(315)
Extras: 15				

Snow 5–92

AUSTRALIA: 324 for 4 declared

Stackpole	c Luckhurst	b Snow	12	(15–1)
Edwards	not out		170	
Chappell. I*	lbw	b Illingworth	50	(139–2)
Chappell. G		b Snow	72	(285–3)
Walters	c Gifford	b Snow	7	(295–4)
Marsh	not out		7	
Extras: 6				

Snow 3–94

ENGLAND: 189

Luckhurst	lbw	b Lillee	23	(55–1)
Edrich	c Marsh	b Colley	37	(74–3)
Parfitt		b Massie	0	(60–2)
Smith		b Lillee	17	(111–4)
D'Oliveira	lbw	b Lillee	29	(133–5)
Gifford	c Marsh	b Massie	16	(145–6)
Greig	c Marsh	b Massie	7	(155–8)
Knott	c Marsh	b Massie	0	(145–7)
Illingworth*	not out		24	
Snow	c Marsh	b Lillee	6	(166–9)
Lever	c Walters	b Colley	9	(189)
Extras: 21				

Lillee 4–35; Massie 4–43

ENGLAND: 290 for 4

Luckhurst	c Chappell. G	b Chappell. I	96	(167–2)
Edrich		b Massie	15	(50–1)
Parfitt		b Lillee	46	(201–4)
Smith	lbw	b Lillee	15	(200–3)
D'Oliveira	not out		50	
Greig	not out		36	
Extras: 32				

Ross Edwards was moved up to open the second innings and responded with his highest first class score. However England comfortably played out a draw.

MATCH DRAWN. The series remained level at 1–1.

4TH TEST: at Leeds; July 27, 28, and 29 1972;
Australia won the toss

AUSTRALIA: 146

Stackpole	c Knott	b Underwood	52	(79–2)
Edwards	c Knott	b Snow	0	(10–1)
Chappell. I*	c &	b Illingworth	26	(93–4)
Chappell. G	lbw	b Underwood	12	(93–3)
Sheahan	c Illingworth	b Underwood	0	(98–7)
Walters		b Illingworth	4	(97–5)
Marsh	c Illingworth	b Underwood	1	(98–6)
Inverarity	not out		26	
Mallett	lbw	b Snow	20	(145–8)
Massie		b Arnold	0	(146–9)
Lillee	c Greig	b Arnold	0	(146)
Extras: 5				

Underwood 4–37

AUSTRALIA: 136

Stackpole	lbw	b Underwood	28	(51–4)
Edwards	c Knott	b Arnold	0	(5–1)
Chappell. I*	c Knott	b Arnold	0	(7–2)
Chappell. G	c D'Oliveira	b Underwood	13	(31–3)
Sheahan	not out		41	
Walters	c Parfitt	b Underwood	3	(63–5)
Marsh	c Knott	b Underwood	1	(69–6)
Inverarity	c Illingworth	b Underwood	0	(69–7)
Mallett		b Illingworth	9	(93–8)
Lillee		b Underwood	7	(111–9)
Massie		b Illingworth	18	(136)
Extras: 16				

Underwood 6–45

ENGLAND: 263

Luckhurst	c Chappell. G	b Mallett	18	(43–1)
Edrich	c Chappell. I	b Mallett	45	(76–4)
Parfitt	c Marsh	b Lillee	2	(52–2)
Fletcher	lbw	b Mallett	5	(66–3)
D'Oliveira		b Mallett	12	(108–5)
Greig	c Chappell. G	b Inverarity	24	(128–7)
Knott	st Marsh	b Mallett	0	(108–6)
Illingworth*	lbw	b Lillee	57	(263)
Snow	st Marsh	b Inverarity	48	(232–8)
Underwood	c Chappell. I	b Inverarity	5	(246–9)
Arnold	not out		1	
Extras: 46				

Mallett 5–114; Inverarity 3–26

ENGLAND: 21 for 1

Luckhurst	not out		12	
Edrich	lbw	b Lillee	4	(7–1)
Parfitt	not out		0	
Extras: 5				

The away team couldn't cope with Derek Underwood who seized ten wickets. Meanwhile, Ray Illingworth recorded the match's highest score on his home ground.

ENGLAND won by 9 wickets to lead the series 2–1.

5TH TEST: at the Oval; August 10, 11, 12, 14, 15, and 16 1972; England won the toss

ENGLAND: 284

Wood	c Marsh	b Watson	26	(50–2)
Edrich	lbw	b Lillee	8	(25–1)
Parfitt		b Lillee	51	(145–5)
Hampshire	c Inverarity	b Mallett	42	(133–3)
D'Oliveira	c Chappell. G	b Mallett	4	(142–4)
Greig	c Stackpole	b Mallett	16	(159–7)
Illingworth*	c Chappell. G	b Lillee	0	(145–6)
Knott	c Marsh	b Lillee	92	(284)
Snow	c Marsh	b Lillee	3	(181–8)
Arnold		b Inverarity	22	(262–9)
Underwood	not out		3	
Extras: 17				

Lillee 5–58; Mallett 3–80

ENGLAND: 356

Wood	lbw	b Massie	90	(194–4)
Edrich		b Lillee	18	(56–1)
Parfitt		b Lillee	18	(81–2)
Hampshire	c Chappell. I	b Watson	20	(114–3)
D'Oliveira	c Chappell. I	b Massie	43	(205–5)
Greig	c Marsh	b Lillee	29	(270–6)
Illingworth*	lbw	b Lillee	31	(271–7)
Knott		b Lillee	63	(356)
Snow	c Stackpole	b Mallett	14	(333–8)
Arnold	lbw	b Mallett	4	(356–9)
Underwood	not out		0	
Extras: 26				

Lillee 5–123

AUSTRALIA: 399

Watson	c Knott	b Arnold	13	(24–1)
Stackpole		b Snow	18	(34–2)
Chappell. I*	c Snow	b Arnold	118	(296–4)
Chappell. G	c Greig	b Illingworth	113	(235–3)
Edwards		b Underwood	79	(383–7)
Sheahan	c Hampshire	b Underwood	5	(310–5)
Marsh		b Underwood	0	(310–6)
Inverarity	c Greig	b Underwood	28	(387–8)
Mallett	run out		5	(399)
Massie		b Arnold	4	(399–9)
Lillee	not out		0	
Extras: 16				

Underwood 4–90; Arnold 3–87

AUSTRALIA; 242 for 5

Watson	lbw	b Arnold	6	(16–1)
Stackpole	c Knott	b Greig	79	(132–2)
Chappell. I*	c sub	b Underwood	37	(136–3)
Chappell. G	lbw	b Underwood	16	(171–5)
Edwards	lbw	b Greig	1	(137–4)
Sheahan	not out		44	
Marsh	not out		43	
Extras: 16				

The Chappell brothers shared in a 201-run stand and collected centuries in the process while Dennis Lillee registered a match haul of ten wickets.

AUSTRALIA won by 5 wickets to level the series at 2–2.

AUSTRALIA: 309

Batsman	Fielder	Bowler	Runs	Fall
Redpath		b Willis	5	(10–2)
Edwards. W	c Amiss	b Hendrick	4	(7–1)
Chappell. I*	c Greig	b Willis	90	(110–3)
Chappell. G	c Fletcher	b Underwood	58	(197–4)
Edwards. R	c Knott	b Underwood	32	(205–6)
Walters	c Lever	b Willis	3	(202–5)
Marsh	c Denness	b Hendrick	14	(229–8)
Jenner	c Lever	b Willis	12	(228–7)
Lillee	c Knott	b Greig	15	(257–9)
Walker	not out		41	
Thomson	run out		23	(309)
Extras: 12				

Willis 4–56

AUSTRALIA: 288 for 5 declared

Batsman	Fielder	Bowler	Runs	Fall
Redpath		b Willis	25	(59–3)
Edwards. W	c Knott	b Willis	5	(15–1)
Chappell. I*	c Fletcher	b Underwood	11	(39–2)
Chappell. G		b Underwood	71	(173–4)
Edwards. R	c Knott	b Willis	53	(190–5)
Walters	not out		62	
Marsh	not out		46	
Extras: 15				

Willis 3–45

ENGLAND: 265

Batsman	Fielder	Bowler	Runs	Fall
Amiss	c Jenner	b Thomson	7	(10–2)
Luckhurst	c Marsh	b Thomson	1	(9–1)
Edrich	c Chappell. I	b Thomson	48	(130–5)
Denness*	lbw	b Walker	6	(33–3)
Fletcher		b Lillee	17	(57–4)
Greig	c Marsh	b Lillee	110	(248–9)
Knott	c Jenner	b Walker	12	(162–6)
Lever	c Chappell. I	b Walker	4	(168–7)
Underwood	c Redpath	b Walters	25	(226–8)
Willis	not out		13	
Hendrick	c Redpath	b Walker	4	(265)
Extras: 18				

Walker 4–73; Thomson 3–59

ENGLAND: 166

Batsman	Fielder	Bowler	Runs	Fall
Amiss	c Walters	b Thomson	25	(44–3)
Luckhurst	c Chappell. I	b Lillee	3	(18–1)
Edrich		b Thomson	6	(40–2)
Denness*	c Walters	b Thomson	27	(92–4)
Fletcher	c Chappell. G	b Jenner	19	(94–5)
Greig		b Thomson	2	(94–6)
Knott		b Thomson	19	(163–9)
Lever	c Redpath	b Lillee	14	(115–7)
Underwood	c Walker	b Jenner	30	(162–8)
Willis	not out		3	
Hendrick		b Thomson	0	(166)
Extras: 18				

Thomson 6–46

Aside from a remarkable century from Tony Greig, the tourists had no answer to the ferocious exhibition of pace from Jeff Thomson. Worse was to come.

AUSTRALIA won by 166 runs to lead the series 1–0.

ENGLAND: 208

Lloyd	c Chappell. G	b Thomson	49	(99–2)
Luckhurst	c Mallett	b Walker	27	(44–1)
Cowdrey		b Thomson	22	(119–3)
Greig	c Mallett	b Walker	23	(132–6)
Fletcher	c Redpath	b Lillee	4	(128–4)
Denness*	c Chappell. G	b Lillee	2	(132–5)
Knott	c Redpath	b Walters	51	(194–7)
Titmus	c Redpath	b Walters	10	(208)
Old	c Chappell. G	b Chappell. I	7	(201–8)
Arnold	run out		1	(202–9)
Willis	not out		4	
Extras: 8				

ENGLAND: 293

Lloyd	c Chappell. G	b Walker	35	(156–6)
Cowdrey	lbw	b Thomson	41	(62–1)
Denness*	c Redpath	b Thomson	20	(124–3)
Greig	c Chappell. G	b Thomson	32	(106–2)
Fletcher	c Marsh	b Thomson	0	(124–4)
Knott	c Chappell. G	b Lillee	18	(154–5)
Luckhurst	c Mallett	b Lillee	23	(219–7)
Titmus	c Chappell. G	b Mallett	61	(293)
Old	c Thomson	b Mallett	43	(285–8)
Arnold	c Mallett	b Thomson	4	(293–9)
Willis	not out		0	
Extras: 16				
Thomson 5–93				

AUSTRALIA: 481

Redpath	st Knott	b Titmus	41	(101–2)
Edwards. W	c Lloyd	b Greig	30	(64–1)
Chappell. I*	c Knott	b Arnold	25	(113–3)
Chappell. G	c Greig	b Willis	62	(192–4)
Edwards. R		b Arnold	115	(416–6)
Walters	c Fletcher	b Willis	103	(362–5)
Marsh	c Lloyd	b Titmus	41	(449–7)
Walker	c Knott	b Old	19	(481)
Lillee		b Old	11	(462–8)
Mallett	c Knott	b Old	0	(462–9)
Thomson	not out		11	
Extras: 23				
Old 3–85				

AUSTRALIA: 23 for 1

Redpath	not out		12	
Edwards. W	lbw	b Arnold	0	(4–1)
Chappell. I*	not out		11	
Extras: 0				

Edwards and Walters were the only centurions in this contest as England fell foul of Jeff Thomson again. Greg Chappell took an astonishing haul of seven catches.

AUSTRALIA won by 9 wickets to lead the series 2–0.

3RD TEST: at Melbourne; December 26, 27, 28, 30, and 31 1974; Australia won the toss

ENGLAND: 242

Amiss	c Walters	b Lillee	4	(4–1)
Lloyd	c Mallett	b Thomson	14	(34–2)
Cowdrey	lbw	b Thomson	35	(110–3)
Edrich	c Marsh	b Mallett	49	(110–4)
Denness*	c Marsh	b Mallett	8	(141–5)
Greig	run out		28	(157–6)
Knott		b Thomson	52	(242)
Titmus	c Mallett	b Lillee	10	(176–7)
Underwood	c Marsh	b Walker	9	(213–8)
Willis	c Walters	b Thomson	13	(232–9)
Hendrick	not out		8	
Extras: 12				

Thomson 4–72

ENGLAND: 244

Amiss	c Chappell. I	b Mallett	90	(158–5)
Lloyd	c &	b Mallett	44	(115–1)
Cowdrey	c Chappell. G	b Lillee	8	(134–2)
Edrich	c Marsh	b Thomson	4	(152–3)
Denness*	c Chappell. I	b Thomson	2	(156–4)
Greig	c Chappell. G	b Lillee	60	(238–9)
Knott	c Marsh	b Thomson	4	(165–6)
Titmus		b Mallett	0	(178–7)
Underwood	c Chappell. I	b Mallett	4	(182–8)
Willis		b Thomson	15	(244)
Hendrick	not out		0	
Extras: 13				

Mallett 4–60; Thomson 4–71

AUSTRALIA: 241

Redpath	c Knott	b Greig	55	(126–5)
Edwards. W	c Denness	b Willis	29	(65–1)
Chappell. G	c Greig	b Willis	2	(67–2)
Edwards. R	c Cowdrey	b Titmus	1	(68–3)
Walters	c Lloyd	b Greig	36	(121–4)
Chappell. I*	lbw	b Willis	36	(173–6)
Marsh	c Knott	b Titmus	44	(237–7)
Walker	c Knott	b Willis	30	(237–8)
Lillee	not out		2	
Mallett	run out		0	(238–9)
Thomson		b Willis	2	(241)
Extras: 4				

Willis 5–61

AUSTRALIA: 238 for 8

Redpath	run out		39	(121–5)
Edwards. W	lbw	b Greig	0	(4–1)
Chappell. I*	lbw	b Willis	0	(5–2)
Chappell. G	lbw	b Titmus	61	(106–3)
Edwards. R	c Lloyd	b Titmus	10	(120–4)
Walters	c Denness	b Greig	32	(171–6)
Marsh	c Knott	b Greig	40	(208–7)
Walker	not out		23	
Lillee	c Denness	b Greig	14	(235–8)
Mallett	not out		0	
Extras: 18				

Greig 4–56

Not for the last time, Melbourne produced one of the closest encounters imaginable. An extra fifteen minutes of play would surely have decided this match.

MATCH DRAWN: Australia still lead the series 2–0.

4TH TEST: at Sydney; January 4, 5, 6, 8, and 9 1975; Australia won the toss

AUSTRALIA: 405

Redpath	hit wicket	b Titmus	33	(96–1)
McCosker	c Knott	b Greig	80	(142–2)
Chappell. I*	c Knott	b Arnold	53	(199–3)
Chappell. G	c Greig	b Arnold	84	(310–7)
Edwards		b Greig	15	(251–4)
Walters	lbw	b Arnold	1	(255–5)
Marsh		b Greig	30	(305–6)
Walker	c Greig	b Arnold	30	(368–9)
Lillee		b Arnold	8	(332–8)
Mallett	lbw	b Greig	31	(405)
Thomson	not out		24	
Extras: 16				

Arnold 5–86; Greig 4–104

AUSTRALIA: 289 for 4 declared

Redpath	c sub	b Underwood	105	(280–4)
Chappell. I*	c Lloyd	b Willis	5	(15–1)
Chappell. G	c Lloyd	b Arnold	144	(235–2)
Walters		b Underwood	5	(242–3)
Edwards	not out		17	
Marsh	not out		7	
Extras: 6				

ENGLAND: 295

Amiss	c Mallett	b Walker	12	(36–1)
Lloyd	c Thomson	b Lillee	19	(46–2)
Cowdrey	c McCosker	b Thomson	22	(69–3)
Edrich*	c Marsh	b Walters	50	(180–6)
Fletcher	c Redpath	b Walker	24	(108–4)
Greig	c Chappell. G	b Thomson	9	(123–5)
Knott		b Thomson	82	(273–8)
Titmus	c Marsh	b Walters	22	(240–7)
Underwood	c Walker	b Lillee	27	(295)
Willis		b Thomson	2	(285–9)
Arnold	not out		3	
Extras: 23				

Thomson 4–74

ENGLAND: 228

Amiss	c Marsh	b Lillee	37	(70–2)
Lloyd	c Chappell. G	b Thomson	26	(68–1)
Cowdrey	c Chappell. I	b Walker	1	(74–3)
Edrich*	not out		33	
Fletcher	c Redpath	b Thomson	11	(103–4)
Greig	st Marsh	b Mallett	54	(158–7)
Knott	c Redpath	b Mallett	10	(136–5)
Titmus	c Thomson	b Mallett	4	(156–6)
Underwood	c &	b Walker	5	(175–8)
Willis		b Lillee	12	(201–9)
Arnold	c Chappell. G	b Mallett	14	(228)
Extras: 21				

Mallett 4–21

Ian Redpath and Greg Chappell were the only two century-makers in this one-sided contest. Chappell actually amassed 228 runs as Australia triumphed again.

AUSTRALIA won by 171 runs to lead the series 3–0.

5TH TEST: at Adelaide; January 25, 26, 27, 29, and 30 1975; England won the toss

AUSTRALIA: 304

Redpath	c Greig	b Underwood	21	(77–4)
McCosker	c Cowdrey	b Underwood	35	(52–1)
Chappell. I*	c Knott	b Underwood	0	(52–2)
Chappell. G	lbw	b Underwood	5	(58–3)
Walters	c Willis	b Underwood	55	(164–6)
Marsh	c Greig	b Underwood	6	(84–5)
Jenner		b Underwood	74	(241–7)
Walker	run out		41	(259–8)
Lillee		b Willis	26	(295–9)
Mallett	not out		23	
Thomson		b Arnold	5	(304)
Extras: 13				
Underwood 7–113				

AUSTRALIA: 272 for 5 declared

Redpath		b Underwood	52	(128–3)
McCosker	c Knott	b Arnold	11	(16–1)
Chappell. I*	c Knott	b Underwood	41	(92–2)
Chappell. G	c Greig	b Underwood	18	(133–4)
Walters	not out		71	
Marsh	c Greig	b Underwood	55	(245–5)
Jenner	not out		14	
Extras: 10				
Underwood 4–102				

ENGLAND: 172

Amiss	c Chappell. I	b Lillee	0	(2–1)
Lloyd	c Marsh	b Lillee	4	(19–2)
Cowdrey	c Walker	b Thomson	26	(66–3)
Denness*	c Marsh	b Thomson	51	(90–4)
Fletcher	c Chappell. I	b Thomson	40	(155–7)
Greig	c Marsh	b Lillee	19	(130–5)
Knott	c Lillee	b Mallett	5	(147–6)
Titmus	c Chappell. G	b Mallett	11	(161–9)
Underwood	c Lillee	b Mallett	0	(156–8)
Arnold		b Lillee	0	(172)
Willis	not out		11	
Extras: 5				
Lillee 4–49; Mallett 3–14; Thomson 3–58				

ENGLAND: 241

Amiss	c Marsh	b Lillee	0	(0–1)
Lloyd	c Walters	b Walker	5	(8–2)
Cowdrey	c Mallett	b Lillee	3	(10–3)
Denness*	c Jenner	b Lillee	14	(33–4)
Fletcher	lbw	b Lillee	63	(144–6)
Greig	lbw	b Walker	20	(76–5)
Knott	not out		106	
Titmus	lbw	b Jenner	20	(212–7)
Underwood	c Chappell. I	b Mallett	0	(213–8)
Arnold		b Mallett	0	(217–9)
Willis		b Walker	3	(241)
Extras: 7				
Lillee 4–69; Walker 3–89				

Derek Underwood grabbed eleven wickets and his Kent county colleague Alan Knott hit the only ton of the match, and yet Australia still won comfortably.

AUSTRALIA won by 163 runs to lead the series 4–0.

6TH TEST: at Melbourne; February 8, 9, 10, 12, and 13 1975; Australia won the toss

AUSTRALIA: 152

Redpath	c Greig	b Lever	1	(5–2)
McCosker	c Greig	b Lever	0	(0–1)
Chappell. I*	c Knott	b Old	65	(104–6)
Chappell. G	c Denness	b Lever	1	(19–3)
Edwards	c Amiss	b Lever	0	(23–4)
Walters	c Edrich	b Old	12	(50–5)
Marsh		b Old	29	(115–7)
Walker	not out		20	
Lillee	c Knott	b Lever	12	(141–8)
Mallett		b Lever	7	(149–9)
Dymock	c Knott	b Greig	0	(152)
Extras: 5				

Lever 6–38; Old 3–50

AUSTRALIA: 373

Redpath	c Amiss	b Greig	83	(248–3)
McCosker	c Cowdrey	b Arnold	76	(111–1)
Chappell. I*	c Knott	b Greig	50	(215–2)
Chappell. G		b Lever	102	(373–8)
Edwards	c Knott	b Arnold	18	(289–4)
Walters		b Arnold	3	(297–5)
Marsh	c Denness	b Lever	1	(306–6)
Walker	c &	b Greig	17	(367–7)
Mallett	c Edrich	b Greig	0	(373)
Dymock	c Knott	b Lever	0	(373–9)
Lillee	not out		0	
Extras: 23				

Greig 4–88; Lever 3–65; Arnold 3–83

ENGLAND: 529

Amiss	lbw	b Lillee	0	(4–1)
Cowdrey	c Marsh	b Walker	7	(18–2)
Edrich	c Chappell. I	b Walker	70	(167–3)
Denness*	c &	b Walker	188	(359–4)
Fletcher	c Redpath	b Walker	146	(507–6)
Greig	c sub	b Walker	89	(507–5)
Knott	c Marsh	b Walker	5	(514–8)
Old		b Dymock	0	(508–7)
Underwood		b Walker	11	(529)
Arnold	c Marsh	b Walker	0	(514–9)
Lever	not out		6	
Extras: 7				

Walker 8–143

Ian Chappell hit two fifties but suffered the embarrassment of an innings defeat after having won the toss. Mike Denness recorded his highest test score in reply.

ENGLAND won by an innings and 4 runs. AUSTRALIA win the series 4–1.

1ST TEST: at Birmingham; July 10, 11, 12, and 14 1975; England won the toss

AUSTRALIA: 359

McCosker		b Arnold	59	(126–2)
Turner	c Denness	b Snow	37	(80–1)
Chappell. I*	c Fletcher	b Snow	52	(161–4)
Chappell. G	lbw	b Old	0	(135–3)
Edwards	c Gooch	b Old	56	(332–8)
Walters	c Old	b Greig	14	(186–5)
Marsh	c Fletcher	b Arnold	61	(265–6)
Walker	c Knott	b Snow	7	(286–7)
Thomson	c Arnold	b Underwood	49	(359)
Lillee	c Knott	b Arnold	3	(343–9)
Mallett	not out		3	
Extras: 18				

Snow 3–86; Arnold 3–91

ENGLAND: 101

Edrich	lbw	b Lillee	34	(78–7)
Amiss	c Thomson	b Lillee	4	(9–1)
Fletcher	c Mallett	b Walker	6	(24–2)
Denness*	c Chappell. G	b Walker	3	(46–3)
Gooch	c Marsh	b Walker	0	(46–4)
Greig	c Marsh	b Walker	8	(54–5)
Knott		b Lillee	14	(75–6)
Underwood		b Lillee	10	(87–8)
Old	c Chappell. G	b Walker	13	(101)
Snow	lbw	b Lillee	0	(97–9)
Arnold	not out		0	
Extras: 9				

Lillee 5–15; Walker 5–48

ENGLAND: 173

Edrich	c Marsh	b Walker	5	(7–1)
Amiss	c sub	b Thomson	5	(122–7)
Fletcher	c Walters	b Lillee	51	(90–5)
Denness*		b Thomson	8	(18–2)
Gooch	c Marsh	b Thomson	0	(20–3)
Greig	c Marsh	b Walker	7	(52–4)
Knott	c McCosker	b Thomson	38	(151–8)
Old	c Walters	b Lillee	7	(100–6)
Snow	c Marsh	b Thomson	34	(167–9)
Underwood		b Mallett	3	(173)
Arnold	not out		6	
Extras: 9				

Thomson 5–38

England were crushed by the pace trio of Lillee, Thomson, and Walker. Gooch was twice caught by Marsh for a debut pair. His two innings lasted a total of 10 balls.

AUSTRALIA won by an innings and 85 runs to lead the series 1–0.

2ND TEST: at Lord's; July 31, August 1, 2, 4, and 5 1975; England won the toss

ENGLAND: 315

Wood	lbw	b Lillee	6	(10–1)
Edrich	lbw	b Lillee	9	(29–2)
Steele		b Thomson	50	(145–5)
Amiss	lbw	b Lillee	0	(31–3)
Gooch	c Marsh	b Lillee	6	(49–4)
Greig*	c Chappell. I	b Walker	96	(222–6)
Knott	lbw	b Thomson	69	(288–7)
Woolmer	c Turner	b Mallett	33	(310–9)
Snow	c Walker	b Mallett	11	(309–8)
Underwood	not out		0	
Lever	lbw	b Walker	4	(315)
Extras: 31				

Lillee 4–84

ENGLAND: 436 for 7 declared

Wood	c Marsh	b Thomson	52	(111–1)
Edrich	c Thomson	b Mallett	175	(387–6)
Steele	c &	b Walters	45	(215–2)
Amiss	c Chappell. G	b Lillee	10	(249–3)
Gooch		b Mallett	31	(315–4)
Greig*	c Walters	b Chappell. I	41	(380–5)
Knott	not out		22	
Woolmer		b Mallett	31	(436–7)
Extras: 29				

Mallett 3–127

AUSTRALIA: 268

McCosker	c &	b Lever	29	(54–4)
Turner	lbw	b Snow	9	(21–1)
Chappell. I*	c Knott	b Snow	2	(29–2)
Chappell. G	lbw	b Snow	4	(37–3)
Edwards	lbw	b Woolmer	99	(199–9)
Walters	c Greig	b Lever	2	(56–5)
Marsh	c Amiss	b Greig	3	(64–6)
Walker		b Snow	5	(81–7)
Thomson		b Underwood	17	(133–8)
Lillee	not out		73	
Mallett	lbw	b Steele	14	(268)
Extras: 11				

Snow 4–66

AUSTRALIA: 329 for 3

McCosker	lbw	b Steele	79	(169–2)
Turner	c Gooch	b Greig	21	(50–1)
Chappell. I*	lbw	b Greig	86	(222–3)
Chappell. G	not out		73	
Edwards	not out		52	
Extras: 18				

Tony Greig's first match as captain was dominated by John Edrich's nine-hour marathon knock. Australia still comfortably secured a draw to stay 1–0 ahead.

MATCH DRAWN. Australia still lead the series 1–0.

ENGLAND: 288

Wood	lbw	b Gilmour	9	(25–1)
Edrich	c Mallett	b Thomson	62	(137–2)
Steele	c Walters	b Thomson	73	(213–5)
Hampshire	lbw	b Gilmour	14	(159–3)
Fletcher	c Mallett	b Lillee	8	(189–4)
Greig*	run out		51	(268–6)
Knott	lbw	b Gilmour	14	(269–7)
Edmonds	not out		13	
Old		b Gilmour	5	(284–8)
Snow	c Walters	b Gilmour	0	(284–9)
Underwood	c Chappell. G	b Gilmour	0	(288)
Extras: 39				
Gilmour 6–85				

ENGLAND: 291

Wood	lbw	b Walker	25	(55–1)
Edrich		b Mallett	35	(70–2)
Steele	c Chappell. G	b Gilmour	92	(272–7)
Fletcher	c Chappell. G	b Lillee	14	(103–3)
Greig*	c &	b Mallett	49	(197–4)
Old	st Marsh	b Mallett	10	(209–5)
Hampshire	c Chappell. G	b Thomson	0	(210–6)
Knott	c Thomson	b Lillee	31	(276–8)
Edmonds	c sub	b Gilmour	8	(285–9)
Snow	c Marsh	b Gilmour	9	(291)
Underwood	not out		0	
Extras: 18				
Mallett 3–50; Gilmour 3–72				

AUSTRALIA: 135

McCosker	c Hampshire	b Old	0	(8–1)
Marsh		b Snow	25	(53–2)
Chappell. I*		b Edmonds	35	(81–5)
Chappell. G	c Underwood	b Edmonds	13	(78–3)
Edwards	lbw	b Edmonds	0	(78–4)
Walters	lbw	b Edmonds	19	(107–8)
Gilmour	c Greig	b Underwood	6	(96–6)
Walker	c Old	b Edmonds	0	(104–7)
Thomson	c Steele	b Snow	16	(135)
Lillee		b Snow	11	(128–9)
Mallett	not out		1	
Extras: 9				
Edmonds 5–28; Snow 3–22				

AUSTRALIA: 220 for 3

McCosker	not out		95	
Marsh		b Underwood	12	(55–1)
Chappell. I*	lbw	b Old	62	(161–2)
Chappell. G	c Steele	b Edmonds	12	(174–3)
Walters	not out		25	
Extras: 14				

Rick McCosker was poised to become the match's first centurion but both teams were denied a result when vandals sabotaged the pitch after Day Four had ended.

MATCH DRAWN. Australia still lead the series 1–0.

4TH TEST: at the Oval; August 28, 29, 30, September 1, 2, and 3 1975; Australia won the toss

AUSTRALIA: 532 for 9 declared

McCosker	c Roope	b Old	127	(284-2)
Turner	c Steele	b Old	2	(7-1)
Chappell. I*	c Greig	b Woolmer	192	(356-4)
Chappell. G	c Knott	b Old	0	(286-3)
Edwards	c Edrich	b Snow	44	(396-5)
Walters		b Underwood	65	(501-9)
Marsh	c &	b Greig	32	(441-6)
Walker	c Steele	b Greig	13	(477-7)
Thomson	c Old	b Greig	0	(477-8)
Lillee	not out		28	
Mallett	not out		5	
Extras: 24				

Old 3–74; Greig 3–107

AUSTRALIA: 40 for 2

McCosker	not out		25	
Turner	c Woolmer	b Greig	8	(22-1)
Edwards	c Old	b Underwood	2	(33-2)
Chappell. G	not out		4	
Extras: 1				

ENGLAND: 191

Wood		b Walker	32	(45-1)
Edrich	lbw	b Walker	12	(78-2)
Steele		b Lillee	39	(96-4)
Roope	c Turner	b Walker	0	(83-3)
Woolmer	c Mallett	b Thomson	5	(103-5)
Greig*	c Marsh	b Lillee	17	(125-6)
Knott	lbw	b Walker	9	(131-7)
Edmonds	c Marsh	b Thomson	4	(147-8)
Old	not out		25	
Snow	c Chappell. G	b Thomson	30	(190-9)
Underwood	c Chappell. G	b Thomson	0	(191)
Extras: 18				

Thomson 4–50; Walker 4–63

ENGLAND: 538

Wood	lbw	b Thomson	22	(77-1)
Edrich		b Lillee	96	(202-2)
Steele	c Marsh	b Lillee	66	(209-3)
Roope		b Lillee	77	(331-4)
Woolmer	lbw	b Walters	149	(538)
Greig*	c Marsh	b Lillee	15	(371-5)
Knott	c Marsh	b Walters	64	(522-6)
Old	c Chappell. I	b Walters	0	(522-7)
Edmonds	run out		7	(533-8)
Snow	c &	b Walters	0	(533-9)
Underwood	not out		3	
Extras: 39				

Walters 4–34; Lillee 4–91

Centuries from Ian Chappell and Rick McCosker ensured a series victory. England at least accumulated their highest-ever second innings score against the Aussies.

MATCH DRAWN. AUSTRALIA win the series 1–0.

1ST TEST: at Lord's; June 16, 17, 18, 20, and 21 1977; England won the toss

ENGLAND: 216

Amiss		b Thomson	4	(12–1)
Brearley*	c Robinson	b Thomson	9	(13–2)
Woolmer	run out		79	(183–8)
Randall	c Chappell	b Walker	53	(111–3)
Greig		b Pascoe	5	(121–4)
Barlow	c McCosker	b Walker	1	(134–5)
Knott	c Walters	b Thomson	8	(155–6)
Old	c Marsh	b Walker	9	(171–7)
Lever		b Pascoe	8	(189–9)
Underwood	not out		11	
Willis		b Thomson	17	(216)
Extras: 12				

Thomson 4–41; Walker 3–66

ENGLAND: 305

Amiss		b Thomson	0	(0–1)
Brearley*	c Robinson	b O'Keeffe	49	(132–2)
Woolmer	c Chappell	b Pascoe	120	(224–3)
Greig	c O'Keeffe	b Pascoe	91	(286–5)
Barlow	lbw	b Pascoe	5	(263–4)
Knott	c Walters	b Walker	8	(286–6)
Randall	c McCosker	b Thomson	0	(286–8)
Old	c Walters	b Walker	0	(286–7)
Lever	c Marsh	b Thomson	3	(305–9)
Underwood	not out		12	
Willis	c Marsh	b Thomson	0	(305)
Extras: 17				

Thomson 4–86; Pascoe 3–96

AUSTRALIA: 296

Robinson		b Lever	11	(25–1)
McCosker		b Old	23	(51–2)
Chappell*	c Old	b Willis	66	(135–3)
Serjeant	c Knott	b Willis	81	(238–4)
Walters	c Brearley	b Willis	53	(256–5)
Hookes	c Brearley	b Old	11	(264–6)
Marsh	lbw	b Willis	1	(265–7)
O'Keeffe	c sub	b Willis	12	(290–9)
Walker	c Knott	b Willis	4	(284–8)
Thomson		b Willis	6	(296)
Pascoe	not out		3	
Extras: 25				

Willis 7–78

AUSTRALIA: 114 for 6

Robinson	c Woolmer	b Old	4	(5–1)
McCosker		b Willis	1	(5–2)
Chappell*	c Lever	b Old	24	(48–3)
Hookes	c &	b Willis	50	(102–6)
Walters	c sub	b Underwood	10	(64–4)
Serjeant	c Amiss	b Underwood	3	(71–5)
Marsh	not out		6	
O'Keeffe	not out		8	
Extras: 8				

Bob Willis helped himself to nine wickets against a new-look Australia while the other Bob, Woolmer took care of their bowlers with two impressive innings.

MATCH DRAWN. The series remained level at 0–0.

2ND TEST: at Manchester; July 7, 8, 9, 11, and 12 1977; Australia won the toss

AUSTRALIA: 297

McCosker	c Old	b Willis	2	(4–1)
Davis	c Knott	b Old	34	(96–3)
Chappell*	c Knott	b Greig	44	(80 2)
Serjeant	lbw	b Lever	14	(125–4)
Walters	c Greig	b Miller	88	(246–7)
Hookes	c Knott	b Lever	5	(140–5)
Marsh	c Amiss	b Miller	36	(238–6)
Bright	c Greig	b Lever	12	(272–9)
O'Keeffe	c Knott	b Willis	12	(272–8)
Walker		b Underwood	9	(297)
Thomson	not out		14	
Extras: 27				
Lever 3–60				

AUSTRALIA: 218

McCosker	c Underwood	b Willis	0	(0–1)
Davis	c Lever	b Willis	12	(30–2)
Chappell*		b Underwood	112	(202–8)
Serjeant	c Woolmer	b Underwood	8	(74–3)
Walters	lbw	b Greig	10	(92–4)
Hookes	c Brearley	b Miller	28	(146–5)
Marsh	c Randall	b Underwood	1	(147–6)
Bright	c &	b Underwood	0	(147–7)
O'Keeffe	not out		24	
Walker	c Greig	b Underwood	6	(212–9)
Thomson	c Randall	b Underwood	1	(218)
Extras: 16				
Underwood 6–66				

ENGLAND: 437

Amiss	c Chappell	b Walker	11	(23–2)
Brearley*	c Chappell	b Thomson	6	(19–1)
Woolmer	c Davis	b O'Keeffe	137	(325–4)
Randall	lbw	b Bright	79	(165–3)
Greig	c &	b Walker	76	(348–5)
Knott	c O'Keeffe	b Thomson	39	(377–7)
Miller	c Marsh	b Thomson	6	(366–6)
Old	c Marsh	b Walker	37	(435–9)
Lever		b Bright	10	(404–8)
Underwood		b Bright	10	(437)
Willis	not out		1	
Extras: 25				
Bright 3–69; Thomson 3–73; Walker 3–131				

ENGLAND: 82 for 1

Amiss	not out		28	
Brearley*	c Walters	b O'Keeffe	44	(75–1)
Woolmer	not out		0	
Extras: 10				

England made light work of the Aussies courtesy of another ton from Woolmer and a 6-wicket haul in Australia's second innings from his Kent colleague, Underwood.

ENGLAND won by 9 wickets to lead the series 1–0.

3RD TEST: at Nottingham; July 28, 29, 30, August 1, and 2 1977; Australia won the toss

AUSTRALIA: 243

McCosker	c Brearley	b Hendrick	51	(101–2)
Davis	c Botham	b Underwood	33	(79–1)
Chappell*		b Botham	19	(131–3)
Hookes	c Hendrick	b Willis	17	(133–4)
Walters	c Hendrick	b Botham	11	(153–5)
Robinson	c Brearley	b Greig	11	(153–6)
Marsh	lbw	b Botham	0	(153–7)
O'Keeffe	not out		48	
Walker	c Hendrick	b Botham	0	(155–8)
Thomson	c Knott	b Botham	21	(196–9)
Pascoe	c Greig	b Hendrick	20	(243)
Extras: 12				

Botham 5–74

AUSTRALIA: 309

McCosker	c Brearley	b Willis	107	(240–5)
Davis	c Greig	b Willis	9	(18–1)
Chappell*		b Hendrick	27	(60–2)
Hookes	lbw	b Hendrick	42	(154–3)
Walters	c Randall	b Greig	28	(204–4)
Robinson	lbw	b Underwood	34	(270–7)
Marsh	c Greig	b Willis	0	(240–6)
O'Keeffe	not out		21	
Walker		b Willis	17	(307–8)
Thomson		b Willis	0	(308–9)
Pascoe	c Hendrick	b Underwood	0	(309)
Extras: 24				

Willis 5–88

ENGLAND: 364

Brearley*	c Hookes	b Pascoe	15	(34–1)
Boycott	c McCosker	b Thomson	107	(297–6)
Woolmer	lbw	b Pascoe	0	(34–2)
Randall	run out		13	(52–3)
Greig		b Thomson	11	(64–4)
Miller	c Robinson	b Pascoe	13	(82–5)
Knott	c Davis	b Thomson	135	(326–7)
Botham		b Walker	25	(357–9)
Underwood		b Pascoe	7	(357–8)
Hendrick		b Walker	1	(364)
Willis	not out		2	
Extras: 35				

Pascoe 4–80; Thomson 3–103

ENGLAND: 189 for 3

Brearley*		b Walker	81	(154–1)
Boycott	not out		80	
Knott	c O'Keeffe	b Walker	2	(156–2)
Greig		b Walker	0	(158–3)
Randall	not out		19	
Extras: 7				

Walker 3–40

Ian Botham took five wickets on his debut while Boycott returned from his self-imposed exile to stoutly resist Australia and lay the foundations for an easy win.

ENGLAND won by 7 wickets to lead the series 2–0.

4TH TEST: at Leeds; August 11, 12, 13, and 15 1977; England won the toss

ENGLAND: 436

Brearley*	c Marsh	b Thomson	0	(0–1)
Boycott	c Chappell	b Pascoe	191	(436)
Woolmer	c Chappell	b Thomson	37	(82–2)
Randall	lbw	b Pascoe	20	(105–3)
Greig		b Thomson	43	(201–4)
Roope	c Walters	b Thomson	34	(275–5)
Knott	lbw	b Bright	57	(398–6)
Botham		b Bright	0	(398–7)
Underwood	c Bright	b Pascoe	6	(412–8)
Hendrick	c Robinson	b Pascoe	4	(422–9)
Willis	not out		5	
Extras: 39				

Pascoe 4–91; Thomson 4–113

AUSTRALIA: 103

McCosker	run out		27	(52–3)
Davis	lbw	b Hendrick	0	(8–1)
Chappell*	c Brearley	b Hendrick	4	(26–2)
Hookes	lbw	b Botham	24	(57–4)
Walters	c Hendrick	b Botham	4	(66–5)
Robinson	c Greig	b Hendrick	20	(87–7)
Marsh	c Knott	b Botham	2	(77–6)
Bright	not out		9	
Walker	c Knott	b Botham	7	(100–8)
Thomson		b Botham	0	(100–9)
Pascoe		b Hendrick	0	(103)
Extras: 6				

Botham 5–21; Hendrick 4–41

AUSTRALIA: 248

McCosker	c Knott	b Greig	12	(35–2)
Davis	c Knott	b Greig	19	(31–1)
Chappell*	c Greig	b Willis	36	(130–5)
Hookes	lbw	b Hendrick	21	(63–3)
Walters	lbw	b Woolmer	15	(97–4)
Robinson		b Hendrick	20	(167–6)
Marsh	c Randall	b Hendrick	63	(248)
Bright	c Greig	b Hendrick	5	(179–7)
Walker		b Willis	30	(244–8)
Thomson		b Willis	0	(245–9)
Pascoe	not out		0	
Extras: 27				

Hendrick 4–54; Willis 3–32

After Mike Brearley had been dismissed on the third ball of the innings, Boycott proceeded to record his one hundredth first class century in front of his home crowd.

ENGLAND won by an innings and 85 runs to lead the series 3–0.

5TH TEST: at the Oval; August 25, 26, 27, 29, and 30 1977; Australia won the toss

ENGLAND: 214

Brearley*	c Marsh	b Malone	39	(88–2)
Boycott	c McCosker	b Walker	39	(86–1)
Woolmer	lbw	b Thomson	15	(104–4)
Randall	c Marsh	b Malone	3	(104–3)
Greig	c Bright	b Malone	0	(106–5)
Roope		b Thomson	38	(169–8)
Knott	c McCosker	b Malone	6	(122–6)
Lever	lbw	b Malone	3	(130–7)
Underwood		b Thomson	20	(174–9)
Hendrick		b Thomson	15	(214)
Willis	not out		24	
Extras: 12				

Malone 5–63; Thomson 4–87

ENGLAND: 57 for 2

Brearley*	c Serjeant	b Thomson	4	(5–1)
Boycott	not out		25	
Woolmer	c Marsh	b Malone	6	(16–2)
Randall	not out		20	
Extras: 2				

AUSTRALIA: 385

Serjeant	lbw	b Willis	0	(0–1)
McCosker	lbw	b Willis	32	(84–4)
Chappell*	c &	b Underwood	39	(54–2)
Hughes	c Willis	b Hendrick	1	(67–3)
Hookes	c Knott	b Greig	85	(184–6)
Walters		b Willis	4	(104–5)
Marsh	lbw	b Hendrick	57	(236–7)
Bright	lbw	b Willis	16	(252–8)
Walker	not out		78	
Malone		b Lever	46	(352–9)
Thomson		b Willis	17	(385)
Extras: 10				

Willis 5–102

Kim Hughes on his debut spent more than 50 minutes accumulating a mere single. Max Walker's unbeaten 78 was his highest first-class score.

MATCH DRAWN. ENGLAND win the series 3–0.

1ST TEST: at Brisbane; December 1, 2, 3, 5, and 6 1978; Australia won the toss

AUSTRALIA: 116

Wood	c Taylor	b Old	7	(14–3)
Cosier	run out		1	(2–1)
Toohey		b Willis	1	(5–2)
Yallop*	c Gooch	b Willis	7	(22–4)
Hughes	c Taylor	b Botham	4	(24–5)
Laughlin	c sub	b Willis	2	(26–6)
Maclean	not out		33	
Yardley	c Taylor	b Willis	17	(53–7)
Hogg	c Taylor	b Botham	36	(113–8)
Hurst	c Taylor	b Botham	0	(113–9)
Higgs		b Old	1	(116)
Extras: 7				

Willis 4–44; Botham 3–40

AUSTRALIA: 339

Wood	lbw	b Old	19	(49–3)
Cosier		b Willis	0	(0–1)
Toohey	lbw	b Botham	1	(2–2)
Yallop*	c &	b Willis	102	(219–4)
Hughes	c Edmonds	b Willis	129	(339)
Laughlin	lbw	b Old	5	(228–5)
Maclean	lbw	b Miller	15	(261–6)
Yardley	c Brearley	b Miller	16	(310–7)
Hogg		b Botham	16	(339–8)
Hurst		b Botham	0	(339–9)
Higgs	not out		0	
Extras: 36				

Willis 3–69; Botham 3–95

ENGLAND: 286

Boycott	c Hughes	b Hogg	13	(38–2)
Gooch	c Laughlin	b Hogg	2	(2–1)
Randall	c Laughlin	b Hurst	75	(111–3)
Taylor	lbw	b Hurst	20	(120–5)
Brearley*	c Maclean	b Hogg	6	(120–4)
Gower	c Maclean	b Hurst	44	(219–7)
Botham	c Maclean	b Hogg	49	(215–6)
Miller	lbw	b Hogg	27	(266–9)
Edmonds	c Maclean	b Hogg	1	(226–8)
Old	not out		29	
Willis	c Maclean	b Hurst	8	(286)
Extras: 12				

Hogg 6–74; Hurst 4–93

ENGLAND: 170 for 3

Boycott	run out		16	(37–2)
Gooch	c Yardley	b Hogg	2	(16–1)
Randall	not out		74	
Brearley*	c Maclean	b Yardley	13	(74–3)
Gower	not out		48	
Extras: 17				

The hosts' cause was ruined when they were reduced to 26 for 6 in the first innings. Kim Hughes and Graham Yallop at least made amends in the second innings.

ENGLAND won by 7 wickets to lead the series 1–0.

ENGLAND: 309

Boycott	lbw	b Hurst	77	(224–6)
Gooch	c Maclean	b Hogg	1	(3–1)
Randall	c Wood	b Hogg	0	(3–2)
Brearley*	c Maclean	b Dymock	17	(41–3)
Gower		b Hogg	102	(199–4)
Botham	lbw	b Hurst	11	(219–5)
Miller		b Hogg	40	(300–9)
Taylor	c Hurst	b Yardley	12	(253–7)
Lever	c Cosier	b Hurst	14	(295–8)
Willis	c Yallop	b Hogg	2	(309)
Hendrick	not out		7	
Extras: 26				

Hogg 5–65; Hurst 3–70

ENGLAND: 208

Boycott	lbw	b Hogg	23	(58–1)
Gooch	lbw	b Hogg	43	(93–2)
Randall	c Cosier	b Yardley	45	(135–4)
Brearley*	c Maclean	b Hogg	0	(93–3)
Gower	c Maclean	b Hogg	12	(151–5)
Botham	c Wood	b Yardley	30	(176–6)
Miller	c Toohey	b Yardley	25	(201–8)
Lever	c Maclean	b Hurst	10	(201–7)
Taylor	c Maclean	b Hogg	2	(206–9)
Willis	not out		3	
Hendrick		b Dymock	1	(208)
Extras: 14				

Hogg 5–57; Yardley 3–41

AUSTRALIA: 190

Wood	lbw	b Lever	5	(8–1)
Darling	run out		25	(60–4)
Hughes		b Willis	16	(34–2)
Yallop*		b Willis	3	(38–3)
Toohey	not out		81	
Cosier	c Gooch	b Willis	4	(78–5)
Maclean	c Gooch	b Miller	0	(79–6)
Yardley	c Taylor	b Hendrick	12	(100–7)
Hogg	c Taylor	b Willis	18	(128–8)
Dymock		b Hendrick	11	(185–9)
Hurst	c Taylor	b Willis	5	(190)
Extras: 10				

Willis 5–44

AUSTRALIA: 161

Wood	c Taylor	b Lever	64	(143–6)
Darling	c Boycott	b Lever	5	(8–1)
Hughes	c Gooch	b Willis	12	(36–2)
Yallop*	c Taylor	b Hendrick	3	(58–3)
Toohey	c Taylor	b Hendrick	0	(58–4)
Cosier	lbw	b Miller	47	(141–5)
Maclean	c Brearley	b Miller	1	(143–7)
Yardley	c Botham	b Lever	7	(151–9)
Hogg		b Miller	0	(147–8)
Dymock	not out		6	
Hurst		b Lever	5	(161)
Extras: 11				

Lever 4–28; Miller 3–21

Rodney Hogg took ten wickets in only his second test, including David Gower twice, but the latter was the only centurion in another easy triumph for England.

ENGLAND won by 166 runs to lead the series 2–0.

3RD TEST: at Melbourne; December 29 and 30 1978, January 1, 2, and 3 1979; Australia won the toss

AUSTRALIA: 258

Wood	c Emburey	b Miller	100	(250–6)
Darling	run out		33	(65–1)
Hughes	c Taylor	b Botham	0	(65–2)
Yallop*	c Hendrick	b Botham	41	(126–3)
Toohey	c Randall	b Miller	32	(189–4)
Border	c Brearley	b Hendrick	29	(247–5)
Maclean		b Botham	8	(258)
Hogg	c Randall	b Miller	0	(250–7)
Dymock		b Hendrick	0	(251–8)
Hurst		b Hendrick	0	(252–9)
Higgs	not out		1	
Extras: 14				

Miller 3–35; Hendrick 3–50; Botham 3–68

AUSTRALIA: 167

Wood		b Botham	34	(81–2)
Darling	c Randall	b Miller	21	(55–1)
Hughes	c Gower	b Botham	48	(152–6)
Yallop*	c Taylor	b Miller	16	(101–3)
Toohey	c Botham	b Emburey	20	(136–4)
Border	run out		0	(136–5)
Maclean	c Hendrick	b Emburey	10	(167–8)
Hogg		b Botham	1	(157–7)
Dymock	c Brearley	b Hendrick	6	(167–9)
Higgs	st Taylor	b Emburey	0	(167)
Hurst	not out		0	
Extras: 11				

Emburey 3–30; Botham 3–41

ENGLAND: 143

Boycott		b Hogg	1	(2–1)
Brearley*	lbw	b Hogg	1	(3–2)
Randall	lbw	b Hurst	13	(40–3)
Gooch	c Border	b Dymock	25	(52–4)
Gower	lbw	b Dymock	29	(81–5)
Botham	c Darling	b Higgs	22	(100–6)
Miller		b Hogg	7	(120–9)
Taylor		b Hogg	1	(101–7)
Emburey		b Hogg	0	(101–8)
Willis	c Darling	b Dymock	19	(143)
Hendrick	not out		6	
Extras: 19				

Hogg 5–30; Dymock 3–38

ENGLAND: 179

Boycott	lbw	b Hurst	38	(122–4)
Brearley*	c Maclean	b Dymock	0	(1–1)
Randall	lbw	b Hogg	2	(6–2)
Gooch	lbw	b Hogg	40	(71–3)
Gower	lbw	b Dymock	49	(163–6)
Botham	c Maclean	b Higgs	10	(163–5)
Miller	c Hughes	b Higgs	1	(167–7)
Taylor	c Maclean	b Hogg	5	(171–8)
Emburey	not out		7	
Willis	c Yallop	b Hogg	3	(179–9)
Hendrick		b Hogg	0	(179)
Extras: 24				

Hogg 5–36

Graeme Wood was the only person who exceeded fifty while Rodney Hogg's ten-wicket haul this time was in a winning cause against a fragile England.

AUSTRALIA won by 103 runs. England lead the series 2–1.

4TH TEST: at Sydney; January 6, 7, 8, 10, and 11 1979; England won the toss

ENGLAND: 152

Boycott	c Border	b Hurst	8	(18–1)
Brearley*		b Hogg	17	(35–3)
Randall	c Wood	b Hurst	0	(18–2)
Gooch	c Toohey	b Higgs	18	(66–5)
Gower	c Maclean	b Hurst	7	(51–4)
Botham	c Yallop	b Hogg	59	(141–9)
Miller	c Maclean	b Hurst	4	(70–6)
Taylor	c Border	b Higgs	10	(94–7)
Emburey	c Wood	b Higgs	0	(98–8)
Willis	not out		7	
Hendrick		b Hurst	10	(152)
Extras: 12				

Hurst 5–28; Higgs 3–42

ENGLAND: 346

Boycott	lbw	b Hogg	0	(0–1)
Brearley*		b Border	53	(111–2)
Randall	lbw	b Hogg	150	(292–6)
Gooch	c Wood	b Higgs	22	(169–3)
Gower	c Maclean	b Hogg	34	(237–4)
Botham	c Wood	b Higgs	6	(267–5)
Miller	lbw	b Hogg	17	(307–7)
Taylor	not out		21	
Emburey	c Darling	b Higgs	14	(334–8)
Willis	c Toohey	b Higgs	0	(334–9)
Hendrick	c Toohey	b Higgs	7	(346)
Extras: 22				

Higgs 5–148; Hogg 4–67

AUSTRALIA: 294

Wood		b Willis	0	(1–1)
Darling	c Botham	b Miller	91	(178–3)
Hughes	c Emburey	b Willis	48	(126–2)
Yallop*	c Botham	b Hendrick	44	(210–5)
Toohey	c Gooch	b Botham	1	(179–4)
Border	not out		60	
Maclean	lbw	b Emburey	12	(235–6)
Hogg	run out		6	(245–7)
Dymock		b Botham	5	(276–8)
Higgs	c Botham	b Hendrick	11	(290–9)
Hurst	run out		0	(294)
Extras: 16				

AUSTRALIA: 111

Wood	run out		27	(44–2)
Darling	c Gooch	b Hendrick	13	(38–1)
Hughes	c Emburey	b Miller	15	(59–4)
Yallop*	c &	b Hendrick	1	(45–3)
Toohey		b Miller	5	(74–5)
Border	not out		45	
Maclean	c Botham	b Miller	0	(76–6)
Dymock		b Emburey	0	(85–7)
Hogg	c Botham	b Emburey	0	(85–8)
Higgs	lbw	b Emburey	3	(105–9)
Hurst		b Emburey	0	(111)
Extras: 2				

Emburey 4–46; Miller 3–38

When Boycott was dismissed first ball in the second innings, England looked doomed, but Derek 'Arkle' Randall turned the match on its head with his 150.

ENGLAND won by 93 runs to lead the series 3–1.

**5TH TEST: at Adelaide; January 27, 28, 29, 31, and February 1 1979;
Australia won the toss**

ENGLAND: 169

Boycott	c Wright	b Hurst	6	(10–1)
Brearley*	c Wright	b Hogg	2	(12–2)
Randall	c Carlson	b Hurst	4	(18–4)
Gooch	c Hughes	b Hogg	1	(16–3)
Gower	lbw	b Hurst	9	(27–5)
Botham	c Wright	b Higgs	74	(147–9)
Miller	lbw	b Hogg	31	(80–6)
Taylor	run out		4	(113–7)
Emburey		b Higgs	4	(136–8)
Willis	c Darling	b Hogg	24	(169)
Hendrick	not out		0	
Extras: 10				

Hogg 4–26; Hurst 3–65

ENGLAND: 360

Boycott	c Hughes	b Hurst	49	(106–4)
Brearley*	lbw	b Carlson	9	(31–1)
Randall	c Yardley	b Hurst	15	(57–2)
Gooch		b Carlson	18	(97–3)
Gower	lbw	b Higgs	21	(132–6)
Botham	c Yardley	b Hurst	7	(130–5)
Miller	c Wright	b Hurst	64	(267–7)
Taylor	c Wright	b Hogg	97	(336–8)
Emburey		b Hogg	42	(347–9)
Willis	c Wright	b Hogg	12	(360)
Hendrick	not out		3	
Extras: 23				

Hurst 4–97; Hogg 3–59

AUSTRALIA: 164

Darling	c Willis	b Botham	15	(94–6)
Wood	c Randall	b Emburey	35	(114–7)
Hughes	c Emburey	b Hendrick	4	(5–1)
Yallop*		b Hendrick	0	(10–2)
Border	c Taylor	b Botham	11	(22–3)
Carlson	c Taylor	b Botham	0	(24–4)
Yardley		b Botham	28	(72–5)
Wright	lbw	b Emburey	29	(133–9)
Hogg		b Willis	0	(116–8)
Higgs	run out		16	(164)
Hurst	not out		17	
Extras: 9				

Botham 4–42

AUSTRALIA: 160

Darling		b Botham	18	(31–1)
Wood	run out		9	(36–2)
Hughes	c Gower	b Hendrick	46	(120–4)
Yallop*		b Hendrick	36	(115–3)
Border		b Willis	1	(121–5)
Carlson	c Gower	b Hendrick	21	(147–9)
Yardley	c Brearley	b Willis	0	(121–6)
Wright	c Emburey	b Miller	0	(124–7)
Hogg		b Miller	2	(130–8)
Higgs	not out		3	
Hurst		b Willis	13	(160)
Extras: 11				

Hendrick 3–19; Willis 3–41

Australia's weak batting capitulated again with no-one reaching 50 in either innings. Bob Taylor meanwhile recorded his highest test innings, falling just short of 100.

ENGLAND won by 205 runs to lead the series 4–1.

6TH TEST: at Sydney; February 10, 11, 12, and 14 1979; Australia won the toss

AUSTRALIA: 198

Wood	c Botham	b Hendrick	15	(19–2)
Hilditch	run out		3	(18–1)
Hughes	c Botham	b Willis	16	(67–3)
Yallop*	c Gower	b Botham	121	(198–9)
Toohey	c Taylor	b Botham	8	(101–4)
Carlson	c Gooch	b Botham	2	(109–5)
Yardley		b Embury	7	(116–6)
Wright	st Taylor	b Emburey	3	(124–7)
Hogg	c Emburey	b Miller	9	(159–8)
Higgs	not out		9	
Hurst		b Botham	0	(198)
Extras: 5				

Botham 4–57

AUSTRALIA: 143

Wood	c Willis	b Miller	29	(48–3)
Hilditch	c Taylor	b Hendrick	1	(8–1)
Hughes	c Gooch	b Emburey	7	(28–2)
Yallop*	c Taylor	b Miller	17	(82–6)
Toohey	c Gooch	b Emburey	0	(48–4)
Carlson	c Botham	b Emburey	0	(48–5)
Yardley	not out		61	
Wright	c Boycott	b Miller	5	(114–7)
Hogg		b Miller	7	(130–8)
Higgs	c Botham	b Emburey	2	(136–9)
Hurst	c &	b Miller	4	(143)
Extras: 10				

Miller 5–44; Emburey 4–52

ENGLAND: 308

Boycott	c Hilditch	b Hurst	19	(37–1)
Brearley*	c Toohey	b Higgs	46	(115–3)
Randall	lbw	b Hogg	7	(46–2)
Gooch	st Wright	b Higgs	74	(182–4)
Gower	c Wright	b Higgs	65	(247–6)
Botham	c Carlson	b Yardley	23	(233–5)
Miller	lbw	b Hurst	18	(270–7)
Taylor	not out		36	
Emburey	c Hilditch	b Hurst	0	(280–8)
Willis		b Higgs	10	(306–9)
Hendrick	c &	b Yardley	0	(308)
Extras: 10				

Higgs 4–69; Hurst 3–58

ENGLAND: 35 for 1

Boycott	c Hughes	b Higgs	13	(31–1)
Brearley*	not out		20	
Randall	not out		0	
Extras: 2				

Yallop hit the match's only century but hapless Australia were undone by the spin of Emburey and Miller in their second innings and suffered another huge defeat.

ENGLAND won by 9 wickets to win the series 5–1.

ENGLAND: 185

Gooch	c Wood	b Lillee	10	(13–1)
Boycott	c Border	b Alderman	27	(57–3)
Woolmer	c Wood	b Lillee	0	(13–2)
Gower	c Yallop	b Lillee	26	(67–4)
Gatting	lbw	b Hogg	52	(159–8)
Willey	c Border	b Alderman	10	(92–5)
Botham*		b Alderman	1	(96–6)
Downton	c Yallop	b Alderman	8	(116–7)
Dilley		b Hogg	34	(185)
Willis	c Marsh	b Hogg	0	(159–9)
Hendrick	not out		6	
Extras: 11				

Alderman 4–68; Lillee 3–34; Hogg 3–47

ENGLAND: 125

Gooch	c Yallop	b Lillee	6	(12–1)
Boycott	c Marsh	b Alderman	4	(12–2)
Woolmer	c Marsh	b Alderman	0	(13–3)
Gower	c sub	b Lillee	28	(94–6)
Gatting	lbw	b Alderman	15	(39–4)
Willey	lbw	b Lillee	13	(61–5)
Botham*	c Border	b Lillee	33	(113–8)
Downton	lbw	b Alderman	3	(109–7)
Dilley	c Marsh	b Alderman	13	(125–9)
Willis	c Chappell	b Lillee	1	(125)
Hendrick	not out		0	
Extras: 9				

Lillee 5–46; Alderman 5–62

AUSTRALIA: 179

Wood	lbw	b Dilley	0	(0–1)
Dyson	c Woolmer	b Willis	5	(21–2)
Yallop		b Hendrick	13	(21–3)
Hughes*	lbw	b Willis	7	(33–4)
Chappell		b Hendrick	17	(64–5)
Border	c &	b Botham	63	(179)
Marsh	c Boycott	b Willis	19	(89–6)
Lawson	c Gower	b Botham	14	(110–7)
Lillee	c Downton	b Dilley	12	(147–8)
Hogg	c Boycott	b Dilley	0	(153–9)
Alderman	not out		12	
Extras: 17				

Dilley 3–38; Willis 3–47

AUSTRALIA: 132 for 6

Wood	c Woolmer	b Willis	8	(20–1)
Dyson	c Downton	b Dilley	38	(80–4)
Yallop	c Gatting	b Botham	6	(40–2)
Hughes*	lbw	b Dilley	22	(77–3)
Chappell	not out		20	
Border		b Dilley	20	(122–5)
Marsh	lbw	b Dilley	0	(122–6)
Lawson	not out		5	
Extras: 13				

Dilley 4–24

Only Allan Border and Mike Gatting reached 50 as neither team could exceed 200 in either innings. For once, Australia just about managed to cope with a small target.

AUSTRALIA won by 4 wickets to lead the series 1–0.

2ND TEST: at Lord's; July 2, 3, 4, 6, and 7 1981; Australia won the toss

ENGLAND: 311

Gooch	c Yallop	b Lawson	44	(60–1)
Boycott	c Alderman	b Lawson	17	(65–2)
Woolmer	c Marsh	b Lawson	21	(298–9)
Gower	c Marsh	b Lawson	27	(134–3)
Gatting	lbw	b Bright	59	(187–4)
Willey	c Border	b Alderman	82	(284–5)
Emburey	run out		31	(293–6)
Botham*	lbw	b Lawson	0	(293–7)
Taylor	c Hughes	b Lawson	0	(293–8)
Dilley	not out		7	
Willis	c Wood	b Lawson	5	(311)
Extras: 18				

Lawson 7–81

ENGLAND: 265 for 8 declared

Gooch	lbw	b Lawson	20	(31–1)
Boycott	c Marsh	b Lillee	60	(178–3)
Woolmer	lbw	b Alderman	9	(55–2)
Gower	c Alderman	b Lillee	89	(217–5)
Gatting	c Wood	b Bright	16	(217–4)
Botham*		b Bright	0	(217–6)
Willey	c Chappell	b Bright	12	(242–7)
Dilley	not out		27	
Taylor		b Lillee	9	(265–8)
Extras: 23				

Bright 3–67; Lillee 3–82

AUSTRALIA: 345

Wood	c Taylor	b Willis	44	(62–1)
Dyson	c Gower	b Botham	7	(62–2)
Yallop		b Dilley	1	(69–3)
Hughes*	c Willis	b Emburey	42	(167–5)
Chappell	c Taylor	b Dilley	2	(81–4)
Border	c Gatting	b Botham	64	(244–6)
Marsh	lbw	b Dilley	47	(257–7)
Bright	lbw	b Emburey	33	(314–9)
Lawson	lbw	b Willis	5	(268–8)
Lillee	not out		40	
Alderman	c Taylor	b Willis	5	(345)
Extras: 55				

Willis 3–50; Dilley 3–106

AUSTRALIA: 90 for 4

Wood	not out		62	
Dyson	lbw	b Dilley	1	(2–1)
Yallop	c Botham	b Willis	3	(11–2)
Hughes*	lbw	b Dilley	4	(17–3)
Chappell	c Taylor	b Botham	5	(62–4)
Border	not out		12	
Extras: 3				

Ian Botham lasted a total of 4 balls en route to a pair and was then relieved of the captaincy. Nobody managed to hit a ton at English cricket's headquarters.

MATCH DRAWN. AUSTRALIA still lead the series 1–0.

3RD TEST: at Leeds; July 16, 17, 18, 20, and 21 1981;
Australia won the toss

AUSTRALIA: 401 for 9 declared

Dyson		b Dilley	102	(196–3)
Wood	lbw	b Botham	34	(55–1)
Chappell	c Taylor	b Willey	27	(149–2)
Hughes*	c &	b Botham	89	(332–5)
Bright		b Dilley	7	(220–4)
Yallop	c Taylor	b Botham	58	(357–7)
Border	lbw	b Botham	8	(354–6)
Marsh		b Botham	28	(401–9)
Lawson	c Taylor	b Botham	13	(396–8)
Lillee	not out		3	
Alderman	not out		0	
Extras: 32				
Botham 6–95				

AUSTRALIA: 111

Dyson	c Taylor	b Willis	34	(68–6)
Wood	c Taylor	b Botham	10	(13–1)
Chappell	c Taylor	b Willis	8	(56–2)
Hughes*	c Botham	b Willis	0	(58–3)
Yallop	c Gatting	b Willis	0	(58–4)
Border		b Old	0	(65–5)
Marsh	c Dilley	b Willis	4	(74–7)
Bright		b Willis	19	(111)
Lawson	c Taylor	b Willis	1	(75–8)
Lillee	c Gatting	b Willis	17	(110–9)
Alderman	not out		0	
Extras: 18				
Willis 8–43				

ENGLAND: 174

Gooch	lbw	b Alderman	2	(12–1)
Boycott		b Lawson	12	(42–3)
Brearley*	c Marsh	b Alderman	10	(40–2)
Gower	c Marsh	b Lawson	24	(84–4)
Gatting	lbw	b Lillee	15	(87–5)
Willey		b Lawson	8	(112–6)
Botham	c Marsh	b Lillee	50	(166–8)
Taylor	c Marsh	b Lillee	5	(148–7)
Dilley	c &	b Lillee	13	(174)
Old	c Border	b Alderman	0	(167–9)
Willis	not out		1	
Extras: 34				
Lillee 4–49; Lawson 3–32; Alderman 3–59				

ENGLAND: 356

Gooch	c Alderman	b Lillee	0	(0–1)
Boycott	lbw	b Alderman	46	(133–6)
Brearley*	c Alderman	b Lillee	14	(18–2)
Gower	c Border	b Alderman	9	(37–3)
Gatting	lbw	b Alderman	1	(41–4)
Willey	c Dyson	b Lillee	33	(105–5)
Botham	not out		149	
Taylor	c Bright	b Alderman	1	(135–7)
Dilley		b Alderman	56	(252–8)
Old		b Lawson	29	(319–9)
Willis	c Border	b Alderman	2	(356)
Extras: 16				
Alderman 6–135; Lillee 3–94				

For all of Botham's heroics, Australia were poised for success at 56 for 1 in the second innings. Then Bob Willis ripped them apart as they slumped to 75 for 8.

ENGLAND won by 18 runs to level the series at 1–1.

ENGLAND: 189

Boycott	c Marsh	b Alderman	13	(29–1)
Brearley*	c Border	b Lillee	48	(101–4)
Gower	c Hogg	b Alderman	0	(29–2)
Gooch	c Marsh	b Bright	21	(60–3)
Gatting	c Alderman	b Lillee	21	(126–5)
Willey		b Bright	16	(145–6)
Botham		b Alderman	26	(161–7)
Emburey		b Hogg	3	(165–9)
Taylor		b Alderman	0	(161–8)
Old	not out		11	
Willis	c Marsh	b Alderman	13	(189)
Extras: 17				
Alderman 5–42				

ENGLAND: 219

Boycott	c Marsh	b Bright	29	(89–3)
Brearley*	lbw	b Lillee	13	(18–1)
Gower	c Border	b Bright	23	(52–2)
Gooch		b Bright	21	(98–4)
Gatting		b Bright	39	(167–8)
Willey		b Bright	5	(110–5)
Botham	c Marsh	b Lillee	3	(115–6)
Old	c Marsh	b Alderman	23	(154–7)
Emburey	not out		37	
Taylor	lbw	b Alderman	8	(217–9)
Willis	c Marsh	b Alderman	2	(219)
Extras: 16				
Bright 5–68; Alderman 3–65				

AUSTRALIA: 258

Wood	run out		38	(115–4)
Dyson		b Old	1	(5–1)
Border	c Taylor	b Old	2	(14–2)
Bright	lbw	b Botham	27	(62–3)
Hughes*	lbw	b Old	47	(166–5)
Yallop		b Emburey	30	(203–6)
Kent	c Willis	b Emburey	46	(253–8)
Marsh		b Emburey	2	(220–7)
Lillee		b Emburey	18	(258)
Hogg	run out		0	(253–9)
Alderman	not out		3	
Extras: 44				
Emburey 4–43; Old 3–44				

AUSTRALIA: 121

Wood	lbw	b Old	2	(2–1)
Dyson	lbw	b Willis	13	(19–2)
Border	c Gatting	b Emburey	40	(105–5)
Hughes*	c Emburey	b Willis	5	(29–3)
Yallop	c Botham	b Emburey	30	(87–4)
Kent		b Botham	10	(121–9)
Marsh		b Botham	4	(114–6)
Bright	lbw	b Botham	0	(114–7)
Lillee	c Taylor	b Botham	3	(120–8)
Hogg	not out		0	
Alderman		b Botham	0	(121)
Extras: 14				
Botham 5–11				

Mike Brearley was actually the match's top scorer with 48, but it took inspired bowling from Botham to dispose of the tourists. Botham ended with 5 for 1 in 28 balls.

ENGLAND won by 29 runs to lead the series 2–1.

5TH TEST: at Manchester; August 13, 14, 15, 16, and 17 1981; England won the toss

ENGLAND: 231

Gooch	lbw	b Lillee	10	(25–2)
Boycott	c Marsh	b Alderman	10	(19–1)
Tavare	c Alderman	b Whitney	69	(175–9)
Gower	c Yallop	b Whitney	23	(57–3)
Brearley*	lbw	b Alderman	2	(62–4)
Gatting	c Border	b Lillee	32	(109–5)
Botham	c Bright	b Lillee	0	(109–6)
Knott	c Border	b Alderman	13	(131–7)
Emburey	c Border	b Alderman	1	(137–8)
Allott	not out		52	
Willis	c Hughes	b Lillee	11	(231)
Extras: 8				

Lillee 4–55; Alderman 4–88

ENGLAND: 404

Gooch		b Alderman	5	(7–1)
Boycott	lbw	b Alderman	37	(79–2)
Tavare	c Kent	b Alderman	78	(282–7)
Gower	c Bright	b Lillee	1	(80–3)
Gatting	lbw	b Alderman	11	(98–4)
Brearley*	c Marsh	b Alderman	3	(104–5)
Botham	c Marsh	b Whitney	118	(253–6)
Knott	c Dyson	b Lillee	59	(356–8)
Emburey	c Kent	b Whitney	57	(396–9)
Allott	c Hughes	b Bright	14	(404)
Willis	not out		5	
Extras: 16				

Alderman 5–109

AUSTRALIA: 130

Wood	lbw	b Allott	19	(24–4)
Dyson	c Botham	b Willis	0	(20–1)
Hughes*	lbw	b Willis	4	(24–2)
Yallop	c Botham	b Willis	0	(24–3)
Kent	c Knott	b Emburey	52	(104–7)
Border	c Gower	b Botham	11	(58–5)
Marsh	c Botham	b Willis	1	(59–6)
Bright	c Knott	b Botham	22	(130)
Lillee	c Gooch	b Botham	13	(125–8)
Whitney		b Allott	0	(126–9)
Alderman	not out		2	
Extras: 6				

Willis 4–63; Botham 3–28

AUSTRALIA: 402

Dyson	run out		5	(7–1)
Wood	c Knott	b Allott	6	(24–2)
Hughes*	lbw	b Botham	43	(119–3)
Yallop		b Emburey	114	(198–4)
Border	not out		123	
Kent	c Brearley	b Emburey	2	(206–5)
Marsh	c Knott	b Willis	47	(296–6)
Bright	c Knott	b Willis	5	(322–7)
Lillee	c Botham	b Allott	28	(373–8)
Alderman	lbw	b Botham	0	(378–9)
Whitney	c Gatting	b Willis	0	(402)
Extras: 29				

Willis 3–96

Two hugely contrasting innings from Botham and Tavare paved the way for victory, but a Border-inspired Australia made a bold attempt at chasing the target of 502.

ENGLAND won by 103 runs to lead the series 3–1.

6TH TEST: at the Oval; August 27, 28, 29, 31, and September 1 1981; England won the toss

AUSTRALIA: 352

Wood	c Brearley	b Botham	66	(120–1)
Kent	c Gatting	b Botham	54	(125–2)
Hughes*	hit wicket	b Botham	31	(199–4)
Yallop	c Botham	b Willis	26	(169–3)
Border	not out		106	
Wellham		b Willis	24	(260–5)
Marsh	c Botham	b Willis	12	(280–6)
Bright	c Brearley	b Botham	3	(303–7)
Lillee		b Willis	11	(319–8)
Alderman		b Botham	0	(320–9)
Whitney		b Botham	4	(352)
Extras: 15				

Botham 6–125; Willis 4–91

AUSTRALIA: 344 for 9 declared

Wood	c Knott	b Hendrick	21	(41–3)
Kent	c Brearley	b Botham	7	(26–1)
Hughes*	lbw	b Hendrick	6	(36–2)
Yallop		b Hendrick	35	(104–4)
Border	c Tavare	b Emburey	84	(205–5)
Wellham	lbw	b Botham	103	(343–8)
Marsh	c Gatting	b Botham	52	(291–6)
Bright		b Botham	11	(332–7)
Lillee	not out		8	
Whitney	c Botham	b Hendrick	0	(344–9)
Extras: 17				

Hendrick 4–82; Botham 4–128

ENGLAND: 314

Boycott	c Yallop	b Lillee	137	(293–7)
Larkins	c Alderman	b Lillee	34	(61–1)
Tavare	c Marsh	b Lillee	24	(131–2)
Gatting		b Lillee	53	(246–3)
Brearley*	c Bright	b Alderman	0	(248–4)
Parker	c Kent	b Alderman	0	(248–5)
Botham	c Yallop	b Lillee	3	(256–6)
Knott		b Lillee	36	(314)
Emburey	lbw	b Lillee	0	(293–8)
Willis		b Alderman	3	(302–9)
Hendrick	not out		0	
Extras: 24				

Lillee 7–89; Alderman 3–84

ENGLAND: 261 for 7

Boycott	lbw	b Lillee	0	(0–1)
Larkins	c Alderman	b Lillee	24	(88–3)
Tavare	c Kent	b Whitney	8	(18–2)
Gatting	c Kent	b Lillee	56	(101–4)
Parker	c Kent	b Alderman	13	(127–5)
Brearley*	c Marsh	b Lillee	51	(237–7)
Botham	lbw	b Alderman	16	(144–6)
Knott	not out		70	
Emburey	not out		5	
Extras: 18				

Lillee 4–70

Botham took 10 wickets, Lillee grabbed 11 and Dirk Wellham hit a century on his debut in this fascinating end to an historic summer, dubbed 'Botham's Ashes'.

MATCH DRAWN. ENGLAND win the series 3–1.

1ST TEST: at Perth; November 12, 13, 14, 16, and 17 1982; Australia won the toss

ENGLAND: 411

Cook	c Dyson	b Lillee	1	(14–1)
Tavare	c Hughes	b Yardley	89	(304–5)
Gower	c Dyson	b Alderman	72	(109–2)
Lamb	c Marsh	b Yardley	46	(189–3)
Botham	c Marsh	b Lawson	12	(204–4)
Randall	c Wood	b Yardley	78	(323–6)
Miller	c Marsh	b Lillee	30	(357–8)
Pringle		b Lillee	0	(342–7)
Taylor	not out		29	
Willis*	c Lillee	b Yardley	26	(406–9)
Cowans		b Yardley	4	(411)

Extras: 24

Yardley 5–107; Lillee 3–96

ENGLAND: 358

Cook	c Border	b Lawson	7	(10–1)
Tavare	c Chappell	b Yardley	9	(77–3)
Gower	lbw	b Lillee	28	(51–2)
Lamb	c Marsh	b Lawson	56	(151–5)
Botham		b Lawson	0	(80–4)
Randall		b Lawson	115	(292–8)
Taylor		b Yardley	31	(228–6)
Miller	c Marsh	b Yardley	0	(242–7)
Pringle	not out		47	
Willis*		b Lawson	0	(292–9)
Cowans	lbw	b Chappell	36	(358)

Extras: 29

Lawson 5–108; Yardley 3–101

AUSTRALIA: 424 for 9

Wood	c &	b Willis	29	(63–1)
Dyson	lbw	b Miller	52	(123–3)
Border	c Taylor	b Botham	8	(76–2)
Chappell*	c Lamb	b Willis	117	(311–5)
Hughes	c Willis	b Miller	62	(264–4)
Hookes	lbw	b Miller	56	(374–7)
Marsh	c Cook	b Botham	0	(311–6)
Lawson		b Miller	50	(414–8)
Yardley	c Lamb	b Willis	17	(424–9)
Lillee	not out		2	

Extras: 31

Miller 4–70; Willis 3–95

AUSTRALIA: 73 for 2

Wood	c Taylor	b Willis	0	(2–1)
Dyson	c Cowans	b Willis	12	(22–2)
Border	not out		32	
Chappell*	not out		22	

Extras: 7

Terry Alderman's Ashes were ruined when he foolishly tackled a pitch invader. Meanwhile, Tavare irritated the hosts with an unprecedented display of slow scoring.

MATCH DRAWN. The series remained level at 0–0.

2ND TEST: at Brisbane; November 26, 27, 28, 30, and December 1 1982; Australia won the toss

ENGLAND: 219

Tavare	c Hughes	b Lawson	1	(13–2)
Fowler	c Yardley	b Lawson	7	(8–1)
Gower	c Wessels	b Lawson	18	(63–3)
Lamb	c Marsh	b Lawson	72	(152–5)
Botham	c Rackemann	b Yardley	40	(141–4)
Randall	c Lawson	b Rackemann	37	(191–8)
Miller	c Marsh	b Lawson	0	(152–6)
Taylor	c Lawson	b Rackemann	1	(178–7)
Hemmings	not out		15	
Willis*	c Thomson	b Yardley	1	(195–9)
Cowans	c Marsh	b Lawson	10	(219)
Extras: 17				

Lawson 6–47

ENGLAND: 309

Tavare	c Marsh	b Lawson	13	(54–1)
Fowler	c Marsh	b Thomson	83	(194–5)
Gower	c Marsh	b Thomson	34	(144–2)
Lamb	c Wessels	b Thomson	12	(165–3)
Randall	c Yardley	b Thomson	4	(169–4)
Botham	c Marsh	b Thomson	15	(201–6)
Miller	c Marsh	b Lawson	60	(295–9)
Taylor	c Hookes	b Lawson	3	(226–7)
Hemmings		b Lawson	18	(285–8)
Willis*	not out		10	
Cowans	c Marsh	b Lawson	5	(309)
Extras: 52				

Thomson 5–73; Lawson 5–87

AUSTRALIA: 341

Wessels		b Willis	162	(341)
Dyson		b Botham	1	(4–1)
Border	c Randall	b Willis	0	(11–2)
Chappell*	run out		53	(94–3)
Hughes	c Taylor	b Botham	0	(99–4)
Hookes	c Taylor	b Miller	28	(130–5)
Marsh	c Taylor	b Botham	11	(171–6)
Yardley	c Tavare	b Willis	53	(271–7)
Lawson	c Hemmings	b Willis	6	(310–8)
Rackemann		b Willis	4	(332–9)
Thomson	not out		5	
Extras: 18				

Willis 5–66; Botham 3–105

AUSTRALIA: 190 for 3

Wessels		b Hemmings	46	(83–3)
Dyson	retired hurt		4	
Border	c Botham	b Hemmings	15	(60–1)
Chappell*	c Lamb	b Cowans	8	(77–2)
Hughes	not out		39	
Hookes	not out		66	
Extras: 12				

Kepler Wessels scored a century in his debut test innings while Geoff Lawson celebrated the capture of 11 wickets, assisted by Rodney Marsh who took 9 catches.

AUSTRALIA won by 7 wickets to lead the series 1–0.

3RD TEST: at Adelaide; December 10, 11, 12, 14, and 15 1982; England won the toss

AUSTRALIA: 438

Wessels	c Taylor	b Botham	44	(76–1)
Dyson	c Taylor	b Botham	44	(138–2)
Chappell*	c Gower	b Willis	115	(264–3)
Hughes	run out		88	(315–5)
Lawson	c Botham	b Willis	2	(270–4)
Border	c Taylor	b Pringle	26	(355–6)
Hookes	c Botham	b Hemmings	37	(391–8)
Marsh	c Hemmings	b Pringle	3	(359–7)
Yardley	c Gower	b Botham	38	(430–9)
Hogg	not out		14	
Thomson	c &	b Botham	3	(438)
Extras: 24				

Botham 4–112

AUSTRALIA: 83 for 2

Wessels	c Taylor	b Botham	1	(3–1)
Dyson	not out		37	
Lawson	c Randall	b Willis	14	(37–2)
Chappell*	not out		26	
Extras: 5				

ENGLAND: 216

Tavare	c Marsh	b Hogg	1	(1–1)
Fowler	c Marsh	b Lawson	11	(21–2)
Gower	c Marsh	b Lawson	60	(140–3)
Lamb	c Marsh	b Lawson	82	(181–4)
Botham	c Wessels	b Thomson	35	(213–8)
Randall		b Lawson	0	(181–5)
Miller	c Yardley	b Hogg	7	(194–6)
Taylor	c Chappell	b Yardley	2	(199–7)
Pringle	not out		1	
Hemmings		b Thomson	0	(213–9)
Willis*		b Thomson	1	(216)
Extras: 16				

Lawson 4–56; Thomson 3–51

ENGLAND: 304

Tavare	c Wessels	b Thomson	0	(11–1)
Fowler	c Marsh	b Lawson	37	(90–2)
Gower		b Hogg	114	(247–5)
Lamb	c Chappell	b Yardley	8	(118–3)
Botham	c Dyson	b Yardley	58	(236–4)
Randall	c Marsh	b Lawson	17	(272–6)
Miller	lbw	b Lawson	17	(277–7)
Pringle	c Marsh	b Thomson	9	(289–8)
Taylor	not out		3	
Hemmings	c Wessels	b Lawson	0	(290–9)
Willis*	c Marsh	b Lawson	10	(304)
Extras: 31				

Lawson 5–66

Lawson could only manage nine wickets this time, while Marsh had to settle for eight catches as England were forced to follow on, en route to a heavy defeat.

AUSTRALIA won by 8 wickets to lead the series 2–0.

4TH TEST: at Melbourne; December 26, 27, 28, 29, and 30 1982; Australia won the toss

ENGLAND: 284

Cook	c Chappell	b Thomson	10	(25–2)
Fowler	c Chappell	b Hogg	4	(11–1)
Tavare	c Yardley	b Thomson	89	(217–4)
Gower	c Marsh	b Hogg	18	(56–3)
Lamb	c Dyson	b Yardley	83	(227–5)
Botham	c Wessels	b Yardley	27	(259–6)
Miller	c Border	b Yardley	10	(262–7)
Pringle	c Wessels	b Hogg	9	(278–9)
Taylor	c Marsh	b Yardley	1	(268–8)
Willis*	not out		6	
Cowans	c Lawson	b Hogg	3	(284)

Extras: 24

Hogg 4–69; Yardley 4–89

ENGLAND: 294

Cook	c Yardley	b Thomson	26	(40–1)
Fowler		b Hogg	65	(128–4)
Tavare		b Hogg	0	(41–2)
Gower	c Marsh	b Lawson	3	(45–3)
Lamb	c Marsh	b Hogg	26	(129–5)
Botham	c Chappell	b Thomson	46	(201–7)
Miller	lbw	b Lawson	14	(160–6)
Pringle	c Marsh	b Lawson	42	(280–9)
Taylor	lbw	b Thomson	37	(262–8)
Willis*	not out		8	
Cowans		b Lawson	10	(294)

Extras: 17

Lawson 4–66; Hogg 3–64; Thomson 3–74

AUSTRALIA: 287

Wessels		b Willis	47	(83–3)
Dyson	lbw	b Cowans	21	(55–1)
Chappell*	c Lamb	b Cowans	0	(55–2)
Hughes		b Willis	66	(261–6)
Border		b Botham	2	(89–4)
Hookes	c Taylor	b Pringle	53	(180–5)
Marsh		b Willis	53	(276–7)
Yardley		b Miller	9	(276–8)
Lawson	c Fowler	b Miller	0	(278–9)
Hogg	not out		8	
Thomson		b Miller	1	(287)

Extras: 27

Willis 3–38; Miller 3–44

AUSTRALIA: 288

Wessels		b Cowans	14	(37–1)
Dyson	c Tavare	b Botham	31	(71–3)
Chappell*	c sub	b Cowans	2	(39–2)
Hughes	c Taylor	b Miller	48	(171–4)
Hookes	c Willis	b Cowans	68	(173–5)
Border	not out		62	
Marsh	lbw	b Cowans	13	(190–6)
Yardley		b Cowans	0	(190–7)
Lawson	c Cowans	b Pringle	7	(202–8)
Hogg	lbw	b Cowans	4	(218–9)
Thomson	c Miller	b Botham	21	(288)

Extras: 18

Cowans 6–77

Nobody could muster a ton in this epic clash. Border and Thomson actually declined 29 singles before Thommo succumbed to a bizarre catch by Miller via Tavare.

ENGLAND won by 3 runs. AUSTRALIA still lead the series 2–1.

5TH TEST: at Sydney; January 2, 3, 4, 6, and 7 1983; Australia won the toss

AUSTRALIA: 314

Wessels	c Willis	b Botham	19	(39–1)
Dyson	c Taylor	b Hemmings	79	(210–5)
Chappell*	lbw	b Willis	35	(96–2)
Hughes	c Cowans	b Botham	29	(150–3)
Hookes	c Botham	b Hemmings	17	(173–4)
Border	c Miller	b Hemmings	89	(314)
Marsh	c &	b Miller	3	(219–6)
Yardley		b Cowans	24	(262–7)
Lawson	c &	b Botham	6	(283–8)
Thomson	c Lamb	b Botham	0	(291–9)
Hogg	not out		0	
Extras: 13				

Botham 4–75; Hemmings 3–68

AUSTRALIA: 382

Wessels	lbw	b Botham	53	(82–3)
Dyson	c Gower	b Willis	2	(23–1)
Chappell*	c Randall	b Hemmings	11	(38–2)
Hughes	c Botham	b Hemmings	137	(358–8)
Hookes	lbw	b Miller	19	(113–4)
Border	c Botham	b Cowans	83	(262–5)
Marsh	c Taylor	b Miller	41	(350–6)
Yardley	c Botham	b Hemmings	0	(357–7)
Lawson	not out		13	
Thomson	c Gower	b Miller	12	(382–9)
Hogg	run out		0	(382)
Extras: 11				

Hemmings 3–116; Miller 3–133

ENGLAND: 237

Cook	c Chappell	b Hogg	8	(23–2)
Tavare		b Lawson	0	(8–1)
Gower	c Chappell	b Lawson	70	(169–6)
Lamb		b Lawson	0	(24–3)
Randall		b Thomson	70	(146–4)
Botham	c Wessels	b Thomson	5	(163–5)
Miller	lbw	b Thomson	34	(237)
Taylor	lbw	b Thomson	0	(170–7)
Hemmings	c Border	b Yardley	29	(220–8)
Willis*	c Border	b Thomson	1	(232–9)
Cowans	not out		0	
Extras: 20				

Thomson 5–50; Lawson 3–70

AUSTRALIA: 314 for 7

Cook	lbw	b Lawson	2	(3–1)
Tavare	lbw	b Yardley	16	(55–2)
Hemmings	c Marsh	b Yardley	95	(196–5)
Gower	c Hookes	b Yardley	24	(104–3)
Lamb	c &	b Yardley	29	(155–4)
Randall		b Thomson	44	(260–6)
Botham	lbw	b Thomson	32	(261–7)
Miller	not out		21	
Taylor	not out		28	
Extras: 23				

Yardley 4–139

Kim Hughes, traumatised by the summer of 1981, ironically ensured the re-capture of the Ashes with his century. Eddie Hemmings recorded his highest test score.

MATCH DRAWN. AUSTRALIA win the series 2–1.

AUSTRALIA: 331

Wood	lbw	b Allott	14	(23–1)
Hilditch	c Downton	b Gooch	119	(201–3)
Wessels	c Botham	b Emburey	36	(155–2)
Border*	c Botham	b Cowans	32	(229–5)
Boon	lbw	b Gooch	14	(229–4)
Ritchie		b Botham	46	(326–7)
Phillips	c Gower	b Emburey	30	(284–6)
McDermott		b Botham	18	(331)
O'Donnell	lbw	b Botham	0	(326–8)
Lawson	c Downton	b Allott	0	(327–9)
Thomson	not out		4	
Extras: 18				

Botham 3–86

AUSTRALIA: 324

Wood	c Lamb	b Botham	3	(5–1)
Hilditch	c Robinson	b Emburey	80	(151–3)
Wessels		b Emburey	64	(144–2)
Border*	c Downton	b Botham	8	(159–4)
Boon		b Cowans	22	(192–6)
Ritchie		b Emburey	1	(160–5)
Phillips	c Lamb	b Botham	91	(307–8)
O'Donnell	c Downton	b Botham	24	(272–7)
Lawson	c Downton	b Emburey	15	(318–9)
McDermott	c Gooch	b Emburey	6	(324)
Thomson	not out		2	
Extras: 8				

Emburey 5–82; Botham 4–107

ENGLAND: 533

Gooch	lbw	b McDermott	5	(14–1)
Robinson	c Boon	b Lawson	175	(417–6)
Gower*	c Phillips	b McDermott	17	(50–2)
Gatting	c Hilditch	b McDermott	53	(186–3)
Lamb		b O'Donnell	38	(264–4)
Botham		b Thomson	60	(344–5)
Willey	c Hilditch	b Lawson	36	(422–7)
Downton	c Border	b McDermott	54	(533)
Emburey		b Lawson	21	(462–8)
Allott	c Boon	b Thomson	12	(484–9)
Cowans	not out		22	
Extras: 40				

McDermott 4–134; Lawson 3–117

ENGLAND: 123 for 5

Gooch	lbw	b O'Donnell	28	(71–3)
Robinson		b Lawson	21	(44–1)
Gower*	c Border	b O'Donnell	5	(59–2)
Gatting	c Phillips	b Lawson	12	(83–4)
Lamb	not out		31	
Botham		b O'Donnell	12	(110–5)
Willey	not out		3	
Extras: 11				

O'Donnell 3–37

Tim Robinson made light work of Australia's pace attack to lay the foundations for first blood. The impressive Andy Hilditch didn't deserve to be on the losing side.

ENGLAND won by 5 wickets to lead the series 1–0.

2ND TEST: at Lord's; June 27, 28, 29, July 1, and 2 1985; Australia won the toss

ENGLAND: 290

Gooch	lbw	b McDermott	30	(51–2)
Robinson	lbw	b McDermott	6	(26–1)
Gower*	c Border	b McDermott	86	(179–4)
Gatting	lbw	b Lawson	14	(99–3)
Lamb	c Phillips	b Lawson	47	(211–6)
Botham	c Ritchie	b Lawson	5	(184–5)
Downton	c Wessels	b McDermott	21	(241–7)
Emburey	lbw	b O'Donnell	33	(273–8)
Edmonds	c Border	b McDermott	21	(290)
Foster	c Wessels	b McDermott	3	(283–9)
Allott	not out		1	
Extras: 23				

McDermott 6–70; Lawson 3–91

ENGLAND: 261

Gooch	c Phillips	b McDermott	17	(32–1)
Robinson		b Holland	12	(34–2)
Emburey		b Lawson	20	(57–4)
Allott		b Lawson	0	(38–3)
Gower*	c Phillips	b McDermott	22	(77–5)
Gatting	not out		75	
Lamb	c Holland	b Lawson	9	(98–6)
Botham	c Border	b Holland	85	(229–7)
Downton	c Boon	b Holland	0	(229–8)
Edmonds	c Boon	b Holland	1	(261–9)
Foster	c Border	b Holland	0	(261)
Extras: 20				

Holland 5–68; Lawson 3–86

AUSTRALIA: 425

Wood	c Emburey	b Allott	8	(11–1)
Hilditch		b Foster	14	(24–2)
Wessels	lbw	b Botham	11	(80–3)
Border*	c Gooch	b Botham	196	(398–7)
Boon	c Downton	b Botham	4	(101–4)
Ritchie	lbw	b Botham	94	(317–5)
Phillips	c Edmonds	b Botham	21	(347–6)
O'Donnell	c Lamb	b Edmonds	48	(414–8)
Lawson	not out		5	
McDermott	run out		9	(425–9)
Holland		b Edmonds	0	(425)
Extras: 15				

Botham 5–109

AUSTRALIA: 127 for 6

Wood	c Lamb	b Botham	6	(9–2)
Hilditch	c Lamb	b Botham	0	(0–1)
Wessels	run out		28	(63–4)
Ritchie		b Allott	2	(22–3)
Border*	not out		41	
Boon		b Edmonds	1	(65–5)
Phillips	c Edmonds	b Emburey	29	(116–6)
O'Donnell	not out		9	
Extras: 11				

Allan Border's harvest of 237 runs was the difference between the two teams, though his troops characteristically struggled to overcome the small target of 127.

AUSTRALIA won by 4 wickets to level the series 1–1.

3RD TEST: at Nottingham; July 11, 12, 13, 15, and 16 1985; England won the toss

ENGLAND: 456

Gooch	c Wessels	b Lawson	70	(171–2)
Robinson	c Border	b Lawson	38	(55–1)
Gower*	c Phillips	b O'Donnell	166	(365–4)
Gatting	run out		74	(358–3)
Lamb	lbw	b Lawson	17	(416–5)
Botham	c O'Donnell	b McDermott	38	(416–6)
Downton	c Ritchie	b McDermott	0	(419–7)
Sidebottom	c O'Donnell	b Lawson	2	(419–8)
Emburey	not out		16	
Edmonds		b Holland	12	(443–9)
Allott	c Border	b Lawson	7	(456)
Extras: 16				

Lawson 5–103

ENGLAND: 196 for 2

Gooch	c Ritchie	b McDermott	48	(79–1)
Robinson	not out		77	
Gower*	c Phillips	b McDermott	17	(107–2)
Gatting	not out		35	
Extras: 19				

AUSTRALIA: 539

Wood	c Robinson	b Botham	172	(424–6)
Hilditch	lbw	b Allott	47	(87–1)
Holland	lbw	b Sidebottom	10	(128–2)
Wessels	c Downton	b Emburey	33	(205–3)
Border*	c Botham	b Edmonds	23	(234–4)
Boon	c &	b Emburey	15	(263–5)
Ritchie		b Edmonds	146	(491–8)
Phillips		b Emburey	2	(437–7)
O'Donnell	c Downton	b Botham	46	(539–9)
Lawson	c Gooch	b Botham	18	(539)
McDermott	not out		0	
Extras: 27				

Botham 3–107; Emburey 3–129

David Gower, Greg Ritchie and Graeme Wood feasted themselves in this high-scoring, weather-interrupted draw in which Arnie Sidebottom won his only cap.

MATCH DRAWN. The series remained level at 1–1.

4TH TEST: at Manchester; August 1, 2, 3, 5, and 6 1985; England won the toss

AUSTRALIA: 257

Wessels	c Botham	b Emburey	34	(71–1)
Hilditch	c Gower	b Edmonds	49	(97–2)
Boon	c Lamb	b Botham	61	(198–6)
Border*	st Downton	b Edmonds	8	(118–3)
Ritchie	c &	b Edmonds	4	(122–4)
Phillips	c Downton	b Botham	36	(193–5)
Matthews		b Botham	4	(211–7)
O'Donnell		b Edmonds	45	(257)
Lawson	c Downton	b Botham	4	(223–8)
McDermott	lbw	b Emburey	0	(224–9)
Holland	not out		5	
Extras: 7				

Edmonds 4–40; Botham 4–79

AUSTRALIA: 340 for 5

Hilditch		b Emburey	40	(85–2)
Matthews	c &	b Edmonds	17	(38–1)
Wessels	c &	b Emburey	50	(126–3)
Border*	not out		146	
Boon		b Emburey	7	(138–4)
Ritchie		b Emburey	31	(213–5)
Phillips	not out		39	
Extras: 10				

Emburey 4–99

ENGLAND: 482 for 9 declared

Gooch	lbw	b McDermott	74	(142–2)
Robinson	c Border	b McDermott	10	(21–1)
Gower*	c Hilditch	b McDermott	47	(148–3)
Gatting	c Phillips	b McDermott	160	(430–6)
Lamb	run out		67	(304–4)
Botham	c O'Donnell	b McDermott	20	(339–5)
Downton		b McDermott	23	(448–7)
Emburey	not out		31	
Edmonds		b McDermott	1	(450–8)
Allott		b McDermott	7	(470–9)
Agnew	not out		2	
Extras: 40				

McDermott 8–141

Craig McDermott's 8 wickets were impressive but they came at a huge cost. It needed the ever-reliable Allan Border to ensure that his team salvaged a draw.

MATCH DRAWN. The series remained level at 1–1.

5TH TEST: at Birmingham; August 15, 16, 17, 19, and 20 1985; England won the toss

AUSTRALIA: 335

Wood	c Edmonds	b Botham	19	(44–1)
Hilditch	c Downton	b Edmonds	39	(92–2)
Wessels	c Downton	b Ellison	83	(191–4)
Border*	c Edmonds	b Ellison	45	(189–3)
Ritchie	c Botham	b Ellison	8	(207–5)
Phillips	c Robinson	b Ellison	15	(218–7)
O'Donnell	c Downton	b Taylor	1	(208–6)
Lawson	run out		53	(335–9)
McDermott	c Gower	b Ellison	35	(276–8)
Thomson	not out		28	
Holland	c Edmonds	b Ellison	0	(335)
Extras: 9				
Ellison 6–77				

AUSTRALIA: 142

Hilditch	c Ellison	b Botham	10	(10–1)
Wood	c Robinson	b Ellison	10	(35–4)
Wessels	c Downton	b Ellison	10	(32–2)
Holland	lbw	b Ellison	0	(32–3)
Border*		b Ellison	2	(36–5)
Ritchie	c Lamb	b Emburey	20	(117–7)
Phillips	c Gower	b Edmonds	59	(113–6)
O'Donnell		b Botham	11	(137–9)
Lawson	c Gower	b Edmonds	3	(120–8)
McDermott	c Edmonds	b Botham	8	(142)
Thomson	not out		4	
Extras: 5				
Ellison 4–27; Botham 3–52				

ENGLAND: 595 for 5 declared

Gooch	c Phillips	b Thomson	19	(38–1)
Robinson		b Lawson	148	(369–2)
Gower*	c Border	b Lawson	215	(463–3)
Gatting	not out		100	
Lamb	c Wood	b McDermott	46	(572–4)
Botham	c Thomson	b McDermott	18	(592–5)
Downton	not out		0	
Extras: 49				

Richard Ellison took 10 wickets and David Gower recorded his career best score, but it took a freak catch by Gower off the boot of Lamb to seal a win on the final day.

ENGLAND won by an innings and 118 runs to lead the series 2–1.

6TH TEST: at the Oval; August 29, 30, 31, and September 2 1985; England won the toss

ENGLAND: 464

Gooch	c &	b McDermott	196	(403–4)
Robinson		b McDermott	3	(20–1)
Gower*	c Bennett	b McDermott	157	(371–2)
Gatting	c Border	b Bennett	4	(376–3)
Emburey	c Wellham	b Lawson	9	(405–5)
Lamb	c McDermott	b Lawson	1	(418–6)
Botham	c Phillips	b Lawson	12	(425–7)
Downton		b McDermott	16	(452–9)
Ellison	c Phillips	b Gilbert	3	(447–8)
Edmonds	lbw	b Lawson	12	(464)
Taylor	not out		1	
Extras: 50				

Lawson 4–101; McDermott 4–108

AUSTRALIA: 241

Wood	lbw	b Botham	22	(35–1)
Hilditch	c Gooch	b Botham	17	(52–2)
Wessels		b Emburey	12	(56–3)
Border*		b Edmonds	38	(109–5)
Wellham	c Downton	b Ellison	13	(101–4)
Ritchie	not out		64	
Phillips		b Edmonds	18	(144–6)
Bennett	c Robinson	b Ellison	12	(171–7)
Lawson	c Botham	b Taylor	14	(192–8)
McDermott	run out		25	(235–9)
Gilbert		b Botham	1	(241)
Extras: 5				

Botham 3–64

AUSTRALIA: 129

Wood		b Botham	6	(13–1)
Hilditch	c Gower	b Taylor	9	(16–2)
Wessels	c Downton	b Botham	7	(37–3)
Border*	c Botham	b Ellison	58	(114–7)
Wellham	lbw	b Ellison	5	(51–4)
Ritchie	c Downton	b Ellison	6	(71–5)
Phillips	c Downton	b Botham	10	(96–6)
Bennett	c &	b Taylor	11	(129)
Lawson	c Downton	b Ellison	7	(127–8)
McDermott	c Botham	b Ellison	2	(129–9)
Gilbert	not out		0	
Extras: 8				

Ellison 5–46; Botham 3–44

The tourists were forced to follow on after Graham Gooch and David Gower ran riot on the first day. The Aussies never recovered and lost the Ashes in the process.

ENGLAND won by an innings and 94 runs to win the series 3–1.

1ST TEST: At Brisbane; November 14, 15, 16, 18, and 19 1986; Australia won the toss

ENGLAND: 456

Broad	c Zoehrer	b Reid	8	(15–1)
Athey	c Zoehrer	b Matthews. C	76	(198–4)
Gatting*		b Hughes	61	(116–2)
Lamb	lbw	b Hughes	40	(198–3)
Gower	c Ritchie	b Matthews. C	51	(316–5)
Botham	c Hughes	b Waugh	138	(443–8)
Richards		b Matthews. C	0	(324–6)
Emburey	c Waugh	b Hughes	8	(351–7)
DeFreitas	c Matthews. C	b Waugh	40	(451–9)
Edmonds	not out		9	
Dilley	c Boon	b Waugh	0	(456)
Extras: 25				

Waugh 3–76; Matthews. C 3–95; Hughes 3–134

ENGLAND: 77 for 3

Broad	not out		35	
Athey	c Waugh	b Hughes	1	(6–1)
Gatting*	c Matthews. G	b Hughes	12	(25–2)
Lamb	lbw	b Reid	9	(40–3)
Gower	not out		15	
Extras: 5				

AUSTRALIA: 248

Marsh	c Richards	b Dilley	56	(126–4)
Boon	c Broad	b DeFreitas	10	(27–1)
Zoehrer	lbw	b Dilley	38	(97–2)
Jones	lbw	b DeFreitas	8	(114–3)
Border*	c DeFreitas	b Edmonds	7	(159–5)
Ritchie	c Edmonds	b Dilley	41	(198–6)
Matthews. G	not out		56	
Waugh	c Richards	b Dilley	0	(204–7)
Matthews. C	c Gatting	b Botham	11	(239–8)
Hughes		b Botham	0	(239–9)
Reid	c Richards	b Dilley	3	(248)
Extras: 18				

Dilley 5–68

AUSTRALIA: 282

Marsh		b DeFreitas	110	(262–6)
Boon	lbw	b Botham	14	(24–1)
Jones	st Richards	b Emburey	18	(44–2)
Border*	c Lamb	b Emburey	23	(92–3)
Ritchie	lbw	b DeFreitas	45	(205–4)
Matthews. G	c &	b Dilley	13	(224–5)
Waugh		b Emburey	28	(266–7)
Zoehrer	not out		16	
Matthews. C	lbw	b Emburey	0	(266–8)
Hughes		b DeFreitas	0	(275–9)
Reid	c Broad	b Emburey	2	(282)
Extras: 13				

Emburey 5–80; DeFreitas 3–62

Phil DeFreitas made an impressive debut as Australia, required to follow on, failed to reach 300 in either innings. Botham had tormented them again with another ton.

ENGLAND won by 7 wickets to lead the series 1–0.

ENGLAND: 592 for 8 declared

Broad	c Zoehrer	b Reid	162	(333-4)
Athey		b Reid	96	(223-1)
Lamb	c Zoehrer	b Reid	0	(227-2)
Gatting*	c Waugh	b Matthews. C	14	(275-3)
Gower	c Waugh	b Matthews. G	136	(546-6)
Botham	c Border	b Reid	0	(339-5)
Richards	c Waugh	b Matthews. C	133	(592-8)
DeFreitas	lbw	b Matthews. C	11	(585-7)
Emburey	not out		5	
Extras: 35				

Reid 4-115; Matthews. C 3-112

ENGLAND: 199 for 8 declared

Broad	lbw	b Waugh	16	(47-2)
Athey	c Border	b Reid	6	(8-1)
Gatting*		b Waugh	70	(172-6)
Lamb	lbw	b Reid	2	(50-3)
Gower	c Zoehrer	b Waugh	48	(123-4)
Botham	c Matthews. G	b Reid	6	(140-5)
Richards	c Lawson	b Waugh	15	(199-8)
DeFreitas		b Waugh	15	(190-7)
Emburey	not out		4	
Extras: 17				

Waugh 5-69; Reid 3-58

AUSTRALIA: 401

Marsh	c Broad	b Botham	15	(64-2)
Boon		b Dilley	2	(4-1)
Waugh	c Botham	b Emburey	71	(114-3)
Jones	c Athey	b Edmonds	27	(128-4)
Border*	c Richards	b Dilley	125	(401)
Ritchie	c Botham	b Edmonds	33	(198-5)
Matthews. G	c Botham	b Dilley	45	(279-6)
Zoehrer	lbw	b Dilley	29	(334-7)
Lawson		b DeFreitas	13	(360-8)
Matthews. C	c Broad	b Emburey	10	(385-9)
Reid	not out		2	
Extras: 29				

Dilley 4-79

AUSTRALIA: 197 for 4

Boon	c Botham	b Dilley	0	(0-1)
Marsh	lbw	b Emburey	49	(142-3)
Jones	run out		69	(126-2)
Border*	c Lamb	b Edmonds	16	(152-4)
Ritchie	not out		24	
Matthews. G	not out		14	
Extras: 25				

Chris Broad, David Gower, and Jack Richards made a mockery of Australia's bowlers but Border heroically saved the follow-on in this absorbing encounter.

MATCH DRAWN. England still lead the series 1–0.

3RD TEST: at Adelaide; December 12, 13, 14, 15, and 16 1986; Australia won the toss

AUSTRALIA: 514 for 5 declared

Marsh		b Edmonds	43	(113–1)
Boon	c Whitaker	b Emburey	103	(185–2)
Jones	c Richards	b Dilley	93	(333–4)
Border*	c Richards	b Edmonds	70	(311–3)
Ritchie	c Broad	b DeFreitas	36	(368–5)
Matthews	not out		73	
Waugh	not out		79	
Extras: 17				

AUSTRALIA: 201 for 3 declared

Marsh	c &	b Edmonds	41	(77–3)
Boon	lbw	b DeFreitas	0	(1–1)
Jones	c Lamb	b Dilley	2	(8–2)
Border*	not out		100	
Ritchie	not out		46	
Extras: 12				

ENGLAND: 455

Broad	c Marsh	b Waugh	116	(273–2)
Athey		b Sleep	55	(112–1)
Gatting*	c Waugh	b Sleep	100	(283–3)
Lamb	c Matthews	b Hughes	14	(341–4)
Gower	lbw	b Reid	38	(341–5)
Emburey	c Dyer	b Reid	49	(439–8)
Whitaker	c Matthews	b Reid	11	(361–6)
Richards	c Jones	b Sleep	29	(422–7)
DeFreitas	not out		4	
Edmonds	c Border	b Sleep	13	(454–9)
Dilley		b Reid	0	(455)
Extras: 26				

Reid 4–64; Sleep 4–132

ENGLAND: 39 for 2

Broad	not out		15	
Athey	c Dyer	b Hughes	12	(21–2)
Gatting*		b Matthews	0	(22–2)
Lamb	not out		9	
Extras: 3				

The hosts profited from the absence of Botham as they too piled on the runs. In their first innings, Greg Ritchie recorded the lowest score which was 36!

MATCH DRAWN. England still lead the series 1–0.

4TH TEST: at Melbourne; December 26, 27, and 28 1986; England won the toss

AUSTRALIA: 141

Marsh	c Richards	b Botham	17	(44–2)
Boon	c Botham	b Small	7	(16–1)
Jones	c Gower	b Small	59	(118–5)
Border*	c Richards	b Botham	15	(80–3)
Waugh	c Botham	b Small	10	(108–4)
Matthews	c Botham	b Small	14	(141)
Sleep	c Richards	b Small	0	(118–6)
Zoehrer		b Botham	5	(129–7)
McDermott	c Richards	b Botham	0	(133–8)
Hughes	c Richards	b Botham	2	(137–9)
Reid	not out		2	
Extras: 10				

Botham 5–41; Small 5–48

AUSTRALIA: 194

Marsh	run out		60	(153–4)
Boon	c Gatting	b Small	8	(13–1)
Jones	c Gatting	b DeFreitas	21	(48–2)
Border*	c Emburey	b Small	34	(113–3)
Waugh		b Edmonds	49	(185–8)
Matthews		b Emburey	0	(153–5)
Sleep	run out		6	(175–6)
Zoehrer	c Athey	b Edmonds	1	(180–7)
McDermott		b Emburey	1	(189–9)
Hughes	c Small	b Edmonds	8	(194)
Reid	not out		0	
Extras: 6				

Edmonds 3–45

ENGLAND: 349

Broad	c Zoehrer	b Hughes	112	(198–3)
Athey	lbw	b Reid	21	(58–1)
Gatting*	c Hughes	b Reid	40	(163–2)
Lamb	c Zoehrer	b Reid	43	(251–5)
Gower	c Matthews	b Sleep	7	(219–4)
Botham	c Zoehrer	b McDermott	29	(273–6)
Richards	c Marsh	b Reid	3	(277–7)
DeFreitas	c Matthews	b McDermott	7	(289–8)
Emburey	c &	b McDermott	22	(319–9)
Edmonds	lbw	b McDermott	19	(349)
Small	not out		21	
Extras: 25				

Reid 4–78; McDermott 4–83

Chris Broad registered his third ton in three tests as England routed their opponents whose batting collapsed in each innings in this three-day embarrassment.

ENGLAND won by an innings and 14 runs to lead the series 2–0.

5TH TEST: at Sydney; January 10, 11, 12, 14, and 15 1986; Australia won the toss

AUSTRALIA: 343

Marsh	c Gatting	b Small	24	(58–2)
Ritchie	lbw	b Dilley	6	(8–1)
Jones	not out		184	
Border*	c Botham	b Edmonds	34	(149–3)
Wellham	c Richards	b Small	17	(184–4)
Waugh	c Richards	b Small	0	(184–5)
Sleep	c Richards	b Small	9	(200–6)
Zoehrer	c Gatting	b Small	12	(232–7)
Taylor	c Emburey	b Edmonds	11	(271–8)
Hughes	c Botham	b Edmonds	16	(338–9)
Reid		b Dilley	4	(343)
Extras: 26				

Small 5–75; Edmonds 3–79

AUSTRALIA: 251

Marsh	c Emburey	b Dilley	14	(29–1)
Ritchie	c Botham	b Edmonds	13	(31–2)
Jones	c Richards	b Emburey	30	(110–4)
Border*		b Edmonds	49	(106–3)
Wellham	c Lamb	b Emburey	1	(115–5)
Waugh	c Athey	b Emburey	73	(243–8)
Sleep	c Lamb	b Emburey	10	(141–6)
Zoehrer	lbw	b Emburey	1	(145–7)
Taylor	c Lamb	b Emburey	42	(248–9)
Hughes		b Emburey	5	(251)
Reid	not out		1	
Extras: 12				

Emburey 7–78

ENGLAND: 275

Broad	lbw	b Hughes	6	(17–3)
Athey	c Zoehrer	b Hughes	5	(16–1)
Gatting*	lbw	b Reid	0	(17–2)
Lamb	c Zoehrer	b Taylor	24	(89–4)
Gower	c Wellham	b Taylor	72	(142–6)
Botham	c Marsh	b Taylor	16	(119–5)
Richards	c Wellham	b Reid	46	(213–7)
Emburey		b Taylor	69	(275)
Edmonds	c Marsh	b Taylor	3	(219–8)
Small		b Taylor	14	(270–9)
Dilley	not out		4	
Extras: 16				

Taylor 6–78

ENGLAND: 264

Broad	c &	b Sleep	17	(24–1)
Athey		b Sleep	31	(91–3)
Gower	c Marsh	b Border	37	(91–2)
Lamb	c Waugh	b Taylor	3	(102–4)
Gatting*	c &	b Waugh	96	(233–6)
Botham	c Wellham	b Taylor	0	(102–5)
Richards		b Sleep	38	(257–7)
Emburey		b Sleep	22	(264)
Edmonds	lbw	b Sleep	0	(257–8)
Small	c Border	b Reid	0	(262–9)
Dilley	not out		2	
Extras: 18				

Sleep 5–72

Dean Jones rescued Australia's first innings and then pride was further restored as the relatively unknown Peter Taylor took six wickets in his first bowling innings.

AUSTRALIA won by 55 runs. ENGLAND win the series 2–1.

1ST TEST: at Leeds; June 8, 9, 10, 12, and 13 1989; England won the toss

AUSTRALIA: 601 for 7 declared

Marsh	lbw	b DeFreitas	16	(44–1)
Taylor	lbw	b Foster	136	(273–4)
Boon	c Russell	b Foster	9	(57–2)
Border*	c Foster	b DeFreitas	66	(174–3)
Jones	c Russell	b Newport	79	(411–5)
Waugh	not out		177	
Healy	c &	b Newport	16	(441–6)
Hughes	c Russell	b Foster	71	(588–7)
Lawson	not out		10	
Extras: 21				

Foster 3–109

AUSTRALIA: 230 for 3 declared

Marsh	c Russell	b Foster	6	(14–1)
Taylor	c Broad	b Pringle	60	(97–2)
Boon	lbw	b DeFreitas	43	(129–3)
Border*	not out		60	
Jones	not out		40	
Extras: 21				

ENGLAND: 430

Gooch	lbw	b Alderman	13	(35–1)
Broad		b Hughes	37	(81–2)
Barnett	lbw	b Alderman	80	(195–3)
Lamb	c Boon	b Alderman	125	(323–5)
Gower*	c Healy	b Lawson	26	(243–4)
Smith	lbw	b Alderman	66	(392–7)
Pringle	lbw	b Campbell	6	(338–6)
Newport	c Boon	b Lawson	36	(421–8)
Russell	c Marsh	b Lawson	15	(430)
DeFreitas	lbw	b Alderman	1	(424–9)
Foster	not out		2	
Extras: 23				

Alderman 5–107; Lawson 3–105

ENGLAND: 191

Gooch	lbw	b Hughes	68	(153–6)
Broad	lbw	b Alderman	7	(17–1)
Barnett	c Taylor	b Alderman	34	(67–2)
Lamb	c Boon	b Alderman	4	(77–3)
Gower*	c Healy	b Lawson	34	(134–4)
Smith	c Border	b Lawson	0	(134–5)
Pringle	c Border	b Alderman	0	(153–7)
Newport	c Marsh	b Alderman	8	(170–9)
Russell	c Healy	b Hughes	2	(166–8)
DeFreitas		b Hughes	21	(191)
Foster	not out		1	
Extras: 12				

Alderman 5–44; Hughes 3–36

Terry Alderman returned to an Ashes tour and quickly tormented the hosts with ten wickets. Mark Taylor and Steve Waugh provided the batting heroics.

AUSTRALIA won by 210 runs to lead the series 1–0.

2ND TEST: at Lord's; June 22, 23, 24, 26, and 27 1989; England won the toss

ENGLAND: 286

Gooch	c Healy	b Waugh	60	(131-4)
Broad	lbw	b Alderman	18	(31-1)
Barnett	c Boon	b Hughes	14	(52-2)
Gatting	c Boon	b Hughes	0	(58-3)
Gower*		b Lawson	57	(180-5)
Smith	c Hohns	b Lawson	32	(191-7)
Emburey		b Alderman	0	(185-6)
Russell	not out		64	
Foster	c Jones	b Hughes	16	(237-8)
Jarvis	c Marsh	b Hughes	6	(253-9)
Dilley	c Border	b Alderman	7	(286)

Extras: 12

Hughes 4-71; Alderman 3-60

ENGLAND: 359

Gooch	lbw	b Alderman	0	(0-1)
Broad		b Lawson	20	(28-3)
Barnett	c Jones	b Alderman	3	(18-2)
Gatting	lbw	b Alderman	22	(84-4)
Gower*	c Border	b Hughes	106	(223-5)
Smith		b Alderman	96	(300-7)
Russell	c Boon	b Lawson	29	(274-6)
Emburey	not out		36	
Foster	lbw	b Alderman	4	(304-8)
Jarvis	lbw	b Alderman	5	(314-9)
Dilley	c Boon	b Hughes	24	(359)

Extras: 14

Alderman 6-128

AUSTRALIA: 528

Marsh	c Russell	b Dilley	3	(6-1)
Taylor	lbw	b Foster	62	(151-2)
Boon	c Gooch	b Dilley	94	(192-3)
Border*	c Smith	b Emburey	35	(221-4)
Jones	lbw	b Foster	27	(235-5)
Waugh	not out		152	
Healy	c Russell	b Jarvis	3	(265-6)
Hughes	c Gooch	b Foster	30	(331-7)
Hohns		b Emburey	21	(381-8)
Lawson	c Broad	b Emburey	74	(511-9)
Alderman	lbw	b Emburey	8	(528)

Extras: 19

Emburey 4-88; Foster 3-129

AUSTRALIA: 119 for 4

Marsh		b Dilley	1	(9-1)
Taylor	c Gooch	b Foster	27	(51-2)
Boon	not out		58	
Border*	c sub	b Foster	1	(61-3)
Jones	c Russell	b Foster	0	(67-4)
Waugh	not out		21	

Extras: 11

Foster 3-39

Alderman could only manage 9 wickets this time as David Boon and Steve Waugh asserted themselves, and England were crushed again after winning the toss.

AUSTRALIA won by 6 wickets to lead the series 2–0.

3RD TEST: at Birmingham; July 6, 7, 8, 10, and 11 1989; Australia won the toss

AUSTRALIA: 424

Marsh	lbw	b Botham	42	(94–2)
Taylor	st Russell	b Emburey	43	(88–1)
Boon	run out		38	(201–4)
Border*		b Emburey	8	(105–3)
Jones	c sub	b Fraser	157	(424)
Waugh		b Fraser	43	(272–5)
Healy		b Fraser	2	(289–6)
Hughes	c Botham	b Dilley	2	(299–7)
Hohns	c Gooch	b Dilley	40	(391–8)
Lawson		b Fraser	12	(421–9)
Alderman	not out		0	
Extras: 37				
Fraser 4–63				

AUSTRALIA: 158 for 2

Marsh		b Jarvis	42	(81–1)
Taylor	c Botham	b Gooch	51	(109–2)
Boon	not out		22	
Healy	not out		33	
Extras: 10				

ENGLAND: 242

Gooch	lbw	b Lawson	8	(17–1)
Curtis	lbw	b Hughes	41	(75–4)
Gower*	lbw	b Alderman	8	(42–2)
Tavare	c Taylor	b Alderman	2	(47–3)
Barnett	c Healy	b Waugh	10	(75–5)
Botham		b Hughes	46	(171–6)
Russell	c Taylor	b Hohns	42	(171–7)
Emburey	c Boon	b Lawson	26	(215–9)
Fraser	run out		12	(185–8)
Dilley	not out		11	
Jarvis	lbw	b Alderman	22	(242)
Extras: 14				
Alderman 3–61				

Dean Jones was the hero of this non-event, which was ruined by the weather. Angus Fraser made an impressive debut as England were grateful for a draw.

MATCH DRAWN. AUSTRALIA still lead the series 2–0.

4TH TEST: at Manchester; July 27, 28, 29, 31, and August 1 1989; England won the toss

ENGLAND: 260

Gooch		b Lawson	11	(23–1)
Curtis		b Lawson	22	(57–3)
Robinson	lbw	b Lawson	0	(23–2)
Smith	c Hohns	b Hughes	143	(260)
Gower*	lbw	b Hohns	35	(132–4)
Botham		b Hohns	0	(140–5)
Russell	lbw	b Lawson	1	(147–6)
Emburey	lbw	b Hohns	5	(158–7)
Foster	c Border	b Lawson	35	(232–8)
Fraser	lbw	b Lawson	2	(252–9)
Cook	not out		0	
Extras: 2				

Lawson 6–72; Hohns 3–59

ENGLAND: 264

Gooch	c Alderman	b Lawson	13	(28–4)
Curtis	c Boon	b Alderman	0	(10–1)
Robinson	lbw	b Lawson	12	(25–2)
Smith	c Healy	b Alderman	1	(27–3)
Gower*	c Marsh	b Lawson	15	(59–6)
Botham	lbw	b Alderman	4	(38–5)
Russell	not out		128	
Emburey		b Alderman	64	(201–7)
Foster		b Alderman	6	(223–8)
Fraser	c Marsh	b Hohns	3	(255–9)
Cook	c Healy	b Hughes	5	(264)
Extras: 13				

Alderman 5–66; Lawson 3–81

AUSTRALIA: 447

Taylor	st Russell	b Emburey	85	(143–2)
Marsh	c Russell	b Botham	47	(135–1)
Boon		b Fraser	12	(154–3)
Border*	c Russell	b Foster	80	(362–5)
Jones		b Botham	69	(274–4)
Waugh	c Curtis	b Fraser	92	(423–9)
Healy	lbw	b Foster	0	(362–6)
Hohns	c Gower	b Cook	17	(413–7)
Hughes		b Cook	3	(423–8)
Lawson		b Fraser	17	(447)
Alderman	not out		6	
Extras: 19				

Fraser 3–95

AUSTRALIA: 81 for 1

Taylor	not out		37	
Marsh	c Robinson	b Emburey	31	(62–1)
Boon	not out		10	
Extras: 3				

Jack Russell and Robin Smith made the only tons of the match, and still England were overpowered, as Geoff Lawson chipped in with nine wickets.

AUSTRALIA won by 9 wickets to lead the series 3–0.

5TH TEST: at Nottingham; August 10, 11, 12, and 14 1989; Australia won the toss

AUSTRALIA: 602 for 6 declared

Marsh	c Botham	b Cook	138	(329–1)
Taylor	st Russell	b Cook	219	(430–2)
Boon	st Russell	b Cook	73	(502–3)
Border*	not out		65	
Jones	c Gower	b Fraser	22	(543–4)
Waugh	c Gower	b Malcolm	0	(553–5)
Healy		b Fraser	5	(560–6)
Hohns	not out		19	
Extras: 61				
Cook 3–91				

ENGLAND: 255

Curtis	lbw	b Alderman	2	(14–3)
Moxon	c Waugh	b Alderman	0	(1–1)
Atherton	lbw	b Alderman	0	(1–2)
Smith	c Healy	b Alderman	101	(172–6)
Gower*	c Healy	b Lawson	11	(37–4)
Russell	c Healy	b Lawson	20	(119–5)
Hemmings		b Alderman	38	(214–7)
Fraser		b Hohns	29	(243–8)
Botham	c Waugh	b Hohns	12	(244–9)
Cook	not out		2	
Malcolm	c Healy	b Hughes	9	(255)
Extras: 31				
Alderman 5–69				

ENGLAND: 167

Gower*		b Lawson	5	(5–1)
Curtis	lbw	b Alderman	6	(13–2)
Atherton	c &	b Hohns	47	(120–6)
Smith		b Hughes	26	(67–3)
Moxon		b Alderman	18	(106–4)
Russell		b Lawson	1	(114–5)
Hemmings	lbw	b Hughes	35	(160–8)
Fraser		b Hohns	1	(134–7)
Cook	not out		7	
Malcolm		b Hughes	5	(167–9)
Botham	absent hurt			
Extras: 16				
Hughes 3–46				

Geoff Marsh and Mark Taylor batted through the whole of Day 1 as debutant Devon Malcolm toiled away. Mike Atherton's first test innings lasted a mere 2 deliveries.

AUSTRALIA won by an innings and 180 runs to lead the series 4–0.

6TH TEST: at the Oval; August 24, 25, 26, 28, and 29 1989; Australia won the toss

AUSTRALIA: 468

Marsh	c Igglesden	b Small	17	(48–1)
Taylor	c Russell	b Igglesden	71	(130–2)
Boon	c Atherton	b Small	46	(149–3)
Border*	c Russell	b Capel	76	(345–4)
Jones	c Gower	b Small	122	(347–5)
Waugh		b Igglesden	14	(386–6)
Healy	c Russell	b Pringle	44	(409–7)
Hohns	c Russell	b Pringle	30	(468)
Hughes	lbw	b Pringle	21	(447–8)
Lawson		b Pringle	2	(453–9)
Alderman	not out		6	
Extras: 19				

Pringle 4–70; Small 3–141

AUSTRALIA: 219 for 4 declared

Marsh	lbw	b Igglesden	4	(7–1)
Taylor	c Russell	b Small	48	(100–2)
Boon	run out		37	(101–3)
Border*	not out		51	
Jones		b Capel	50	(189–4)
Waugh	not out		7	
Extras: 22				

ENGLAND: 285

Gooch	lbw	b Alderman	0	(1–1)
Stephenson	c Waugh	b Alderman	25	(80–4)
Atherton	c Healy	b Hughes	12	(28–2)
Smith		b Lawson	11	(47–3)
Gower*	c Healy	b Alderman	79	(169–7)
Capel	lbw	b Alderman	4	(84–5)
Russell	c Healy	b Alderman	12	(98–6)
Pringle	c Taylor	b Hohns	27	(201–8)
Small	c Jones	b Lawson	59	(274–9)
Cook	c Jones	b Lawson	31	(285)
Igglesden	not out		2	
Extras: 23				

Alderman 5–66; Lawson 3–85

ENGLAND: 143 for 5

Gooch	c &	b Alderman	10	(27–2)
Stephenson	lbw	b Alderman	11	(20–1)
Atherton		b Lawson	14	(51–3)
Smith	not out		77	
Gower*	c Waugh	b Lawson	7	(67–4)
Capel	c Taylor	b Hohns	17	(138–5)
Russell	not out		0	
Extras: 7				

Border and Jones showed no mercy to the England attack, but the home team had the weather to thank for avoiding another humiliation in their summer of woe.

MATCH DRAWN. AUSTRALIA win the series 4–0.

ENGLAND: 194

Atherton	lbw	b Reid	13	(43–2)
Larkins	c Healy	b Hughes	12	(23–1)
Gower	c Healy	b Reid	61	(123–4)
Lamb*	c Hughes	b Matthews	32	(117–3)
Smith		b Reid	7	(134–5)
Stewart	lbw	b Reid	4	(135–6)
Russell	c &	b Alderman	16	(181–8)
Lewis	c Border	b Hughes	20	(167–7)
Small	not out		12	
Fraser	c Healy	b Alderman	1	(187–9)
Malcolm	c Waugh	b Hughes	5	(194)
Extras: 11				

Reid 4–53; Hughes 3–39

ENGLAND: 114

Atherton		b Alderman	15	(42–2)
Larkins	lbw	b Reid	0	(0–1)
Gower		b Hughes	27	(46–3)
Lamb*	lbw	b Alderman	14	(60–4)
Russell	lbw	b Waugh	15	(93–7)
Smith	c Taylor	b Alderman	1	(78–5)
Stewart	c sub	b Alderman	6	(84–6)
Lewis	lbw	b Alderman	14	(112–8)
Small	c Alderman	b Hughes	15	(114)
Fraser	c sub	b Alderman	0	(114–9)
Malcolm	not out		0	
Extras: 7				

Alderman 6–47

AUSTRALIA: 152

Marsh	lbw	b Fraser	9	(22–1)
Taylor	c Lewis	b Fraser	10	(35–2)
Boon	lbw	b Small	18	(60–4)
Border*	c Atherton	b Small	9	(49–3)
Jones	c Small	b Lewis	17	(89–6)
Waugh	c Smith	b Small	1	(64–5)
Matthews	c Small	b Malcolm	35	(135–7)
Healy	c Atherton	b Lewis	22	(150–9)
Hughes	c Russell	b Fraser	9	(150–8)
Reid		b Lewis	0	(152)
Alderman	not out		0	
Extras: 22				

Lewis 3–29; Fraser 3–33; Small 3–34

AUSTRALIA: 157 for 0

Taylor	not out		67
Marsh	not out		72
Extras: 18			

At 42 for 1 in the second innings, England were in a dominant position, but six Alderman wickets saw the tourists' last nine wickets disappear for only 72 runs.

AUSTRALIA won by 10 wickets to lead the series 1–0.

2ND TEST: at Melbourne; December 26, 27, 28, 29, and 30 1990; England won the toss

ENGLAND: 352

Gooch*	lbw	b Alderman	20	(30–2)
Atherton	c Boon	b Reid	0	(12–1)
Larkins	c Healy	b Reid	64	(152–4)
Smith	c Healy	b Hughes	30	(109–3)
Gower	c &	b Reid	100	(274–5)
Stewart	c Healy	b Reid	79	(324–8)
Russell	c Healy	b Hughes	15	(303–6)
DeFreitas	c Healy	b Reid	3	(307–7)
Fraser	c Jones	b Alderman	24	(352)
Malcolm	c Taylor	b Reid	6	(344–9)
Tufnell	not out		0	

Extras: 11

Reid 6–97

ENGLAND: 150

Gooch*	c Alderman	b Reid	58	(103–2)
Atherton	c Healy	b Reid	4	(17–1)
Larkins	c Healy	b Reid	54	(148–6)
Smith	c Taylor	b Reid	8	(115–3)
Gower	c Border	b Matthews	0	(122–4)
Stewart	c Marsh	b Reid	8	(147–5)
Russell	c Jones	b Matthews	1	(150–9)
DeFreitas	lbw	b Reid	0	(148–7)
Fraser	c Taylor	b Reid	0	(148–8)
Malcolm	lbw	b Matthews	1	(150)
Tufnell	not out		0	

Extras: 16

Reid 7–51; Matthews 3–40

AUSTRALIA: 306

Marsh	c Russell	b DeFreitas	36	(63–1)
Taylor	c Russell	b DeFreitas	61	(149–3)
Boon	c Russell	b Malcolm	28	(133–2)
Border*	c Russell	b Fraser	62	(281–6)
Jones	c Russell	b Fraser	44	(224–4)
Waugh		b Fraser	19	(264–5)
Matthews	lbw	b Fraser	12	(298–8)
Healy	c Russell	b Fraser	5	(289–7)
Hughes	lbw	b Malcolm	4	(306)
Alderman		b Fraser	0	(302–9)
Reid	not out		3	

Extras: 32

Fraser 6–82

AUSTRALIA: 197 for 2

Marsh	not out		79	
Taylor	c Atherton	b Malcolm	5	(9–1)
Healy	c Atherton	b Fraser	1	(10–2)
Boon	not out		94	

Extras: 18

It was a case of deja vu as this time Bruce Reid seized 6 wickets that took England from the dominance of 103 for 1 in the second innings to a demoralising 150 all out.

AUSTRALIA won by 8 wickets to lead the series 2–0.

3RD TEST: at Sydney; January 4, 5, 6, 7, and 8 1991; Australia won the toss

AUSTRALIA: 518

Marsh	c Larkins	b Malcolm	13	(21–1)
Taylor	c Russell	b Malcolm	11	(38–2)
Boon	c Atherton	b Gooch	97	(185–3)
Border*		b Hemmings	78	(226–4)
Jones	st Russell	b Small	60	(347–6)
Waugh	c Stewart	b Malcolm	48	(292–5)
Matthews	c Hemmings	b Tufnell	128	(512–9)
Healy	c Small	b Hemmings	35	(442–7)
Rackemann		b Hemmings	1	(457–8)
Alderman	not out		26	
Reid	c Smith	b Malcolm	0	(518)
Extras: 21				

Malcolm 4–128; Hemmings 3–105

AUSTRALIA: 205

Taylor	lbw	b Hemmings	19	(29–2)
Marsh	c Stewart	b Malcolm	4	(21–1)
Healy	c Smith	b Tufnell	69	(166–7)
Boon	c Gooch	b Tufnell	29	(81–3)
Border*	c Gooch	b Tufnell	20	(129–4)
Jones	c &	b Tufnell	0	(129–5)
Waugh	c Russell	b Hemmings	14	(166–6)
Matthews		b Hemmings	19	(189–8)
Rackemann		b Malcolm	9	(205)
Alderman	c Gower	b Tufnell	1	(192–9)
Reid	not out		5	
Extras: 16				

Tufnell 5–61; Hemmings 3–94

ENGLAND: 469 for 8 declared

Gooch*	c Healy	b Reid	59	(95–1)
Atherton	c Boon	b Matthews	105	(295–4)
Larkins	run out		11	(116–2)
Smith	c Healy	b Reid	18	(156–3)
Gower	c Marsh	b Reid	123	(394–5)
Stewart	lbw	b Alderman	91	(426–6)
Russell	not out		30	
Small	lbw	b Alderman	10	(444–7)
Hemmings		b Alderman	0	(444–8)
Tufnell	not out		5	
Extras: 17				

Alderman 3–62; Reid 3–79

ENGLAND: 113 for 4

Gooch*	c Border	b Matthews	54	(100–3)
Gower	c Taylor	b Matthews	36	(84–1)
Larkins	lbw	b Border	0	(84–2)
Stewart	run out		7	(100–4)
Smith	not out		10	
Atherton	not out		3	
Extras: 3				

Phil Tufnell's 5 for 61 off 37 overs in only his second test almost created a rare away win, but England were left with only 28 overs to pursue 255 runs.

MATCH DRAWN. Australia still lead the series 2–0.

4TH TEST: at Adelaide; January 25, 26, 27, 28, and 29 1991; Australia won the toss

AUSTRALIA: 386

Marsh	c Gooch	b Small	37	(62–2)
Taylor	run out		5	(11–1)
Boon	c Fraser	b Malcolm	49	(124–5)
Border*		b DeFreitas	12	(104–3)
Jones	lbw	b DeFreitas	0	(104–4)
Waugh		b Malcolm	138	(295–6)
Matthews	c Stewart	b Gooch	65	(358–8)
Healy	c Stewart	b DeFreitas	1	(298–7)
McDermott	not out		42	
Hughes	lbw	b Small	1	(373–9)
Reid	c Lamb	b DeFreitas	5	(386)
Extras: 31				

DeFreitas 4–56

AUSTRALIA: 314 for 6 declared

Taylor	run out		4	(8–2)
Marsh	c Gooch	b Small	0	(1–1)
Boon		b Tufnell	121	(240–6)
Jones	lbw	b DeFreitas	8	(25–3)
Waugh		b Malcolm	23	(64–4)
Hughes	c Gooch	b Fraser	30	(130–5)
Border*	not out		83	
Matthews	not out		34	
Extras: 11				

ENGLAND: 229

Gooch*	c Healy	b Reid	87	(176–5)
Atherton	lbw	b McDermott	0	(10–1)
Lamb	c Healy	b McDermott	0	(11–2)
Smith	c &	b Hughes	53	(137–3)
Gower	c Hughes	b McDermott	11	(160–4)
Stewart	c Healy	b Reid	11	(179–6)
DeFreitas	c Matthews	b McDermott	45	(229)
Small		b McDermott	1	(198–7)
Fraser	c Healy	b Reid	2	(215–8)
Malcolm	c Healy	b Reid	2	(219–9)
Tufnell	not out		0	
Extras: 17				

McDermott 5–97; Reid 4–53

ENGLAND: 335 for 4

Gooch*	c Marsh	b Reid	117	(203–1)
Atherton	c Waugh	b Reid	87	(246–2)
Lamb		b McDermott	53	(287–3)
Gower	lbw	b Hughes	16	(287–4)
Smith	not out		10	
Stewart	c Jones	b McDermott	9	(297–5)
DeFreitas	not out		19	
Extras: 24				

Graham Gooch enjoyed one of his better matches against Australia as England made a commendable attempt at chasing the daunting target of 472.

MATCH DRAWN. Australia still lead the series 2–0.

5TH TEST: at Perth; February 1, 2, 3, and 5 1991; England won the toss

ENGLAND: 244

Gooch*	c Healy	b McDermott	13	(27–1)
Atherton	c Healy	b McDermott	27	(50–2)
Lamb	c Border	b McDermott	91	(212–4)
Smith	c Taylor	b McDermott	58	(191–3)
Gower	not out		28	
Stewart	lbw	b McDermott	2	(220–5)
DeFreitas	c Marsh	b McDermott	5	(226–6)
Newport	c Healy	b McDermott	0	(226–7)
Small	c Boon	b Hughes	0	(227–8)
Tufnell	c Healy	b Hughes	0	(227–9)
Malcolm	c Marsh	b McDermott	7	(244)
Extras: 13				

McDermott 8–97

ENGLAND: 182

Gooch*	c Alderman	b Hughes	18	(41–1)
Atherton	c Boon	b Hughes	25	(75–3)
Lamb	lbw	b McDermott	5	(49–2)
Smith	lbw	b Alderman	43	(118–6)
Gower	c Taylor	b Alderman	5	(80–4)
Stewart	c Healy	b McDermott	7	(114–5)
DeFreitas	c Healy	b Alderman	5	(125–7)
Newport	not out		40	
Small	c Taylor	b Hughes	4	(134–8)
Tufnell	c Healy	b Hughes	8	(144–9)
Malcolm	c Jones	b McDermott	6	(182)
Extras: 16				

Hughes 4–37; McDermott 3–60; Alderman 3–75

AUSTRALIA: 307

Marsh	c Stewart	b Small	1	(1–1)
Taylor	c Stewart	b Malcolm	12	(44–2)
Boon	c Stewart	b Malcolm	64	(113–4)
Border*	lbw	b DeFreitas	17	(90–3)
Jones		b Newport	34	(161–5)
Waugh	c Small	b Malcolm	26	(168–6)
Matthews	not out		60	
Healy	c Lamb	b Small	42	(230–7)
McDermott		b Tufnell	25	(281–8)
Hughes	c Gooch	b Tufnell	0	(283–9)
Alderman	lbw	b DeFreitas	7	(307)
Extras: 19				

Malcolm 3–94

AUSTRALIA: 120 for 1

Taylor	c Stewart	b DeFreitas	19	(39–1)
Marsh	not out		63	
Boon	not out		30	
Extras: 8				

Craig McDermott recorded his test career best of 8 for 97 as his eleven wickets were instrumental in another savage defeat for hapless England.

AUSTRALIA won by 9 wickets to win the series 3–0.

1ST TEST: at Manchester; June 3, 4, 5, 6, and 7 1993; England won the toss

AUSTRALIA: 289

Taylor	c &	b Such	124	(225–4)
Slater	c Stewart	b DeFreitas	58	(128–1)
Boon	c Lewis	b Such	21	(183–2)
Waugh. M	c &	b Tufnell	6	(221–3)
Border*	st Stewart	b Such	17	(260–6)
Waugh. S		b Such	3	(232–5)
Healy	c Such	b Tufnell	12	(267–9)
Julian	c Gatting	b Such	0	(264–7)
Hughes	c DeFreitas	b Such	2	(266–8)
Warne	not out		15	
McDermott	run out		8	(289)
Extras: 23				

Such 6–67

AUSTRALIA: 432 for 5 declared

Taylor	lbw	b Such	9	(23–1)
Slater	c Caddick	b Such	27	(46–2)
Boon	c Gatting	b DeFreitas	93	(252–5)
Waugh. M		b Tufnell	64	(155–3)
Border*	c &	b Caddick	31	(234–4)
Waugh. S	not out		78	
Healy	not out		102	
Extras: 28				

ENGLAND: 210

Gooch*	c Julian	b Warne	65	(123–4)
Atherton	c Healy	b Hughes	19	(71–1)
Gatting		b Warne	4	(80–2)
Smith	c Taylor	b Warne	4	(84–3)
Hick	c Border	b Hughes	34	(148–5)
Stewart		b Julian	27	(183–8)
Lewis	c Boon	b Hughes	9	(168–6)
DeFreitas	lbw	b Julian	5	(178–7)
Caddick	c Healy	b Warne	7	(203–9)
Such	not out		14	
Tufnell	c Healy	b Hughes	1	(210)
Extras: 21				

Warne 4–51; Hughes 4–59

ENGLAND: 332

Gooch*	handled the ball		133	(223–4)
Atherton	c Taylor	b Warne	25	(73–1)
Gatting		b Hughes	23	(133–2)
Smith		b Warne	18	(171–3)
Hick	c Healy	b Hughes	22	(230–5)
Stewart	c Healy	b Warne	11	(238–6)
Lewis	c Taylor	b Warne	43	(299–8)
DeFreitas	lbw	b Julian	7	(260–7)
Caddick	c Warne	b Hughes	25	(331–9)
Such	c Border	b Hughes	9	(332)
Tufnell	not out		0	
Extras: 16				

Warne 4–86; Hughes 4–92

Shane Warne took 8 wickets including 'that delivery' against Gatting as Australia resumed their mastery of England. Slater hit a half century in his debut knock.

AUSTRALIA won by 179 runs to lead the series 1–0.

2ND TEST: at Lord's; June 17, 18, 19, 20, and 21 1993;
Australia won the toss

AUSTRALIA: 632 for 4 declared

Taylor	st Stewart	b Tufnell	111	(277–2)
Slater	c sub	b Lewis	152	(260–1)
Boon	not out		164	
Waugh. M		b Tufnell	99	(452–3)
Border*		b Lewis	77	(591–4)
Waugh. S	not out		13	
Extras: 16				

ENGLAND: 205

Gooch*	c May	b Hughes	12	(33–1)
Atherton		b Warne	80	(174–8)
Gatting		b May	5	(50–2)
Smith	st Healy	b May	22	(84–3)
Hick	c Healy	b Hughes	20	(123–4)
Stewart	lbw	b Hughes	3	(131–5)
Lewis	lbw	b Warne	0	(132–6)
Foster	c Border	b Warne	16	(167–7)
Caddick	c Healy	b Hughes	21	(205)
Such	c Taylor	b Warne	7	(189–9)
Tufnell	not out		2	
Extras: 17				

Hughes 4–52; Warne 4–57

ENGLAND: 365

Gooch*	c Healy	b Warne	29	(71–1)
Atherton	run out		99	(175–2)
Gatting	lbw	b Warne	59	(244–4)
Smith	c sub	b May	5	(180–3)
Hick	c Taylor	b May	64	(304–5)
Stewart	lbw	b May	62	(361–7)
Lewis	st Healy	b May	0	(312–6)
Foster	c Waugh. M	b Border	20	(361–8)
Caddick	not out		0	
Such		b Warne	4	(365–9)
Tufnell		b Warne	0	(365)
Extras: 23				

May 4–81; Warne 4–102

Atherton twice exceeded 50 runs while Warne weighed in with 8 more wickets. Meanwhile, the Aussies failed narrowly to post 4 centuries at the top of their order.

AUSTRALIA won by an innings and 62 runs to lead the series 2–0.

3RD TEST: at Nottingham; July 1, 2, 3, 5, and 6 1993; England won the toss

ENGLAND: 321

Lathwell	c Healy	b Hughes	20	(28–1)
Atherton	c Boon	b Warne	11	(63–2)
Smith	c &	b Julian	86	(159–4)
Stewart	c Waugh. M	b Warne	25	(153–3)
Gooch*	c Border	b Hughes	38	(220–6)
Thorpe	c Waugh. S	b Hughes	6	(174–5)
Hussain	c Boon	b Warne	71	(321–9)
Caddick	lbw	b Hughes	15	(290–7)
McCague	c Waugh. M	b Hughes	9	(304–8)
Ilott	c Taylor	b May	6	(321)
Such	not out		0	

Extras: 34

Hughes 5–92; Warne 3–74

ENGLAND: 422 for 6 declared

Lathwell	lbw	b Warne	33	(109–3)
Atherton	c Healy	b Hughes	9	(11–1)
Smith	c Healy	b Warne	50	(100–2)
Stewart	lbw	b Hughes	6	(117–4)
Gooch*	c Taylor	b Warne	120	(309–6)
Caddick	c Boon	b Julian	12	(159–5)
Thorpe	not out		114	
Hussain	not out		47	

Extras: 31

Warne 3–108

AUSTRALIA: 373

Slater	lbw	b Caddick	40	(74–2)
Taylor	c Stewart	b McCague	28	(55–1)
Boon		b McCague	101	(284–7)
Waugh. M	c McCague	b Such	70	(197–3)
Waugh. S	c Stewart	b McCague	13	(239–4)
Healy	c Thorpe	b Ilott	9	(250–5)
Julian	c Stewart	b Ilott	5	(262–6)
Border*	c Smith	b Such	38	(356–9)
Hughes		b Ilott	17	(311–8)
Warne	not out		35	
May	lbw	b McCague	1	(373)

Extras: 16

McCague 4–121; Ilott 3–108

AUSTRALIA: 202 for 6

Slater		b Such	26	(46–1)
Taylor	c Atherton	b Such	28	(74–2)
Boon	c Stewart	b Caddick	18	(93–5)
Waugh. M		b Caddick	1	(75–3)
Border*	c Thorpe	b Caddick	2	(81–4)
Waugh. S	not out		47	
Healy	lbw	b Ilott	5	(115–6)
Julian	not out		56	

Extras: 19

Caddick 3–32

England failed narrowly to force a victory after Graham Thorpe scored a ton on his debut. Warne had match figures of 6 for 182 from 90 overs, a herculean effort.

MATCH DRAWN. AUSTRALIA still lead the series 2–0.

AUSTRALIA: 653 for 4 declared

Slater		b Ilott	67	(110–2)
Taylor	lbw	b Bicknell	27	(86–1)
Boon	lbw	b Ilott	107	(321–4)
Waugh. M		b Ilott	52	(216–3)
Border*	not out		200	
Waugh. S	not out		157	
Extras: 43				

Ilott 3–161

ENGLAND: 200

Lathwell	c Healy	b Hughes	0	(0–1)
Atherton		b Reiffel	55	(158–4)
Smith	c &	b May	23	(43–2)
Stewart	c Slater	b Reiffel	5	(50–3)
Gooch*	lbw	b Reiffel	59	(169–6)
Thorpe	c Healy	b Reiffel	0	(158–5)
Hussain		b Reiffel	15	(184–7)
Caddick	c Waugh. M	b Hughes	9	(195–8)
Bicknell	c Border	b Hughes	12	(200)
McCague	c Taylor	b Warne	0	(200–9)
Ilott	not out		0	
Extras: 22				

Reiffel 5–65; Hughes 3–47

ENGLAND: 305

Lathwell		b May	25	(60–1)
Atherton	st Healy	b May	63	(131–2)
Smith	lbw	b Reiffel	35	(149–3)
Stewart	c Waugh. M	b Reiffel	78	(263–6)
Gooch*	st Healy	b May	26	(202–4)
Thorpe	c Taylor	b Reiffel	13	(256–5)
Hussain	not out		18	
Caddick	lbw	b Hughes	12	(279–7)
Bicknell	lbw	b Hughes	0	(279–8)
McCague		b Hughes	11	(295–9)
Ilott	c Border	b May	4	(305)
Extras: 20				

May 4–65; Hughes 3–79; Reiffel 3–87

Atherton recorded another brace of fifties, but England's bowlers were put to the sword as Allan Border and Steve Waugh shared an unbroken stand of 332 runs.

AUSTRALIA won by an innings and 148 runs to lead the series 3–0.

5TH TEST: at Birmingham; August 5, 6, 7, 8, and 9 1993; England won the toss

ENGLAND: 276

Gooch	c Taylor	b Reiffel	8	(17–1)
Atherton*		b Reiffel	72	(156–5)
Smith		b Waugh. M	21	(71–2)
Maynard	c Waugh. S	b May	0	(76–3)
Stewart	c &	b Warne	45	(156–4)
Thorpe	c Healy	b May	37	(215–7)
Hussain		b Reiffel	3	(160–6)
Emburey	not out		55	
Bicknell	c Waugh. M	b Reiffel	14	(262–8)
Such		b Reiffel	1	(264–9)
Ilott	c Healy	b Reiffel	3	(276)
Extras: 17				

Reiffel 6–71

ENGLAND: 251

Gooch		b Warne	48	(115–4)
Atherton*	c Border	b Warne	28	(60–1)
Smith	lbw	b Warne	19	(104–2)
Maynard	c Healy	b May	10	(115–3)
Stewart	lbw	b Warne	5	(124–5)
Thorpe	st Healy	b Warne	60	(229–9)
Hussain	c Waugh. S	b May	0	(125–6)
Emburey	c Healy	b May	37	(229–7)
Bicknell	c Waugh. S	b May	0	(229–8)
Such	not out		7	
Ilott		b May	15	(251)
Extras: 22				

Warne 5–82; May 5–89

AUSTRALIA: 408

Taylor	run out		19	(69–3)
Slater	c Smith	b Such	22	(34–1)
Boon	lbw	b Emburey	0	(39–2)
Waugh. M	c Thorpe	b Ilott	137	(233–5)
Border*	c Hussain	b Such	3	(80–4)
Waugh. S	c Stewart	b Bicknell	59	(263–6)
Healy	c Stewart	b Bicknell	80	(370–7)
Hughes		b Bicknell	38	(379–8)
Reiffel		b Such	20	(408)
Warne	c Stewart	b Emburey	10	(398–9)
May	not out		3	
Extras: 17				

Such 3–90; Bicknell 3–99

AUSTRALIA: 120 for 2

Slater	c Thorpe	b Emburey	8	(12–2)
Taylor	c Thorpe	b Such	4	(12–1)
Boon	not out		38	
Waugh. M	not out		62	
Extras: 8				

Mark Waugh registered the match's only century and followed it up with an unbeaten 62 while Tim May's spin bowling yielded 7 wickets for 121 from 67.2 overs.

AUSTRALIA won by 8 wickets to lead the series 4–0.

6TH TEST: at the Oval; August 19, 20, 21, 22, and 23 1993; England won the toss

ENGLAND: 380

Gooch	c Border	b Waugh. S	56	(88–1)
Atherton*	lbw	b Waugh. S	50	(143–2)
Hick	c Warne	b May	80	(231–4)
Maynard		b Warne	20	(177–3)
Hussain	c Taylor	b Warne	30	(253–5)
Stewart	c Healy	b Hughes	76	(339–7)
Ramprakash	c Healy	b Hughes	6	(272–6)
Fraser		b Reiffel	28	(380)
Watkin	c Waugh. S	b Reiffel	13	(363–8)
Such	c Waugh. M	b Hughes	4	(374–9)
Malcolm	not out		0	
Extras: 17				
Hughes 3–121				

ENGLAND: 313

Gooch	c Healy	b Warne	79	(186–5)
Atherton*	c Warne	b Reiffel	42	(77–1)
Hick	c Boon	b May	36	(157–2)
Maynard	c Reiffel	b Hughes	9	(180–3)
Hussain	c Waugh. M	b Hughes	0	(180–4)
Stewart	c Waugh. M	b Reiffel	35	(254–6)
Ramprakash	c Slater	b Hughes	64	(313)
Fraser	c Healy	b Reiffel	13	(276–7)
Watkin	lbw	b Warne	4	(283–8)
Such	lbw	b Warne	10	(313–9)
Malcolm	not out		0	
Extras: 21				
Reiffel 3–55; Warne 3–78; Hughes 3–110				

AUSTRALIA: 303

Taylor	c Hussain	b Malcolm	70	(132–4)
Slater	c Gooch	b Malcolm	4	(9–1)
Boon	c Gooch	b Malcolm	13	(30–2)
Waugh. M	c Stewart	b Fraser	10	(53–3)
Border*	c Stewart	b Fraser	48	(181–6)
Waugh. S		b Fraser	20	(164–5)
Healy	not out		83	
Hughes	c Ramprakash	b Watkin	7	(196–7)
Reiffel	c Maynard	b Watkin	0	(196–8)
Warne	c Stewart	b Fraser	16	(248–9)
May	c Stewart	b Fraser	15	(303)
Extras: 17				
Fraser 5–87; Malcolm 3–86				

AUSTRALIA: 229

Slater	c Stewart	b Watkin	12	(23–1)
Taylor		b Watkin	8	(30–3)
Boon	lbw	b Watkin	0	(23–2)
Waugh. M	c Ramprakash	b Malcolm	49	(95–5)
Border*	c Stewart	b Malcolm	17	(92–4)
Waugh. S	lbw	b Malcolm	26	(142–7)
Healy	c Maynard	b Watkin	5	(106–6)
Hughes	c Watkin	b Fraser	12	(143–8)
Reiffel	c &	b Fraser	42	(217–9)
Warne	lbw	b Fraser	37	(229)
May	not out		4	
Extras: 17				
Watkin 4–65; Fraser 3–44; Malcolm 3–84				

Eight wickets for Fraser and a pair of half-centuries from Gooch enabled England to end their depressing sequence of 18 tests against Australia without a win.

ENGLAND won by 161 runs. AUSTRALIA win the series 4–1.

1ST TEST: at Brisbane; November 25, 26, 27, 28, and 29 1994; Australia won the toss

AUSTRALIA: 426

Slater	c Gatting	b Gooch	176	(308–3)
Taylor*	run out		59	(99–1)
Boon		b Gough	3	(126–2)
Waugh. M	c Stewart	b Gough	140	(425–9)
Bevan	c Hick	b Gough	7	(326–4)
Warne	c Rhodes	b Gough	2	(352–5)
Waugh. S	c Hick	b DeFreitas	19	(379–6)
Healy	c Hick	b DeFreitas	7	(407–7)
McDermott	c Gough	b McCague	2	(419–8)
May	not out		3	
McGrath	c Gough	b McCague	0	(426)
Extras: 8				
Gough 4–107				

AUSTRALIA: 248 for 8 declared

Taylor*	c Stewart	b Tufnell	58	(117–2)
Slater	lbw	b Gough	45	(109–1)
Boon		b Tufnell	28	(190–6)
Waugh. M		b Tufnell	15	(139–3)
Bevan	c Rhodes	b DeFreitas	21	(174–4)
Waugh. S	c sub	b Tufnell	7	(183–5)
Healy	not out		45	
Warne	c sub	b DeFreitas	0	(191–7)
McDermott	c Rhodes	b Gough	6	(201–8)
May	not out		9	
Extras: 14				
Tufnell 4–79				

ENGLAND: 167

Atherton*	c Healy	b McDermott	54	(140–7)
Stewart	c Healy	b McDermott	16	(22–1)
Hick	c Healy	b McDermott	3	(35–2)
Thorpe	c &	b Warne	28	(82–3)
Gooch	c Healy	b May	20	(105–4)
Gatting	lbw	b McDermott	10	(131–5)
McCague		b McDermott	1	(133–6)
Rhodes	lbw	b McDermott	4	(151–9)
DeFreitas	c Healy	b Warne	7	(147–8)
Gough	not out		17	
Tufnell	c Taylor	b Warne	0	(167)
Extras: 7				
McDermott 6–53; Warne 3–39				

ENGLAND: 323

Atherton*	lbw	b Warne	23	(59–2)
Stewart		b Warne	33	(50–1)
Hick	c Healy	b Warne	80	(220–4)
Thorpe		b Warne	67	(219–3)
Gooch	c Healy	b Warne	56	(309–7)
Gatting	c Healy	b McDermott	13	(250–5)
Rhodes	c Healy	b McDermott	2	(280–6)
DeFreitas		b Warne	11	(310–8)
Gough	c Waugh. M	b Warne	10	(323)
McCague	lbw	b Warne	0	(310–9)
Tufnell	not out		2	
Extras: 26				
Warne 8–71				

Swashbuckling innings from Slater and Mark Waugh wrecked the tourists' bowling before the unplayable Warne stepped forth to deliver 11 for 110 from 71 overs.

AUSTRALIA won by 184 runs to lead the series 1–0.

2ND TEST: at Melbourne; December 24, 26, 27, 28, and 29 1994;
England won the toss

AUSTRALIA: 279

Slater	run out		3	(10–1)
Taylor*	lbw	b DeFreitas	9	(39–2)
Boon	c Hick	b Tufnell	41	(91–3)
Waugh. M	c Thorpe	b DeFreitas	71	(171–5)
Bevan	c Atherton	b Gough	3	(100–4)
Waugh. S	not out		94	
Healy	c Rhodes	b Tufnell	17	(208–6)
Warne	c Hick	b Gough	6	(220–7)
May	lbw	b Gough	9	(242–8)
McDermott		b Gough	0	(242–9)
Fleming	c Hick	b Malcolm	16	(279)
Extras: 10				

Gough 4–60

AUSTRALIA: 320 for 7 declared

Taylor*	lbw	b Gough	19	(61–1)
Slater	st Rhodes	b Tufnell	44	(81–2)
Boon	lbw	b DeFreitas	131	(275–5)
Waugh. M	c &	b Gough	29	(157–3)
Bevan	c sub	b Tufnell	35	(269–4)
Waugh. S	not out		26	
Healy	c Thorpe	b Tufnell	17	(316–6)
Warne	c DeFreitas	b Gough	0	(317–7)
McDermott	not out		2	
Extras: 17				

Gough 3–59; Tufnell 3–90

ENGLAND: 212

Atherton*	lbw	b Warne	44	(119–2)
Stewart	c &	b Warne	16	(185–7)
Hick	c Healy	b McDermott	23	(40–1)
Thorpe	c Waugh. M	b Warne	51	(124–3)
Gooch	c &	b McDermott	15	(148–5)
Gatting	c Waugh. S	b Warne	9	(140–4)
Gough	c Healy	b McDermott	20	(189–8)
Rhodes	c Waugh. M	b Warne	0	(151–6)
DeFreitas	st Healy	b Warne	14	(207–9)
Malcolm	not out		11	
Tufnell	run out		0	(212)
Extras: 9				

Warne 6–64; McDermott 3–72

ENGLAND: 92

Gooch	c Healy	b Fleming	2	(3–1)
Atherton*	c Healy	b McDermott	25	(43–4)
Hick		b Fleming	2	(10–2)
Thorpe	c Healy	b McDermott	9	(23–3)
Gatting	c Taylor	b McDermott	25	(81–5)
Rhodes	c Waugh. M	b McDermott	16	(88–6)
Stewart	not out		8	
DeFreitas	lbw	b Warne	0	(91–7)
Gough	c Healy	b Warne	0	(91–8)
Malcolm	c Boon	b Warne	0	(91–9)
Tufnell	c Healy	b McDermott	0	(92)
Extras: 5				

McDermott 5–42; Warne 3–16

Atherton was the only England batsman to reach double figures in both innings. Warne took a second innings hat-trick as he and McDermott crushed the tourists.

AUSTRALIA won by 295 runs to lead the series 2–0.

3RD TEST: at Sydney; January 1, 2, 3, 4, and 5 1995; England won the toss

ENGLAND: 309

Gooch	c Healy	b Fleming	1	(1–1)
Atherton*		b McDermott	88	(194–4)
Hick		b McDermott	2	(10–2)
Thorpe	lbw	b McDermott	10	(20–3)
Crawley	c Waugh. M	b Fleming	72	(196–6)
Gatting	c Healy	b McDermott	0	(194–5)
Fraser	c Healy	b Fleming	27	(309)
Rhodes	run out		1	(197–7)
Gough	c Fleming	b McDermott	51	(255–8)
Malcolm		b Warne	29	(295–9)
Tufnell	not out		4	
Extras: 24				

McDermott 5–101; Fleming 3–52

ENGLAND: 255 for 2 declared

Gooch	lbw	b Fleming	29	(54–1)
Atherton*	c Taylor	b Fleming	67	(158–2)
Hick	not out		98	
Thorpe	not out		47	
Extras: 14				

AUSTRALIA: 116

Slater		b Malcolm	11	(12–1)
Taylor*	c &	b Gough	49	(116–9)
Boon		b Gough	3	(15–2)
Waugh. M	c Rhodes	b Malcolm	3	(18–3)
Bevan	c Thorpe	b Fraser	8	(38–4)
Waugh. S		b Gough	1	(39–5)
Healy	c Hick	b Gough	10	(57–6)
Warne	c Gatting	b Fraser	0	(62–7)
May	c Hick	b Gough	0	(65–8)
McDermott	not out		21	
Fleming		b Gough	0	(116)
Extras: 10				

Gough 6–49

AUSTRALIA: 344 for 7

Taylor*		b Malcolm	113	(239–2)
Slater	c Tufnell	b Fraser	103	(208–1)
Boon	c Hick	b Gough	17	(265–3)
Waugh. M	lbw	b Fraser	25	(289–6)
Bevan	c Rhodes	b Fraser	7	(282–4)
Waugh. S	c Rhodes	b Fraser	0	(286–5)
Healy	c Rhodes	b Fraser	5	(292–7)
Warne	not out		36	
May	not out		10	
Extras: 28				

Fraser 5–73

Darren Gough and then Angus Fraser humbled the Australian batsmen, but centuries from Slater and Taylor rescued the hosts in an extraordinary match.

MATCH DRAWN. AUSTRALIA still lead the series 2–0.

4TH TEST: at Adelaide; January 26, 27, 28, 29, and 30 1995; England won the toss

ENGLAND: 353

Batsman	Dismissal	Bowler	Runs	(Fall)
Gooch	c Waugh. M	b Fleming	47	(93–1)
Atherton*	c Boon	b Fleming	80	(175–2)
Gatting	c Waugh. S	b McIntyre	117	(353)
Thorpe	c Taylor	b Warne	26	(211–3)
Crawley		b Warne	28	(286–4)
Rhodes	c Taylor	b McDermott	6	(293–5)
Lewis	c Blewett	b McDermott	10	(307–6)
DeFreitas	c Blewett	b McIntyre	21	(334–7)
Fraser	run out		7	(353–8)
Malcolm		b McDermott	0	(353–9)
Tufnell	not out		0	
Extras: 11				
McDermott 3–66				

ENGLAND: 328

Batsman	Dismissal	Bowler	Runs	(Fall)
Gooch	c Healy	b McDermott	34	(83–3)
Atherton*	lbw	b Waugh. M	14	(26–1)
Gatting		b Waugh. M	0	(30–2)
Thorpe	c Warne	b McDermott	83	(154–4)
Crawley	c &	b Waugh. M	71	(270–7)
Rhodes	c Fleming	b Warne	2	(169–5)
Lewis		b Fleming	7	(181–6)
DeFreitas	c Healy	b Waugh. M	88	(317–9)
Fraser	c McDermott	b Waugh. M	5	(317–8)
Malcolm	not out		10	
Tufnell	lbw	b Warne	0	(328)
Extras: 14				
Waugh. M 5–40				

AUSTRALIA: 419

Batsman	Dismissal	Bowler	Runs	(Fall)
Slater	c Atherton	b DeFreitas	67	(128–1)
Taylor*	lbw	b Lewis	90	(202–3)
Boon	c Rhodes	b DeFreitas	0	(130–2)
Waugh. M	c Rhodes	b Fraser	39	(207–4)
Waugh. S	c Atherton	b Lewis	19	(232–5)
Blewett	not out		102	
Healy	c Rhodes	b Malcolm	74	(396–6)
Warne	c Thorpe	b Fraser	7	(405–7)
Fleming	c Rhodes	b Malcolm	0	(406–8)
McIntyre		b Malcolm	0	(414–9)
McDermott	c Crawley	b Fraser	5	(419)
Extras: 16				
Malcolm 3–78; Fraser 3–95				

AUSTRALIA: 156

Batsman	Dismissal	Bowler	Runs	(Fall)
Taylor*	c Thorpe	b Malcolm	13	(17–1)
Slater	c Tufnell	b Malcolm	5	(22–3)
Boon	c Rhodes	b Fraser	4	(22–2)
Waugh. M	c Gatting	b Tufnell	24	(64–5)
Waugh. S		b Malcolm	0	(23–4)
Blewett	c Rhodes	b Lewis	12	(75–6)
Healy	not out		51	
Warne	lbw	b Lewis	2	(83–7)
McDermott	c Rhodes	b Lewis	0	(83–8)
Fleming	lbw	b Lewis	24	(152–9)
McIntyre	lbw	b Malcolm	0	(156)
Extras: 21				
Lewis 4–24; Malcolm 4–39				

Greg Blewett scored a century on his debut test innings but 7 Malcolm wickets contributed to an away win, as Australia's discomfort with run chases re-surfaced.

ENGLAND won by 106 runs. AUSTRALIA still lead the series 2–1.

5TH TEST: at Perth; February 3, 4, 5, 6, and 7 1995; Australia won the toss

AUSTRALIA: 402

Slater	c Lewis	b DeFreitas	124	(238–3)
Taylor*	c Rhodes	b Lewis	9	(47–1)
Boon	c Ramprakash	b Lewis	1	(55–2)
Waugh. M	c DeFreitas	b Lewis	88	(247–4)
Waugh. S	not out		99	
Blewett	c Rhodes	b Fraser	20	(287–5)
Healy	c Lewis	b DeFreitas	12	(320–6)
Warne	c Rhodes	b DeFreitas	1	(328–7)
Angel	run out		11	(386–8)
McGrath	run out		0	(388–9)
McDermott	run out		6	(402)
Extras: 31				

Lewis 3–73; DeFreitas 3–91

AUSTRALIA: 345 for 8 declared

Taylor*		b Fraser	52	(123–5)
Slater	c Atherton	b Fraser	45	(75–1)
Angel	run out		0	(79–2)
Boon	c Rhodes	b Malcolm	18	(102–3)
Waugh. M	c Rhodes	b DeFreitas	1	(115–4)
Waugh. S	c Ramprakash	b Lewis	80	(326–6)
Blewett	c Malcolm	b Lewis	115	(333–7)
Healy	not out		11	
Warne	c Lewis	b Malcolm	6	(345–8)
Extras: 17				

ENGLAND: 295

Gooch	lbw	b Waugh. M	37	(77–3)
Atherton*	c Healy	b McGrath	4	(5–1)
Gatting		b McGrath	0	(5–2)
Thorpe	st Healy	b Warne	123	(235–5)
Crawley	c Warne	b Waugh. M	0	(77–4)
Ramprakash		b Warne	72	(246–7)
Rhodes		b Angel	2	(246–6)
Lewis	c Blewett	b McGrath	40	(293–9)
DeFreitas		b Angel	0	(247–8)
Fraser	c Warne	b Angel	9	(295)
Malcolm	not out		0	
Extras: 8				

Angel 3–65; McGrath 3–88

ENGLAND: 123

Gooch	c &	b McDermott	4	(4–1)
Atherton*	c Healy	b McGrath	8	(27–6)
Gatting		b McDermott	8	(17–2)
Fraser	lbw	b McGrath	5	(26–3)
Thorpe	c Taylor	b McGrath	0	(26–4)
Crawley	c Waugh. M	b McDermott	0	(27–5)
Ramprakash	c Waugh. S	b Waugh. M	42	(95–7)
Rhodes	not out		39	
Lewis	lbw	b McDermott	11	(121–8)
DeFreitas	c Taylor	b McDermott	0	(123–9)
Malcolm		b McDermott	0	(123)
Extras: 6				

McDermott 6–38; McGrath 3–40

McDermott and McGrath shared 12 wickets en route to a comfortable success. Blewett became only the fifth test batsman to score two tons in his first 2 matches.

AUSTRALIA won by 329 runs to win the series 3–1.

1ST TEST: at Birmingham; June 5, 6, 7, and 8 1997; Australia won the toss

AUSTRALIA: 118

Taylor*	c Butcher	b Malcolm	7	(15–2)
Elliott		b Gough	6	(11–1)
Blewett	c Hussain	b Gough	7	(28–4)
Waugh. M		b Gough	5	(26–3)
Waugh. S	c Stewart	b Caddick	12	(48–5)
Bevan	c Ealham	b Malcolm	8	(48–7)
Healy	c Stewart	b Caddick	0	(48–6)
Gillespie	lbw	b Caddick	4	(54–8)
Warne	c Malcolm	b Caddick	47	(118)
Kasprowicz	c Butcher	b Caddick	17	(110–9)
McGrath	not out		1	
Extras: 4				

Caddick 5–50; Gough 3–43

AUSTRALIA: 477

Elliott		b Croft	66	(133–1)
Taylor*	c &	b Croft	129	(327–2)
Blewett	c Butcher	b Croft	125	(354–3)
Waugh. S	lbw	b Gough	33	(431–6)
Bevan	c Hussain	b Gough	24	(393–4)
Waugh. M	c Stewart	b Gough	1	(399–5)
Healy	c Atherton	b Ealham	30	(465–7)
Warne	c &	b Ealham	32	(477)
Kasprowicz	c Butcher	b Ealham	0	(465–8)
Gillespie	run out		0	(477–9)
McGrath	not out		0	
Extras: 37				

Ealham 3–60; Gough 3–123; Croft 3–125

ENGLAND: 478 for 9 declared

Butcher	c Healy	b Kasprowicz	8	(16–2)
Atherton*	c Healy	b McGrath	2	(8–1)
Stewart	c Elliott	b Gillespie	18	(50–3)
Hussain	c Healy	b Warne	207	(416–6)
Thorpe	c Bevan	b McGrath	138	(338–4)
Crawley	c Healy	b Kasprowicz	1	(345–5)
Ealham	not out		53	
Croft	c Healy	b Kasprowicz	24	(460–7)
Gough	c Healy	b Kasprowicz	0	(463–8)
Caddick	lbw	b Bevan	0	(478–9)
Extras: 27				

Kasprowicz 4–113

ENGLAND: 119 for 1

Butcher	lbw	b Kasprowicz	14	(29–1)
Atherton*	not out		57	
Stewart	not out		40	
Extras: 8				

England enjoyed a rare comprehensive win after Australia were reduced to 54 for 8 in the first innings, before Hussain and Thorpe put on 288 runs in their reply.

ENGLAND won by 9 wickets to lead the series 1–0.

2ND TEST: at Lord's; June 19, 20, 21, 22, and 23 1997;
Australia won the toss

ENGLAND: 77

Butcher	c Blewett	b McGrath	5	(11–1)
Atherton*	c Taylor	b McGrath	1	(12–2)
Stewart		b McGrath	1	(13–3)
Hussain	lbw	b McGrath	19	(62–6)
Thorpe	c Blewett	b Reiffel	21	(47–4)
Crawley	c Healy	b McGrath	1	(56–5)
Ealham	c Elliott	b Reiffel	7	(77–9)
Croft	c Healy	b McGrath	2	(66–7)
Gough	c Healy	b McGrath	10	(76–8)
Caddick	lbw	b McGrath	1	(77)
Malcolm	not out		0	
Extras: 9				

McGrath 8–38

ENGLAND: 266 for 4

Butcher		b Warne	87	(202–4)
Atherton*	hit wicket	b Kasprowicz	77	(162–1)
Stewart	c Kasprowicz	b McGrath	13	(189–2)
Hussain	c &	b Warne	0	(197–3)
Thorpe	not out		30	
Crawley	not out		29	
Extras: 30				

AUSTRALIA: 213 for 7 declared

Taylor*		b Gough	1	(4–1)
Elliott	c Crawley	b Caddick	112	(212–7)
Blewett	c Hussain	b Croft	45	(73–2)
Waugh. M	c Malcolm	b Caddick	33	(147–3)
Warne	c Hussain	b Gough	0	(147–4)
Waugh. S	lbw	b Caddick	0	(147–5)
Bevan	c Stewart	b Caddick	4	(159–6)
Healy	not out		13	
Reiffel	not out		1	
Extras: 4				

Caddick 4–71

Glenn McGrath's career best 8 for 38 from 20.3 overs took its rightful place amongst history records, but prolonged rain prevented any possibility of a result.

MATCH DRAWN. ENGLAND still lead the series 1–0.

3RD TEST: at Manchester; July 3, 4, 5, 6, and 7 1997; Australia won the toss

AUSTRALIA: 235

Taylor*	c Thorpe	b Headley	2	(9–1)
Elliott	c Stewart	b Headley	40	(85–4)
Blewett		b Gough	8	(22–2)
Waugh. M	c Stewart	b Ealham	12	(42–3)
Waugh. S		b Gough	108	(235–9)
Bevan	c Stewart	b Headley	7	(113–5)
Healy	c Stewart	b Caddick	9	(150–6)
Warne	c Stewart	b Ealham	3	(160–7)
Reiffel		b Gough	31	(230–8)
Gillespie	c Stewart	b Headley	0	(235)
McGrath	not out		0	
Extras: 15				

Headley 4–72; Gough 3–52

AUSTRALIA: 395 for 8 declared

Elliott	c Butcher	b Headley	11	(39–3)
Taylor*	c Butcher	b Headley	1	(5–1)
Blewett	c Hussain	b Croft	19	(33–2)
Waugh. M		b Ealham	55	(131–4)
Waugh. S	c Stewart	b Headley	116	(333–8)
Bevan	c Atherton	b Headley	0	(132–5)
Healy	c Butcher	b Croft	47	(210–6)
Warne	c Stewart	b Caddick	53	(298–7)
Reiffel	not out		45	
Gillespie	not out		28	
Extras: 20				

Headley 4–104

ENGLAND: 162

Butcher	st Healy	b Bevan	51	(94–3)
Atherton*	c Healy	b McGrath	5	(8–1)
Stewart	c Taylor	b Warne	30	(74–2)
Hussain	c Healy	b Warne	13	(110–5)
Thorpe	c Taylor	b Warne	3	(101–4)
Crawley	c Healy	b Warne	4	(111–6)
Ealham	not out		24	
Croft	c Waugh. S	b McGrath	7	(122–7)
Gough	lbw	b Warne	1	(123–8)
Caddick	c Waugh. M	b Warne	15	(161–9)
Headley		b McGrath	0	(162)
Extras: 9				

Warne 6–48; McGrath 3–40

ENGLAND: 200

Butcher	c McGrath	b Gillespie	28	(55–4)
Atherton*	lbw	b Gillespie	21	(44–1)
Stewart		b Warne	1	(45–2)
Hussain	lbw	b Gillespie	1	(50–3)
Thorpe	c Healy	b Warne	7	(84–5)
Crawley	hit wicket	b McGrath	83	(177–8)
Ealham	c Healy	b McGrath	9	(158–6)
Croft	c Reiffel	b McGrath	7	(170–7)
Gough		b McGrath	6	(188–9)
Caddick	c Gillespie	b Warne	17	(200)
Headley	not out		0	
Extras: 20				

McGrath 4–46; Gillespie 3–31; Warne 3–63

Dean Headley made an impressive debut, but he was overshadowed by England's nemesis Steve Waugh whose batting decided the match and turned the series.

AUSTRALIA won by 268 runs to level the series at 1–1.

4TH TEST: at Leeds; July 24, 25, 26, 27, and 28 1997; Australia won the toss

ENGLAND: 172

Butcher	c Blewett	b Reiffel	24	(43–1)
Atherton*	c Gillespie	b McGrath	41	(154–5)
Stewart	c Blewett	b Gillespie	7	(58–2)
Hussain	c Taylor	b McGrath	26	(103–3)
Headley	c Waugh. S	b Gillespie	22	(138–4)
Thorpe		b Gillespie	15	(154–6)
Crawley	c Blewett	b Gillespie	2	(163–7)
Ealham	not out		8	
Croft	c Ponting	b Gillespie	6	(172–8)
Gough		b Gillespie	0	(172–9)
Smith		b Gillespie	0	(172)

Extras: 21

Gillespie 7–37

ENGLAND: 268

Butcher	c Healy	b McGrath	19	(23–1)
Atherton*	c Warne	b McGrath	2	(28–2)
Stewart		b Reiffel	16	(57–3)
Hussain	c Gillespie	b Warne	105	(222–5)
Thorpe	c Waugh. M	b Gillespie	15	(89–4)
Crawley		b Reiffel	72	(256–7)
Ealham	c Waugh. M	b Reiffel	4	(252–6)
Headley	lbw	b Reiffel	3	(263–8)
Croft	c Healy	b Reiffel	5	(268)
Gough	c Waugh. M	b Gillespie	0	(264–9)
Smith	not out		4	

Extras: 23

Reiffel 5–49

AUSTRALIA: 501 for 9 declared

Taylor*	c Stewart	b Gough	0	(0–1)
Elliott		b Gough	199	(444–8)
Blewett	c Stewart	b Gough	1	(16–2)
Waugh. M	c &	b Headley	8	(43–3)
Waugh. S	c Crawley	b Headley	4	(50–4)
Ponting	c Ealham	b Gough	127	(318–5)
Healy		b Ealham	31	(382–6)
Warne	c Thorpe	b Ealham	0	(383–7)
Reiffel	not out		54	
Gillespie		b Gough	3	(461–9)
McGrath	not out		20	

Extras: 54

Gough 5–149

Jason Gillespie scooped nine wickets while Matthew Elliott fell agonisingly short of a double hundred as Australia won comfortably, with an innings to spare.

AUSTRALIA won by an innings and 61 runs to lead the series 2–1.

5TH TEST: at Nottingham; August 7, 8, 9, and 10 1997;
Australia won the toss

AUSTRALIA: 427

Elliott	c Stewart	b Headley	69	(117–1)
Taylor*		b Caddick	76	(160–2)
Blewett	c Stewart	b Hollioake. B	50	(225–3)
Waugh. M	lbw	b Caddick	68	(311–4)
Waugh. S		b Malcolm	75	(386–8)
Ponting		b Headley	9	(325–5)
Healy	c Hollioake. A	b Malcolm	16	(355–6)
Warne	c Thorpe	b Malcolm	0	(363–7)
Reiffel	c Thorpe	b Headley	26	(419–9)
Gillespie	not out		18	
McGrath		b Headley	1	(427)
Extras: 19				

Headley 4–87; Malcolm 3–100

AUSTRALIA: 336

Taylor*	c Hussain	b Hollioake. B	45	(105–2)
Elliott	c Crawley	b Caddick	37	(51–1)
Blewett	c Stewart	b Caddick	60	(156–4)
Waugh. M	lbw	b Headley	7	(134–3)
Waugh. S	c Hollioake. A	b Caddick	14	(171–5)
Ponting	c Stewart	b Hollioake. A	45	(292–7)
Healy	c Stewart	b Hollioake. A	63	(276–6)
Warne	c Thorpe	b Croft	20	(314–8)
Reiffel	c Hollioake. B	b Croft	22	(336)
Gillespie	c Thorpe	b Headley	4	(326–9)
McGrath	not out		1	
Extras: 18				

Caddick 3–85

ENGLAND: 313

Atherton*	c Healy	b Warne	27	(106–1)
Stewart	c Healy	b Warne	87	(129–2)
Crawley	c Healy	b McGrath	18	(141–4)
Hussain		b Warne	2	(135–3)
Thorpe	c Blewett	b Warne	53	(243–6)
Hollioake. A	c Taylor	b Reiffel	45	(243–5)
Hollioake. B	c Waugh. M	b Reiffel	28	(290–8)
Croft	c Blewett	b McGrath	18	(272–7)
Caddick	c Healy	b McGrath	0	(290–9)
Headley	not out		10	
Malcolm		b McGrath	12	(313)
Extras: 13				

McGrath 4–71; Warne 4–86

ENGLAND: 186

Atherton*	c Healy	b McGrath	8	(25–1)
Stewart	c Waugh. S	b Reiffel	16	(25–2)
Crawley	c Healy	b Gillespie	33	(99–4)
Hussain		b Gillespie	21	(78–3)
Thorpe	not out		82	
Hollioake. A	lbw	b Gillespie	2	(121–5)
Hollioake. B	lbw	b Warne	2	(144–6)
Croft	c McGrath	b Warne	6	(150–7)
Caddick	lbw	b Warne	0	(166–8)
Headley	c Healy	b McGrath	4	(186–9)
Malcolm	c Waugh. M	b McGrath	0	(186)
Extras: 12				

McGrath 3–36; Warne 3–43; Gillespie 3–65

McGrath and Warne shared fourteen wickets while the first five Australian batsmen all reached fifty in their first innings to secure another Ashes series triumph.

AUSTRALIA won by 264 runs to lead the series 3–1.

ENGLAND: 180

Butcher		b McGrath	5	(18–1)
Atherton*	c Healy	b McGrath	8	(24–2)
Stewart	lbw	b McGrath	36	(97–3)
Hussain	c Elliott	b McGrath	35	(128–4)
Thorpe		b McGrath	27	(131–5)
Ramprakash	c Blewett	b McGrath	4	(132–7)
Hollioake		b Warne	0	(132–6)
Caddick	not out		26	
Martin		b McGrath	20	(158–8)
Tufnell	c Blewett	b Warne	1	(175–9)
Malcolm	lbw	b Kasprowicz	0	(180)
Extras: 18				
McGrath 7–76				

ENGLAND: 163

Butcher	lbw	b Waugh. M	13	(26–3)
Atherton*	c Waugh. S	b Kasprowicz	8	(20–1)
Stewart	lbw	b Kasprowicz	3	(24–2)
Hussain	c Elliott	b Warne	2	(52–4)
Thorpe	c Taylor	b Kasprowicz	62	(131–5)
Ramprakash	st Healy	b Warne	48	(160–7)
Hollioake	lbw	b Kasprowicz	4	(138–6)
Caddick	not out		0	
Martin	c &	b Kasprowicz	3	(163–8)
Tufnell	c Healy	b Kasprowicz	0	(163–9)
Malcolm		b Kasprowicz	0	(163)
Extras: 20				
Kasprowicz 7–36				

AUSTRALIA: 220

Elliott		b Tufnell	12	(49–1)
Taylor*	c Hollioake	b Tufnell	38	(54–2)
Blewett	c Stewart	b Tufnell	47	(150–5)
Waugh. M	c Butcher	b Tufnell	19	(94–3)
Waugh. S	lbw	b Caddick	22	(140–4)
Ponting	c Hussain	b Tufnell	40	(220)
Healy	c Stewart	b Tufnell	2	(164–6)
Young	c Stewart	b Tufnell	0	(164–7)
Warne		b Caddick	30	(205–8)
Kasprowicz	lbw	b Caddick	0	(205–9)
McGrath	not out		1	
Extras: 9				
Tufnell 7–66; Caddick 3–76				

AUSTRALIA: 104

Taylor*	lbw	b Caddick	18	(36–2)
Elliott	lbw	b Malcolm	4	(5–1)
Blewett	c Stewart	b Caddick	19	(49–4)
Waugh. M	c Hussain	b Tufnell	1	(42–3)
Waugh. S	c Thorpe	b Caddick	6	(54–5)
Ponting	lbw	b Tufnell	20	(88–6)
Healy	c &	b Caddick	14	(92–7)
Young	not out		4	
Warne	c Martin	b Tufnell	3	(95–8)
Kasprowicz	c Hollioake	b Caddick	4	(99–9)
McGrath	c Thorpe	b Tufnell	1	(104)
Extras: 10				
Caddick 5–42; Tufnell 4–27				

Tufnell took 11 for 93 from 47.4 overs and Caddick chipped in with 8 wickets. Thorpe was the only player to pass fifty on his home ground in this nailbiting win.

ENGLAND won by 19 runs. AUSTRALIA win the series 3–2.

1ST TEST: at Brisbane; November 20, 21, 22, 23, and 24 1998; Australia won the toss

AUSTRALIA: 485

Taylor*	c Hussain	b Cork	46	(106–4)
Slater	c Butcher	b Mullally	16	(30–1)
Langer	lbw	b Gough	8	(59–2)
Waugh. M	c Stewart	b Mullally	31	(106–3)
Waugh. S	c Stewart	b Mullally	112	(365–6)
Ponting	c Butcher	b Cork	21	(178–5)
Healy	c Mullally	b Fraser	134	(420–8)
Kasprowicz	c Stewart	b Mullally	0	(365–7)
Fleming	not out		71	
MacGill	c Stewart	b Mullally	20	(445–9)
McGrath	c Atherton	b Croft	5	(485)
Extras: 21				

Mullally 5–105

AUSTRALIA: 237 for 3 declared

Slater	c &	b Fraser	113	(182–2)
Taylor*		b Cork	0	(20–1)
Langer	c Mullally	b Croft	74	(199–3)
Waugh. M	not out		27	
Waugh. S	not out		16	
Extras: 7				

ENGLAND: 375

Butcher	c &	b Waugh. M	116	(240–4)
Atherton	c Waugh. M	b McGrath	0	(11–1)
Hussain	c Healy	b Kasprowicz	59	(145–2)
Stewart*	c Kasprowicz	b MacGill	8	(168–3)
Thorpe	c Langer	b McGrath	77	(315–5)
Ramprakash	not out		69	
Cork	c MacGill	b McGrath	0	(319–6)
Croft		b Kasprowicz	23	(360–7)
Gough	lbw	b McGrath	0	(373–8)
Mullally	c Kasprowicz	b McGrath	0	(373–9)
Fraser	c Waugh. M	b McGrath	1	(375)
Extras: 22				

McGrath 6–85

ENGLAND: 179 for 6

Butcher	lbw	b MacGill	40	(96–2)
Atherton	c Fleming	b McGrath	28	(46–1)
Hussain		b MacGill	47	(148–5)
Stewart*	c Ponting	b Waugh. M	3	(103–3)
Thorpe	c Langer	b Waugh. M	9	(133–4)
Ramprakash	st Healy	b MacGill	14	(161–6)
Cork	not out		21	
Croft	not out		4	
Extras: 13				

MacGill 3–51

A thunderstorm saved England from a likely defeat after Ian Healy, Michael Slater, and Steve Waugh had all plundered centuries.

MATCH DRAWN. The series remained level at 0–0.

2ND TEST: at Perth; November 28, 29, and 30 1998; Australia won the toss

ENGLAND: 112

Butcher	c Healy	b Fleming	0	(2–1)
Atherton	c Healy	b McGrath	1	(4–2)
Hussain	c Healy	b McGrath	6	(19–3)
Stewart*		b McGrath	38	(62–4)
Ramprakash	c Taylor	b Fleming	26	(90–8)
Crawley	c Waugh. M	b Gillespie	4	(74–5)
Hick	c Healy	b Gillespie	0	(74–6)
Cork	c Taylor	b Fleming	2	(81–7)
Tudor	not out		18	
Gough	c Waugh. M	b Fleming	11	(108–9)
Mullally	c Healy	b Fleming	0	(112)

Extras: 6

Fleming 5–46; McGrath 3–37

ENGLAND: 191

Butcher	c Ponting	b Fleming	1	(5–1)
Atherton	c Taylor	b Fleming	35	(40–4)
Hussain	lbw	b Fleming	1	(11–2)
Stewart*	c Taylor	b Fleming	0	(15–3)
Ramprakash	not out		47	
Crawley	c Langer	b Miller	15	(67–5)
Hick	c Ponting	b Gillespie	68	(158–6)
Cork	lbw	b Gillespie	16	(189–7)
Tudor	c Healy	b Gillespie	0	(189–8)
Gough	lbw	b Gillespie	0	(189–9)
Mullally		b Gillespie	0	(191)

Extras: 8

Gillespie 5–88; Fleming 4–45

AUSTRALIA: 240

Taylor*	c Stewart	b Cork	61	(138–3)
Slater	c Butcher	b Gough	34	(81–1)
Langer	c Crawley	b Ramprakash	15	(115–2)
Waugh. M	c Butcher	b Tudor	36	(214–6)
Gillespie	c Stewart	b Mullally	11	(165–4)
Waugh. S		b Tudor	33	(209–5)
Ponting	c Stewart	b Tudor	11	(239–9)
Healy	lbw	b Gough	12	(228–7)
Fleming	c Hick	b Gough	0	(228–8)
Miller	not out		3	
McGrath	c Cork	b Tudor	0	(240)

Extras: 24

Tudor 4–89; Gough 3–43

AUSTRALIA: 64 for 3

Slater	c &	b Gough	17	(24–2)
Taylor*	c Hick	b Mullally	3	(16–1)
Langer	c Atherton	b Tudor	7	(36–3)
Waugh. M	not out		17	
Waugh. S	not out		15	

Extras: 5

Graeme Hick and Mark Taylor were the only players to record a fifty as Damien Fleming's nine wickets were instrumental in achieving a comfortable test triumph.

AUSTRALIA won by 7 wickets to lead the series 1–0.

3rd TEST: at Adelaide; December 11, 12, 13, 14, and 15 1998; Australia won the toss

AUSTRALIA: 391

Slater	c Stewart	b Headley	17	(28–1)
Taylor*	c Hussain	b Such	59	(140–2)
Langer	not out		179	
Waugh. M	c &	b Such	7	(156–3)
Waugh. S	c Hick	b Gough	59	(264–4)
Ponting	c Hick	b Gough	5	(274–5)
Healy	c Ramprakash	b Headley	13	(311–6)
Fleming	lbw	b Headley	12	(338–7)
MacGill		b Such	0	(339–8)
Miller	lbw	b Headley	11	(354–9)
McGrath	c Stewart	b Gough	10	(391)
Extras: 19				

Headley 4–97; Such 3–99; Gough 3–103

AUSTRALIA: 278 for 5 declared

Taylor*	lbw	b Such	29	(54–1)
Slater	lbw	b Gough	103	(188–2)
Langer	c sub	b Such	52	(216–3)
Waugh. M	not out		51	
Waugh. S	c Hick	b Headley	7	(230–4)
Ponting		b Gough	10	(268–5)
Healy	not out		7	
Extras: 19				

ENGLAND: 227

Butcher	lbw	b Miller	6	(18–1)
Atherton	c Taylor	b MacGill	41	(83–2)
Hussain	not out		89	
Stewart*	c Slater	b Miller	0	(84–3)
Ramprakash	c Waugh. M	b McGrath	61	(187–4)
Crawley		b McGrath	5	(195–5)
Hick	c Taylor	b MacGill	8	(210–6)
Headley	lbw	b MacGill	0	(210–7)
Gough	c Healy	b MacGill	7	(226–8)
Mullally		b Fleming	0	(227–9)
Such	lbw	b Fleming	0	(227)
Extras: 10				

MacGill 4–53

ENGLAND: 237

Butcher	c Healy	b Fleming	19	(27–1)
Atherton	c Waugh. M	b Miller	5	(31–2)
Hussain	lbw	b Miller	41	(120–3)
Ramprakash		b Fleming	57	(163–5)
Headley	c Waugh. M	b Miller	2	(122–4)
Stewart*	not out		63	
Crawley	c Waugh. M	b McGrath	13	(221–6)
Hick	c Ponting	b McGrath	0	(221–7)
Gough	c Healy	b McGrath	3	(231–8)
Mullally	c Healy	b Fleming	4	(236–9)
Such	lbw	b McGrath	0	(237)
Extras: 30				

McGrath 4–50; Fleming 3–56; Miller 3–57

Mark Ramprakash recorded a brace of half centuries but the proceedings were dominated by Justin Langer who helped himself to more than 230 runs in the match.

AUSTRALIA won by 205 runs to lead the series 2–0.

ENGLAND: 270

Atherton	c Healy	b McGrath	0	(0–1)
Stewart*		b MacGill	107	(200–4)
Butcher	c Langer	b McGrath	0	(4–2)
Hussain	c Healy	b Nicholson	19	(81–3)
Ramprakash	c McGrath	b Waugh. S	63	(202–5)
Hick	c Fleming	b MacGill	39	(266–8)
Hegg	c Healy	b Waugh. S	3	(206–6)
Headley	c Taylor	b McGrath	14	(244–7)
Gough		b MacGill	11	(270–9)
Fraser	not out		0	
Mullally	lbw	b MacGill	0	(270)
Extras: 14				

MacGill 4–61; McGrath 3–64

ENGLAND: 244

Atherton		b Fleming	0	(5–1)
Stewart*	c Slater	b MacGill	52	(78–4)
Butcher	c Slater	b MacGill	14	(61–2)
Headley		b McGrath	1	(66–3)
Hussain	c Slater	b Nicholson	50	(178–6)
Ramprakash		b Nicholson	14	(127–5)
Hick		b Fleming	60	(221–9)
Hegg	c MacGill	b Nicholson	9	(202–7)
Gough	c Slater	b MacGill	4	(221–8)
Fraser	not out		7	
Mullally	c &	b McGrath	16	(244)
Extras: 17				

Nicholson 3–56; MacGill 3–81

AUSTRALIA: 340

Taylor*	c Hick	b Gough	7	(26–2)
Slater	lbw	b Gough	1	(13–1)
Langer	c Hussain	b Gough	44	(127–4)
Waugh. M	lbw	b Fraser	36	(98–3)
Waugh. S	not out		122	
Lehmann	c Hegg	b Gough	13	(151–5)
Healy	c Headley	b Fraser	36	(209–6)
Fleming	c Hick	b Mullally	12	(235–7)
Nicholson		b Gough	5	(252–8)
MacGill	c Hegg	b Mullally	43	(340–9)
McGrath		b Mullally	0	(340)
Extras: 21				

Gough 5–96; Mullally 3–64

AUSTRALIA: 162

Slater	lbw	b Headley	18	(31–1)
Taylor*	c Headley	b Mullally	19	(41–2)
Langer	c Ramprakash	b Mullally	30	(103–3)
Waugh. M	c Hick	b Headley	43	(130–4)
Waugh. S	not out		30	
Lehmann	c Hegg	b Headley	4	(140–5)
Healy	c Hick	b Headley	0	(140–6)
Fleming	lbw	b Headley	0	(140–7)
Nicholson	c Hegg	b Headley	9	(161–8)
MacGill		b Gough	0	(162–9)
McGrath	lbw	b Gough	0	(162)
Extras: 9				

Headley 6–60

The hosts were cruising to victory at 130 for 3 before five wickets from Dean Headley triggered a collapse in which the last seven wickets fell for just 32 runs.

ENGLAND won by 12 runs. AUSTRALIA still lead the series 2–1.

AUSTRALIA: 322

Taylor*	c Hick	b Headley	2	(4–1)
Slater	c Hegg	b Headley	18	(52–2)
Langer	c Ramprakash	b Tudor	26	(52–3)
Waugh. M	c Hegg	b Headley	121	(319–6)
Waugh. S		b Such	96	(242–4)
Lehmann	c Hussain	b Tudor	32	(284–5)
Healy	c Hegg	b Gough	14	(321–7)
Warne	not out		2	
MacGill		b Gough	0	(321–8)
Miller		b Gough	0	(321–9)
McGrath	c Hick	b Headley	0	(322)
Extras: 11				

Headley 4–62; Gough 3–61

AUSTRALIA: 184

Slater	c Hegg	b Headley	123	(180–8)
Taylor*	c Stewart	b Gough	2	(16–1)
Langer	lbw	b Headley	1	(25–2)
Waugh. M	c Ramprakash	b Headley	24	(64–3)
Lehmann	c Crawley	b Such	0	(73–4)
Healy	c Crawley	b Such	5	(91–5)
Waugh. S		b Headley	8	(110–6)
Warne	c Ramprakash	b Such	8	(141–7)
MacGill	c Butcher	b Such	6	(184–9)
Miller	not out		3	
McGrath	c Stewart	b Such	0	(184)
Extras: 4				

Such 5–81; Headley 4–40

ENGLAND: 220

Butcher	lbw	b Warne	36	(56–2)
Stewart*	c Warne	b McGrath	3	(18–1)
Hussain	c Waugh. M	b Miller	42	(139–5)
Ramprakash	c MacGill	b McGrath	14	(88–3)
Hick	c Warne	b MacGill	23	(137–4)
Crawley	c Taylor	b MacGill	44	(213–8)
Hegg		b Miller	15	(171–6)
Tudor		b MacGill	14	(204–7)
Headley	c McGrath	b MacGill	8	(220)
Gough	lbw	b MacGill	0	(213–9)
Such	not out		0	
Extras: 21				

MacGill 5–57

ENGLAND: 188

Butcher	st Healy	b Warne	27	(57–1)
Stewart*	st Healy	b MacGill	42	(77–2)
Hussain	c &	b MacGill	53	(162–7)
Ramprakash	c Taylor	b McGrath	14	(110–3)
Hick		b MacGill	7	(131–4)
Crawley	lbw	b Miller	5	(150–5)
Hegg	c Healy	b MacGill	3	(157–6)
Tudor		b MacGill	3	(175–8)
Headley	c Healy	b MacGill	16	(180–9)
Gough	not out		7	
Such	c &	b MacGill	2	(188)
Extras: 9				

MacGill 7–50

Darren Gough grabbed a hat-trick before Michael Slater rescued Australia's second innings from disaster, and then Stuart MacGill stole the show with 12 for 107.

AUSTRALIA won by 98 runs to win the series 3–1.

1ST TEST: at Birmingham; July 5, 6, 7, and 8 2001; Australia won the toss

ENGLAND: 294

Atherton	c Waugh. M	b Gillespie	57	(123–3)
Trescothick	c Warne	b Gillespie	0	(2–1)
Butcher	c Ponting	b Warne	38	(106–2)
Hussain*	lbw	b McGrath	13	(136–4)
Ward		b McGrath	23	(159–5)
Stewart	lbw	b McGrath	65	(294)
Afzaal		b Warne	4	(170–6)
White	lbw	b Warne	4	(174–7)
Giles	c Gilchrist	b Warne	7	(191–8)
Gough	c Gillespie	b Warne	0	(191–9)
Caddick	not out		49	

Extras: 34

Warne 5–71; McGrath 3–67

ENGLAND: 164

Atherton	c Waugh. M	b McGrath	4	(4–1)
Trescothick	c Waugh. M	b Warne	76	(155–7)
Butcher	c Gilchrist	b Lee	41	(99–2)
Hussain*	retired hurt		9	
Ward		b Lee	3	(142–3)
Stewart	c Warne	b Gillespie	5	(148–4)
Afzaal	lbw	b Gillespie	2	(150–5)
White		b Gillespie	0	(154–6)
Giles	c Waugh. M	b Warne	0	(164–9)
Gough	lbw	b Warne	0	(155–8)
Caddick	not out		6	

Extras: 18

Warne 3–29; Gillespie 3–52

AUSTRALIA: 576

Slater		b Gough	77	(134–3)
Hayden	c White	b Giles	35	(98–1)
Ponting	lbw	b Gough	11	(130–2)
Waugh. M	c Stewart	b Caddick	49	(267–4)
Waugh. S*	lbw	b Gough	105	(336–5)
Martyn	c Trescothick	b Butcher	105	(496–6)
Gilchrist	c Caddick	b White	152	(576)
Warne	c Atherton	b Butcher	8	(511–7)
Lee	c Atherton	b Butcher	0	(513–8)
Gillespie	lbw	b Butcher	0	(513–9)
McGrath	not out		1	

Extras: 33

Butcher 4–42; Gough 3–152

Having been reduced to 134 for 3, the tourists' middle order then went on the rampage. The chief destroyer was Adam Gilchrist who hammered 25 boundaries.

AUSTRALIA won by an innings and 118 runs to lead the series 1–0.

2ND TEST: at Lord's; July 19, 20, 21, and 22 2001;
Australia won the toss

ENGLAND: 187

Atherton*	lbw	b McGrath	37	(96–3)
Trescothick	c Gilchrist	b Gillespie	15	(33–1)
Butcher	c Waugh. M	b McGrath	21	(75–2)
Thorpe	c Gilchrist	b McGrath	20	(129–6)
Ramprakash		b Lee	14	(121–4)
Stewart	c Gilchrist	b McGrath	0	(126–5)
Ward	not out		23	
White	c Hayden	b McGrath	0	(131–7)
Cork	c Ponting	b Gillespie	24	(178–8)
Caddick		b Warne	0	(181–9)
Gough		b Warne	5	(187)
Extras: 28				

McGrath 5–54

ENGLAND: 227

Atherton*		b Warne	20	(47–2)
Trescothick	c Gilchrist	b Gillespie	3	(8 1)
Butcher	c Gilchrist	b Gillespie	83	(188–7)
Thorpe	lbw	b Lee	2	(50–3)
Ramprakash	lbw	b Gillespie	40	(146–4)
Stewart	lbw	b McGrath	28	(188–5)
Ward	c Ponting	b McGrath	0	(188–6)
White	not out		27	
Cork	c Warne	b McGrath	2	(193–8)
Caddick	c Gilchrist	b Gillespie	7	(225–9)
Gough	c Waugh. M	b Gillespie	1	(227)
Extras: 14				

Gillespie 5–53; McGrath 3–60

AUSTRALIA: 401

Slater	c Stewart	b Caddick	25	(105–3)
Hayden	c Butcher	b Caddick	0	(5–1)
Ponting	c Thorpe	b Gough	14	(27–2)
Waugh. M	run out		108	(212–4)
Waugh. S*	c Stewart	b Cork	45	(230–5)
Martyn	c Stewart	b Caddick	52	(308–6)
Gilchrist	c Stewart	b Gough	90	(387–8)
Warne	c Stewart	b Caddick	5	(322–7)
Lee		b Caddick	20	(401)
Gillespie		b Gough	9	(401–9)
McGrath	not out		0	
Extras: 33				

Caddick 5–101; Gough 3–115

AUSTRALIA: 14 for 2

Hayden	not out		6	
Slater	c Butcher	b Caddick	4	(6–1)
Ponting	lbw	b Gough	4	(13–2)
Waugh. M	not out		0	
Extras: 0				

Mark Butcher was the only home batsman to pass fifty in this drubbing, as Glenn McGrath finished with match figures of eight wickets for 114 runs from 43 overs.

AUSTRALIA won by 8 wickets to lead the series 2–0.

ENGLAND: 185

Atherton*	c Waugh. M	b McGrath	0	(0–1)
Trescothick	c Gilchrist	b Gillespie	69	(117–4)
Butcher	c Ponting	b McGrath	13	(30–2)
Ramprakash	c Gilchrist	b Gillespie	14	(63–3)
Stewart	c Waugh. M	b McGrath	46	(180–9)
Ward	c Gilchrist	b McGrath	6	(142–5)
White	c Hayden	b McGrath	0	(147–6)
Tudor	lbw	b Warne	3	(158–7)
Croft	c Ponting	b Warne	3	(168–8)
Caddick		b Lee	13	(185)
Gough	not out		0	
Extras: 18				
McGrath 5–49				

ENGLAND: 162

Atherton*	c Gilchrist	b Warne	51	(115–3)
Trescothick	c Gilchrist	b Warne	32	(57–1)
Butcher	lbw	b Lee	1	(59–2)
Ramprakash	st Gilchrist	b Warne	26	(126–5)
Stewart		b Warne	0	(115–4)
Ward	lbw	b Gillespie	13	(144–7)
White	c Waugh. S	b Warne	7	(144–6)
Tudor	c Ponting	b Warne	9	(162)
Croft		b Gillespie	0	(146–8)
Caddick	c Gilchrist	b Gillespie	4	(156–9)
Gough	not out		5	
Extras: 14				
Warne 6–33; Gillespie 3–61				

AUSTRALIA: 190

Slater		b Gough	15	(56–2)
Hayden	lbw	b Tudor	33	(48–1)
Ponting	c Stewart	b Gough	14	(69–3)
Waugh. M	c Atherton	b Tudor	15	(94–5)
Waugh. S*	c Atherton	b Caddick	13	(82–4)
Martyn	c Stewart	b Caddick	4	(102–6)
Gilchrist	c Atherton	b Tudor	54	(188–9)
Warne	lbw	b Caddick	0	(102–7)
Lee	c Butcher	b Tudor	4	(122–8)
Gillespie	not out		27	
McGrath	c Butcher	b Tudor	2	(190)
Extras: 9				
Tudor 5–44; Caddick 3–70				

AUSTRALIA: 158 for 3

Hayden	lbw	b Tudor	42	(88–3)
Slater	c Trescothick	b Caddick	12	(36–1)
Ponting	c Stewart	b Croft	17	(72–2)
Waugh. M	not out		42	
Waugh. S*	retired hurt		1	
Martyn	not out		33	
Extras: 11				

Both England's openers recorded half centuries but Shane Warne continued to torture his opponents with eight wickets for 70 runs from 34 overs.

AUSTRALIA won by 7 wickets to lead the series 3–0.

Australia won the toss

AUSTRALIA: 447

Slater	lbw	b Caddick	21	(39–1)
Hayden	lbw	b Caddick	15	(42–2)
Ponting	c Stewart	b Tudor	144	(263–3)
Waugh	c Ramprakash	b Caddick	72	(288–4)
Martyn	c Stewart	b Gough	118	(447)
Katich		b Gough	15	(355–5)
Gilchrist*	c Trescothick	b Gough	19	(396–6)
Warne	c Stewart	b Gough	0	(412–7)
Lee	c Ramprakash	b Mullally	0	(422–8)
Gillespie	c Atherton	b Gough	5	(438–9)
McGrath	not out		8	
Extras: 30				

Gough 5–103; Caddick 3–143

AUSTRALIA: 176 for 4 declared

Hayden	c Stewart	b Mullally	35	(141–3)
Slater		b Gough	16	(25–1)
Ponting	lbw	b Gough	72	(129–2)
Waugh	not out		24	
Martyn	lbw	b Caddick	6	(171–4)
Katich	not out		0	
Extras: 23				

ENGLAND: 309

Atherton	c Gilchrist	b McGrath	22	(50–1)
Trescothick	c Gilchrist	b McGrath	37	(67–2)
Butcher	run out		47	(158–4)
Hussain*	lbw	b McGrath	46	(158–3)
Ramprakash	c Gilchrist	b Lee	40	(252–6)
Afzaal	c Warne	b McGrath	14	(174–5)
Stewart	not out		76	
Tudor	c Gilchrist	b McGrath	2	(267–7)
Caddick	c Gilchrist	b Lee	5	(289–8)
Gough	c Slater	b McGrath	8	(299–9)
Mullally	c Katich	b McGrath	0	(309)
Extras: 12				

McGrath 7–76

ENGLAND: 315 for 4

Atherton	c Gilchrist	b McGrath	8	(8–1)
Trescothick	c Hayden	b Gillespie	10	(33–2)
Butcher	not out		173	
Hussain*	c Gilchrist	b Gillespie	55	(214–3)
Ramprakash	c Waugh	b Warne	32	(289–4)
Afzaal	not out		4	
Extras: 33				

Gilchrist, deputising for the injured Steve Waugh. Made a tempting declaration and against the odds Mark Butcher gratefully obliged with a remarkable 173 not out.

ENGLAND won by 6 wickets. AUSTRALIA still lead the series 3–1.

5TH TEST: at the Oval; August 23, 24, 25, 26, and 27 2001; Australia won the toss

AUSTRALIA: 641 for 4 declared

Hayden	c Trescothick	b Tufnell	68	(158–1)
Langer	retired hurt		102	
Ponting	c Atherton	b Ormond	62	(292–2)
Waugh. M		b Gough	120	(489–3)
Waugh. S*	not out		157	
Gilchrist	c Ramprakash	b Afzaal	25	(534–4)
Martyn	not out		64	
Extras: 43				

ENGLAND: 432

Atherton		b Warne	13	(58–1)
Trescothick		b Warne	55	(85–2)
Butcher	c Langer	b Warne	25	(104–3)
Hussain*		b Waugh. M	52	(166–4)
Ramprakash	c Gilchrist	b McGrath	133	(424–9)
Afzaal	c Gillespie	b McGrath	54	(255–5)
Stewart	c Gilchrist	b Warne	29	(313–6)
Caddick	lbw	b Warne	0	(313–7)
Ormond		b Warne	18	(350–8)
Gough	st Gilchrist	b Warne	24	(432)
Tufnell	not out		7	
Extras: 22				

Warne 7–165

ENGLAND: 184

Atherton	c Warne	b McGrath	9	(17–1)
Trescothick	c &	b McGrath	24	(48–3)
Butcher	c Waugh. S	b Warne	14	(46–2)
Hussain*	lbw	b Warne	2	(50–4)
Ramprakash	c Hayden	b Warne	19	(95–6)
Afzaal	c Ponting	b McGrath	5	(55–5)
Stewart		b Warne	34	(126–7)
Caddick		b Lee	17	(126–8)
Ormond	c Gilchrist	b McGrath	17	(184–9)
Gough	not out		39	
Tufnell	c Warne	b McGrath	0	(184)
Extras: 4				

McGrath 5–43; Warne 4–64

Warne seized 11 wickets, but the damage had already been inflicted by the Aussie batsmen, with six of them passing 60 runs, and 3 of them going on to three figures.

AUSTRALIA won by an innings and 25 runs to win the series 4–1.

1ST TEST: at Brisbane; November 7, 8, 9, and 10 2002;
England won the toss

AUSTRALIA: 492

Langer	c Stewart	b Jones	32	(67–1)
Hayden	c Stewart	b Caddick	197	(378–3)
Ponting		b Giles	123	(339–2)
Martyn	c Trescothick	b White	26	(399–4)
Waugh*	c Crawley	b Caddick	7	(408–5)
Lehmann	c Butcher	b Giles	30	(478–7)
Gilchrist	c Giles	b White	0	(415–6)
Warne	c Butcher	b Caddick	57	(492–9)
Bichel	lbw	b Giles	0	(478–8)
Gillespie	not out		0	
McGrath	lbw	b Giles	0	(492)
Extras: 20				

Giles 4–101; Caddick 3–108

AUSTRALIA: 296 for 5 declared

Langer	c Stewart	b Caddick	22	(30–1)
Hayden	c &	b Giles	103	(192–3)
Ponting	c Trescothick	b Caddick	3	(39–2)
Martyn	c Hussain	b Giles	64	(213–4)
Gilchrist	not out		60	
Waugh*	c Trescothick	b Caddick	12	(242–5)
Lehmann	not out		20	
Extras: 12				

Caddick 3–95

ENGLAND: 325

Trescothick	c Ponting	b McGrath	72	(171–3)
Vaughan	c Gilchrist	b McGrath	33	(49–1)
Butcher	c Hayden	b McGrath	54	(170–2)
Hussain*	c Gilchrist	b Gillespie	51	(268–4)
Crawley	not out		69	
Stewart		b Gillespie	0	(270–5)
White		b McGrath	12	(283–6)
Giles	c Gilchrist	b Bichel	13	(308–7)
Caddick	c Ponting	b Bichel	0	(308–8)
Hoggard	c Hayden	b Warne	4	(325–9)
Jones	absent hurt			
Extras: 17				

McGrath 4–87

ENGLAND: 79

Trescothick	c Gilchrist	b Gillespie	1	(3–2)
Vaughan	lbw	b McGrath	0	(1–1)
Butcher	c Ponting	b Warne	40	(74–8)
Hussain*	c Ponting	b McGrath	11	(33–3)
Crawley	run out		0	(34–4)
Stewart	c Hayden	b Warne	0	(35–5)
White	c Hayden	b McGrath	13	(66–6)
Giles	c Gilchrist	b McGrath	4	(74–7)
Caddick	c Lehmann	b Warne	4	(79–9)
Hoggard	not out		1	
Jones	absent hurt			
Extras: 5				

McGrath 4–36; Warne 3–29

This match was over after Day One when Hussain put Australia in to bat and the home team reached 364 for 2 at stumps, courtesy of tons from Hayden and Ponting.

AUSTRALIA won by 384 runs to lead the series 1–0.

2ND TEST: at Adelaide; November 21, 22, 23, and 24 2002; England won the toss

ENGLAND: 342

Trescothick		b McGrath	35	(88–1)
Vaughan	c Warne	b Bichel	177	(295–4)
Key	c Ponting	b Warne	1	(106–2)
Hussain*	c Gilchrist	b Warne	47	(246–3)
Butcher	c Gilchrist	b Gillespie	22	(295–5)
Stewart	lbw	b Gillespie	29	(337–9)
White	c Bichel	b Gillespie	1	(308–6)
Dawson	lbw	b Warne	6	(325–7)
Caddick		b Warne	0	(325–8)
Hoggard	c Gilchrist	b Gillespie	6	(342)
Harmison	not out		3	
Extras: 15				

Gillespie 4–78; Warne 4–93

ENGLAND: 159

Trescothick	lbw	b Gillespie	0	(5–1)
Vaughan	c McGrath	b Warne	41	(114–5)
Butcher	lbw	b McGrath	4	(17–2)
Hussain*		b Bichel	10	(36–3)
Key	c Lehmann	b Bichel	1	(40–4)
Stewart	lbw	b Warne	57	(130–7)
White	c sub	b McGrath	5	(130–6)
Dawson	c Gilchrist	b McGrath	19	(159)
Hoggard		b McGrath	1	(132–8)
Harmison	lbw	b Warne	0	(134–9)
Caddick	not out		6	
Extras: 15				

McGrath 4–41; Warne 3–36

AUSTRALIA: 552 for 9 declared

Langer	c Stewart	b Dawson	48	(114–2)
Hayden	c Caddick	b White	46	(101–1)
Ponting	c Dawson	b White	154	(397–4)
Martyn	c Hussain	b Harmison	95	(356–3)
Waugh*	c Butcher	b White	34	(423–6)
Lehmann	c sub	b White	5	(414–5)
Gilchrist	c Stewart	b Harmison	54	(552–9)
Warne	c &	b Dawson	25	(471–7)
Bichel		b Hoggard	48	(548–8)
Gillespie	not out		0	
Extras: 43				

White 4–106

England's first innings was rescued by a swashbuckling effort from Michael Vaughan but 7 more wickets for Warne and another Ponting century decided this contest.

AUSTRALIA won by an innings and 51 runs to lead the series 2–0.

3RD TEST: at Perth; November 29, 30, and December 1 2002; England won the toss

ENGLAND: 185

Trescothick	c Gilchrist	b Lee	34	(47–1)
Vaughan	c Gilchrist	b McGrath	34	(101–4)
Butcher	run out		9	(69–2)
Hussain*	c Gilchrist	b Lee	8	(83–3)
Key		b Martyn	47	(156–8)
Stewart	c Gilchrist	b McGrath	7	(111–5)
White	c Martyn	b Lee	2	(121–6)
Tudor	c Martyn	b Warne	0	(135–7)
Dawson	not out		19	
Silverwood	c Hayden	b Gillespie	10	(173–9)
Harmison		b Gillespie	6	(185)
Extras: 9				
Lee 3–78				

ENGLAND: 223

Trescothick	c Gilchrist	b Lee	4	(13–1)
Vaughan	run out		9	(34–3)
Dawson	c Waugh	b Gillespie	8	(33–2)
Butcher	lbw	b McGrath	0	(34–4)
Hussain*	c Gilchrist	b Warne	61	(169–6)
Key	lbw	b McGrath	23	(102–5)
Stewart	not out		66	
White	st Gilchrist	b Warne	15	(208–7)
Tudor	retired hurt		3	
Harmison		b Lee	5	(223–8)
Silverwood	absent hurt			
Extras: 29				

AUSTRALIA: 456

Langer	run out		19	(31–1)
Hayden	c Tudor	b Harmison	30	(85–2)
Ponting		b White	68	(159–3)
Martyn	c Stewart	b Tudor	71	(264–5)
Lehmann	c Harmison	b White	42	(226–4)
Waugh*		b Tudor	53	(348–7)
Gilchrist	c Tudor	b White	38	(316–6)
Warne	run out		35	(416–8)
Lee	c Key	b White	41	(423–9)
Gillespie		b White	27	(456)
McGrath	not out		8	
Extras: 24				
White 5–127				

McGrath was left stranded on 8 not out, as he narrowly failed to make it a perfect eleven of Aussie batsmen who reached double figures in this latest stroll.

AUSTRALIA won by an innings and 48 runs to lead the series 3–0.

4TH TEST: at Melbourne; December 26, 27, 28, 29, and 30 2002; Australia won the toss

AUSTRALIA: 551 for 6 declared

Langer	c Caddick	b Dawson	250	(545–5)
Hayden	c Crawley	b Caddick	102	(195–1)
Ponting		b White	21	(235–2)
Martyn	c Trescothick	b White	17	(265–3)
Waugh*	c Foster	b White	77	(394–4)
Love	not out		62	
Gilchrist		b Dawson	1	(551–6)
Extras: 21				
White 3–133				

AUSTRALIA: 107 for 5

Langer	lbw	b Caddick	24	(90–5)
Hayden	c sub	b Caddick	1	(8–1)
Ponting	c Foster	b Harmison	30	(58–2)
Martyn	c Foster	b Harmison	0	(58–3)
Waugh*	c Butcher	b Caddick	14	(83–4)
Love	not out		6	
Gilchrist	not out		10	
Extras: 22				
Caddick 3–51				

ENGLAND: 270

Trescothick	c Gilchrist	b Lee	37	(73–2)
Vaughan		b McGrath	11	(13–1)
Butcher	lbw	b Gillespie	25	(94–3)
Hussain*	c Hayden	b MacGill	24	(118–6)
Dawson	c Love	b MacGill	6	(111–4)
Key	lbw	b Lee	0	(113–5)
Crawley	c Langer	b Gillespie	17	(172–7)
White	not out		85	
Foster	lbw	b Waugh	19	(227–8)
Caddick		b Gillespie	17	(264–9)
Harmison	c Gilchrist	b Gillespie	2	(270)
Extras: 27				
Gillespie 4–25				

ENGLAND: 387

Trescothick	lbw	b MacGill	37	(67–1)
Vaughan	c Love	b MacGill	145	(236–4)
Butcher	c Love	b Gillespie	6	(89–2)
Hussain*	c &	b McGrath	23	(169–3)
Key	c Ponting	b Gillespie	52	(287–5)
Crawley		b Lee	33	(342–6)
White	c Gilchrist	b MacGill	21	(342–7)
Foster	c Love	b MacGill	6	(356–8)
Dawson	not out		15	
Caddick	c Waugh	b MacGill	10	(378–9)
Harmison		b Gillespie	7	(387)
Extras: 32				
MacGill 5–152; Gillespie 3–71				

Langer recorded his test career best as the hosts piled on the runs again. However, they again made hard work of pursuing a small total in their second innings.

AUSTRALIA won by 5 wickets to lead the series 4–0.

5TH TEST: at Sydney; January 2, 3, 4, 5, and 6 2002; England won the toss

ENGLAND: 362

Trescothick	c Gilchrist	b Bichel	19	(32–2)
Vaughan	c Gilchrist	b Lee	0	(4–1)
Butcher		b Lee	124	(240–5)
Hussain*	c Gilchrist	b Gillespie	75	(198–3)
Key	lbw	b Waugh	3	(210–4)
Crawley	not out		35	
Stewart		b Bichel	71	(332–6)
Dawson	c Gilchrist	b Bichel	2	(337–7)
Caddick		b MacGill	7	(348–8)
Hoggard	st Gilchrist	b MacGill	0	(350–9)
Harmison	run out		4	(362)
Extras: 22				

Bichel 3–86

ENGLAND: 452 for 9 declared

Trescothick		b Lee	22	(37–1)
Vaughan	lbw	b Bichel	183	(345–5)
Butcher	c Hayden	b MacGill	34	(124–2)
Hussain*	c Gilchrist	b Lee	72	(313–3)
Key	c Hayden	b Lee	14	(344–4)
Crawley	lbw	b Gillespie	8	(356–6)
Stewart	not out		38	
Dawson	c &	b Bichel	12	(378–7)
Caddick	c Langer	b MacGill	8	(407–8)
Hoggard		b MacGill	0	(409–9)
Harmison	not out		20	
Extras: 41				

MacGill 3–120; Lee 3–132

AUSTRALIA: 363

Langer	c Hoggard	b Caddick	25	(56–3)
Hayden	lbw	b Caddick	15	(36–1)
Ponting	c Stewart	b Caddick	7	(45–2)
Martyn	c Caddick	b Harmison	26	(146–4)
Waugh*	c Butcher	b Hoggard	102	(241–6)
Love	c Trescothick	b Harmison	0	(150–5)
Gilchrist	c Stewart	b Harmison	133	(349–9)
Bichel	c Crawley	b Hoggard	4	(267–7)
Lee	c Stewart	b Hoggard	0	(267–8)
Gillespie	not out		31	
MacGill	c Hussain	b Hoggard	1	(363)
Extras: 19				

Hoggard 4–92; Harmison 3–70; Caddick 3–121

AUSTRALIA: 226

Langer	lbw	b Caddick	3	(5–1)
Hayden	lbw	b Hoggard	2	(5–2)
Bichel	lbw	b Caddick	49	(93–4)
Ponting	lbw	b Caddick	11	(25–3)
Martyn	c Stewart	b Dawson	21	(109–6)
Waugh*		b Caddick	6	(99–5)
Love		b Harmison	27	(139–7)
Gilchrist	c Butcher	b Caddick	37	(181–8)
Lee	c Stewart	b Caddick	46	(224–9)
Gillespie	not out		3	
MacGill		b Caddick	1	(226)
Extras: 20				

Caddick 7–94

The tourists avoided a whitewash thanks to hundreds from Butcher and Vaughan plus Caddick's ten wickets against a team struggling without McGrath and Warne.

ENGLAND won by 225 runs. AUSTRALIA win the series 4–1.

1ST TEST: at Lord's; July 21, 22, 23, and 24 2005; Australia won the toss

AUSTRALIA: 190

Langer	c Harmison	b Flintoff	40	(66–3)
Hayden		b Hoggard	12	(35–1)
Ponting*	c Strauss	b Harmison	9	(55–2)
Martyn	c Jones. G	b Jones. S	2	(66–4)
Clarke	lbw	b Jones. S	11	(87–5)
Katich	c Jones. G	b Harmison	27	(178–8)
Gilchrist	c Jones. G	b Flintoff	26	(126–6)
Warne		b Harmison	28	(175–7)
Lee	c Jones. G	b Harmison	3	(178–9)
Gillespie	lbw	b Harmison	1	(190)
McGrath	not out		10	

Extras: 21

Harmison 5–43

AUSTRALIA: 384

Langer	run out		6	(18–1)
Hayden		b Flintoff	34	(54–2)
Ponting*	c sub	b Hoggard	42	(100–3)
Martyn	lbw	b Harmison	65	(255–5)
Clarke		b Hoggard	91	(255–4)
Katich	c Jones. S	b Harmison	67	(384)
Gilchrist		b Flintoff	10	(274–6)
Warne	c Giles	b Harmison	2	(279–7)
Lee	run out		8	(289–8)
Gillespie		b Jones. S	13	(341–9)
McGrath	not out		20	

Extras: 26

Harmison 3–54

ENGLAND: 155

Trescothick	c Langer	b McGrath	4	(10–1)
Strauss	c Warne	b McGrath	2	(11–2)
Vaughan*		b McGrath	3	(18–3)
Bell		b McGrath	6	(19–4)
Pietersen	c Martyn	b Warne	57	(122–9)
Flintoff		b McGrath	0	(21–5)
Jones. G	c Gilchrist	b Lee	30	(79–6)
Giles	c Gilchrist	b Lee	11	(92–7)
Hoggard	c Hayden	b Warne	0	(101–8)
Harmison	c Martyn	b Lee	11	(155)
Jones. S	not out		20	

Extras: 11

McGrath 5–53; Lee 3–47

ENGLAND: 180

Trescothick	c Hayden	b Warne	44	(96–2)
Strauss	c &	b Lee	37	(80–1)
Vaughan*		b Lee	4	(112–4)
Bell	lbw	b Warne	8	(104–3)
Pietersen	not out		64	
Flintoff	c Gilchrist	b Warne	3	(119–5)
Jones. G	c Gillespie	b McGrath	6	(158–6)
Giles	c Hayden	b McGrath	0	(158–7)
Hoggard	lbw	b McGrath	0	(164–8)
Harmison	lbw	b Warne	0	(167–9)
Jones. S	c Warne	b McGrath	0	(180)

Extras: 14

McGrath 4–29; Warne 4–64

Only 1 Aussie batsman got beyond 30 runs in their first innings but McGrath reduced England to 21 for 5 as Australia enjoyed yet another successful trip to Lord's.

AUSTRALIA won by 239 runs to lead the series 1–0.

2ND TEST: at Birmingham; August 4, 5, 6, and 7 2005; Australia won the toss

ENGLAND: 407

Trescothick	c Gilchrist	b Kasprowicz	90	(164–2)
Strauss		b Warne	48	(112–1)
Vaughan*	c Lee	b Gillespie	24	(187–4)
Bell	c Gilchrist	b Kasprowicz	6	(170–3)
Pietersen	c Katich	b Lee	71	(348–8)
Flintoff	c Gilchrist	b Gillespie	68	(290–5)
Jones. G	c Gilchrist	b Kasprowicz	1	(293–6)
Giles	lbw	b Warne	23	(342–7)
Hoggard	lbw	b Warne	16	(407)
Harmison		b Warne	17	(375–9)
Jones. S	not out		19	
Extras: 24				

Warne 4–116; Kasprowicz 3–80

ENGLAND: 182

Trescothick	c Gilchrist	b Lee	21	(27–2)
Strauss		b Warne	6	(25–1)
Hoggard	c Hayden	b Lee	1	(31–4)
Vaughan*		b Lee	1	(29–3)
Bell	c Gilchrist	b Warne	21	(75–6)
Pietersen	c Gilchrist	b Warne	20	(72–5)
Flintoff		b Warne	73	(182)
Jones. G	c Ponting	b Lee	9	(101–7)
Giles	c Hayden	b Warne	8	(131–8)
Harmison	c Ponting	b Warne	0	(131–9)
Jones. S	not out		12	
Extras: 10				

Warne 6–46; Lee 4–82

AUSTRALIA: 308

Langer	lbw	b Jones. S	82	(262–6)
Hayden	c Strauss	b Hoggard	0	(0–1)
Ponting*	c Vaughan	b Giles	61	(88–2)
Martyn	run out		20	(118–3)
Clarke	c Jones. G	b Giles	40	(194–4)
Katich	c Jones. G	b Flintoff	4	(208–5)
Gilchrist	not out		49	
Warne		b Giles	8	(273–7)
Lee	c Flintoff	b Jones. S	6	(282–8)
Gillespie	lbw	b Flintoff	7	(308–9)
Kasprowicz	lbw	b Flintoff	0	(308)
Extras: 31				

Flintoff 3–52; Giles 3–78

AUSTRALIA: 279

Langer		b Flintoff	28	(47–1)
Hayden	c Trescothick	b Jones. S	31	(82–3)
Ponting*	c Jones. G	b Flintoff	0	(48–2)
Martyn	c Bell	b Hoggard	28	(107–4)
Clarke		b Harmison	30	(175–8)
Katich	c Trescothick	b Giles	16	(134–5)
Gilchrist	c Flintoff	b Giles	1	(136–6)
Gillespie	lbw	b Flintoff	0	(137–7)
Warne	hit wicket	b Flintoff	42	(220–9)
Lee	not out		43	
Kasprowicz	c Jones. G	b Harmison	20	(279)
Extras: 40				

Flintoff 4–79

Andrew Flintoff took seven wickets and scored a brace of fifties but it was Melbourne 1982 revisited as Australia almost defied the odds and snatched a victory.

ENGLAND won by 2 runs to level the series at 1–1.

3RD TEST: at Manchester; August 11, 12, 13, 14, and 15 2005; England won the toss

ENGLAND: 444

Trescothick	c Gilchrist	b Warne	63	(163–2)
Strauss		b Lee	6	(26–1)
Vaughan*	c McGrath	b Katich	166	(290–3)
Bell	c Gilchrist	b Lee	59	(346–6)
Pietersen	c sub	b Lee	21	(333–4)
Hoggard		b Lee	4	(341–5)
Flintoff	c Langer	b Warne	46	(433–7)
Jones. G		b Gillespie	42	(434–8)
Giles	c Hayden	b Warne	0	(438–9)
Harmison	not out		10	
Jones. S		b Warne	0	(444)
Extras: 27				

Warne 4–99; Lee 4–100

ENGLAND: 280 for 6 declared

Trescothick		b McGrath	41	(64–1)
Strauss	c Martyn	b McGrath	106	(224–3)
Vaughan*	c sub	b Lee	14	(97–2)
Bell	c Katich	b McGrath	65	(264–6)
Pietersen	lbw	b McGrath	0	(225–4)
Flintoff		b McGrath	4	(248–5)
Jones. G	not out		27	
Giles	not out		0	
Extras: 23				

McGrath 5–115

AUSTRALIA: 302

Langer	c Bell	b Giles	31	(58–1)
Hayden	lbw	b Giles	34	(86–3)
Ponting*	c Bell	b Jones. S	7	(73–2)
Martyn		b Giles	20	(133–5)
Katich		b Flintoff	17	(119–4)
Gilchrist	c Jones. G	b Jones. S	30	(186–6)
Warne	c Giles	b Jones. S	90	(287–8)
Clarke	c Flintoff	b Jones. S	7	(201–7)
Gillespie	lbw	b Jones. S	26	(302)
Lee	c Trescothick	b Jones. S	1	(293–9)
McGrath	not out		1	
Extras: 38				

Jones. S 6–53; Giles 3–100

AUSTRALIA: 371 for 9

Langer	c Jones. G	b Hoggard	14	(25–1)
Hayden		b Flintoff	36	(96–2)
Ponting*	c Jones. G	b Harmison	156	(354–9)
Martyn	lbw	b Harmison	19	(129–3)
Katich	c Giles	b Flintoff	12	(165–4)
Gilchrist	c Bell	b Flintoff	4	(182–5)
Clarke		b Jones. S	39	(263–6)
Gillespie	lbw	b Hoggard	0	(264–7)
Warne	c Jones. G	b Flintoff	34	(340–8)
Lee	not out		18	
McGrath	not out		5	
Extras: 34				

Flintoff 4–71

Centuries for Vaughan and Strauss and two half centuries from Bell put England in charge, but a Ponting ton inspired a resolute effort from the Australian tailenders.

MATCH DRAWN. The series remained level at 1–1.

4TH TEST: at Nottingham; August 25, 26, 27, and 28 2005; England won the toss

ENGLAND: 477

Trescothick		b Tait	65	(137–2)
Strauss	c Hayden	b Warne	35	(105–1)
Vaughan*	c Gilchrist	b Ponting	58	(213–4)
Bell	c Gilchrist	b Tait	3	(146–3)
Pietersen	c Gilchrist	b Lee	45	(241–5)
Flintoff	lbw	b Tait	102	(418–6)
Jones. G	c &	b Kasprowicz	85	(450–7)
Giles	lbw	b Warne	15	(450–8)
Hoggard	c Gilchrist	b Warne	10	(477)
Harmison	st Gilchrist	b Warne	2	(454–9)
Jones. S	not out		15	
Extras: 42				

Warne 4–102; Tait 3–97

ENGLAND: 129 for 7

Trescothick	c Ponting	b Warne	27	(32–1)
Strauss	c Clarke	b Warne	23	(57–3)
Vaughan*	c Hayden	b Warne	0	(36–2)
Bell	c Kasprowicz	b Lee	3	(57–4)
Pietersen	c Gilchrist	b Lee	23	(103–5)
Flintoff		b Lee	26	(111–6)
Jones. G	c Kasprowicz	b Warne	3	(116–7)
Giles	not out		7	
Hoggard	not out		8	
Extras: 9				

Warne 4–31; Lee 3–51

AUSTRALIA: 218

Langer	c Bell	b Hoggard	27	(58–4)
Hayden	lbw	b Hoggard	7	(20–1)
Ponting*	lbw	b Jones. S	1	(21–2)
Martyn	lbw	b Hoggard	1	(22–3)
Clarke	lbw	b Harmison	36	(99–5)
Katich	c Strauss	b Jones. S	45	(157–6)
Gilchrist	c Strauss	b Flintoff	27	(163–8)
Warne	c Bell	b Jones. S	0	(157–7)
Lee	c Bell	b Jones. S	47	(218)
Kasprowicz		b Jones. S	5	(175–9)
Tait	not out		3	
Extras: 19				

Jones. S 5–44; Hoggard 3–70

AUSTRALIA: 387

Langer	c Bell	b Giles	61	(129–2)
Hayden	c Giles	b Flintoff	26	(50–1)
Ponting*	run out		48	(155–3)
Martyn	c Jones. G	b Flintoff	13	(161–4)
Clarke	c Jones. G	b Hoggard	56	(261–5)
Katich	lbw	b Harmison	59	(314–7)
Gilchrist	lbw	b Hoggard	11	(277–6)
Warne	st Jones. G	b Giles	45	(342–8)
Lee	not out		26	
Kasprowicz	c Jones. G	b Harmison	19	(373–9)
Tait		b Harmison	4	(387)
Extras: 19				

Harmison 3–93

Australia suffered the humiliation of a follow-on, but it was England's turn to stagger over the finishing line. 'Freddie' Flintoff was the match's only century-maker.

ENGLAND won by 3 wickets to lead the series 2–1.

5TH TEST: at the Oval; September 1, 2, 3, 4, and 5 2005;
England won the toss

ENGLAND: 373

Trescothick	c Hayden	b Warne	43	(82–1)
Strauss	c Katich	b Warne	129	(297–7)
Vaughan*	c Clarke	b Warne	11	(102–2)
Bell	lbw	b Warne	0	(104–3)
Pietersen		b Warne	14	(131–4)
Flintoff	c Warne	b McGrath	72	(274–5)
Collingwood	lbw	b Tait	7	(289–6)
Jones		b Lee	25	(325–8)
Giles	lbw	b Warne	32	(373)
Hoggard	c Martyn	b McGrath	2	(345–9)
Harmison	not out		20	
Extras: 18				

Warne 6–122

ENGLAND: 335

Trescothick	lbw	b Warne	33	(109–4)
Strauss	c Katich	b Warne	1	(2–1)
Vaughan*	c Gilchrist	b McGrath	45	(67–2)
Bell	c Warne	b McGrath	0	(67–3)
Pietersen		b McGrath	158	(308–8)
Flintoff	c &	b Warne	8	(126–5)
Collingwood	c Ponting	b Warne	10	(186–6)
Jones		b Tait	1	(199–7)
Giles		b Warne	59	(335–9)
Hoggard	not out		4	
Harmison	c Hayden	b Warne	0	(335)
Extras: 16				

Warne 6–124; McGrath 3–85

AUSTRALIA: 367

Langer		b Harmison	105	(185–1)
Hayden	lbw	b Flintoff	138	(323–4)
Ponting*	c Strauss	b Flintoff	35	(264–2)
Martyn	c Collingwood	b Flintoff	10	(281–3)
Clarke	lbw	b Hoggard	25	(359–7)
Katich	lbw	b Flintoff	1	(329–5)
Gilchrist	lbw	b Hoggard	23	(356–6)
Warne	c Vaughan	b Flintoff	0	(363–8)
Lee	c Giles	b Hoggard	6	(367)
McGrath	c Strauss	b Hoggard	0	(363–9)
Tait	not out		1	
Extras: 23				

Flintoff 5–78; Hoggard 4–97

AUSTRALIA: 4 for 0

Langer	not out		0
Hayden	not out		0
Extras: 4			

The Ashes remained in the balance until the final afternoon when Kevin Pietersen smashed his team to safety with the help of 7 sixes, assisted by a 50 from Giles.

MATCH DRAWN. ENGLAND win the series 2–1.

THE WHITEWASH SERIES OF 2006–7

This book covers the 60 years from 1945 to the end of 2005, but it would be remiss of me not to record the next series. This page is for the eyes of Australians only!

1ST TEST: at Brisbane; November 23–27 2006;   Australia won the toss

AUSTRALIA: 602 for 9 declared
(Ponting 196; Hussey 86; Langer 82; Clarke 56; Flintoff 4–99)
ENGLAND: 157
(Bell 50; McGrath 6–50; Clark 3–21)
AUSTRALIA: 202 for 1 declared
(Langer 100 not out; Ponting 60 not out)
ENGLAND: 370
(Collingwood 96; Pietersen 92; Clark 4–72; Warne 4–124)
AUSTRALIA won by 277 runs to lead the series 1–0.

2ND TEST: at Adelaide; December 1–5 2006;   England won the toss

ENGLAND: 551 for 6 declared
(Collingwood 206; Pietersen 158; Bell 60; Clark 3–75)
AUSTRALIA: 513
(Ponting 142; Clarke 124; Hussey 91; Gilchrist 64; Hoggard 7–109)
ENGLAND: 129
(Warne 4–49)
AUSTRALIA: 168 for 4
(Hussey 61 not out)
AUSTRALIA won by 6 wickets to lead the series 2–0.

3RD TEST: at Perth; December 14–18 2006;   Australia won the toss

AUSTRALIA: 244
(Hussey 74 not out; Panesar 5–92; Harmison 4–48)
ENGLAND: 215
(Pietersen 70; Clark 3–49)
AUSTRALIA: 527 for 5 declared
(Clarke 135 not out; Hussey 103; Gilchrist 102 not out; Hayden 92; Ponting 75; Panesar 3–145)
ENGLAND: 350
(Cook 116; Bell 87; Pietersen 60 not out; Flintoff 51; Warne 4–115)
AUSTRALIA won by 206 runs to lead the series 3–0.

4TH TEST: at Melbourne; December 26–28 2006;   England won the toss

ENGLAND: 159
(Strauss 50; Warne 5–39)
AUSTRALIA: 419
(Symonds 156; Hayden 153; Mahmood 4–100; Flintoff 3–77)
ENGLAND: 161
(Lee 4–47; Clark 3–30)
AUSTRALIA won by innings and 99 runs to lead the series 4–0.

5TH TEST: at Sydney; January 2–5 2007;   England won the toss

ENGLAND: 291
(Flintoff 89; Bell 71; Clark 3–62; McGrath 3–67; Lee 3–75)
AUSTRALIA: 393
(Warne 71; Gilchrist 62; Anderson 3–98)
ENGLAND: 147
(McGrath 3–38; Lee 3–39)
AUSTRALIA: 46 for 0
AUSTRALIA won by 10 wickets to win the series 5–0.

THE ASHES, 1877–1938

Year	Venue	Result
1877	Australia	1–1. The Ashes were not yet contested.
1879	Australia	1–0 to Australia. The Ashes were not yet contested.
1880	England	1–0 to England. The Ashes were not yet contested.
1881–2	Australia	2–0 to Australia, and 2 draws. The Ashes were not yet contested.
1882	England	1–0 to Australia. The Ashes were not yet contested.
1882–3	Australia	2–2. England won The Ashes 2–1. Australia won an extra test.
1884	England	1–0 to England, and 2 draws.
1884–5	Australia	3–2 to England.
1886	England	3–0 to England.
1887	Australia	2–0 to England.
1888	Australia	1–0 to England.
1888	England	2–1 to England.
1890	England	2–0 to England, and 1 abandoned match.
1892	Australia	2–1 to Australia.
1893	England	1–0 to England, and 2 draws.
1894–5	Australia	3–2 to England.
1896	England	2–1 to England.
1897–8	Australia	4–1 to Australia.
1899	England	1–0 to Australia, and 4 draws.
1901–2	Australia	4–1 to Australia.
1902	England	2–1 to Australia, and 2 draws.
1903–4	Australia	3–2 to England.
1905	England	2–0 to England, and 3 draws.
1907–8	Australia	4–1 to Australia.
1909	England	2–1 to Australia, and 2 draws.
1911–2	Australia	4–1 to England.
1912	England	1–0 to England, and 2 draws.
1920–1	Australia	5–0 to Australia.
1921	England	3–0 to Australia.
1924–5	Australia	4–1 to Australia.
1926	England	1–0 to England, and 4 draws.
1928–9	Australia	4–1 to England.
1930	England	2–1 to Australia, and 2 draws.
1932–3	Australia	4–1 to England.
1934	England	2–1 to Australia, and 2 draws.
1936–7	Australia	3–2 to Australia.
1938	England	1–1, and 2 draws, and 1 abandoned match.

NON-ASHES TEST MATCHES

The following 6 tests were not Ashes contests, but they are listed here, for the record. The matches were drawn, unless stated otherwise.

Centenary Test: at Melbourne; March 12–14 and March 16–17 1977;   England won the toss

AUSTRALIA: 138
(Underwood 3–16; Old 3–39)
ENGLAND: 95
(Lillee 6–26; Walker 4–54)
AUSTRALIA: 419 for 9 declared
(Marsh 110 not out; Davis 68; Walters 66; Hookes 56; Old 4–104)
ENGLAND: 417
(Randall 174; Amiss 64; Lillee 5–139; O'Keeffe 3–108)
AUSTRALIA won by 45 runs.

1ST TEST: at Perth; December 14–16 and December 18–19 1979;   England won the toss

AUSTRALIA: 244
(Hughes 99; Botham 6–78)
ENGLAND: 228
(Brearley 64; Lillee 4–73; Dymock 3–52)
AUSTRALIA: 337
(Border 115; Wiener 58; Botham 5–98; Underwood 3–82)
ENGLAND: 215
(Boycott 99 not out; Dymock 6–34)
AUSTRALIA won by 138 runs to lead the series 1–0.

2ND TEST: at Sydney; January 4–6 and January 8 1980;   Australia won the toss

ENGLAND: 123
(Lillee 4–40; Dymock 4–42)
AUSTRALIA: 145
(Botham 4–29)
ENGLAND: 237
(Gower 98 not out; Dymock 3–48; Pascoe 3–76)
AUSTRALIA: 219 for 4
(Chappell. G 98 not out; Underwood 3–71)
AUSTRALIA won by 6 wickets to lead the series 2–0.

3RD TEST: at Melbourne; February 1–3 and February 5–6 1980;   England won the toss

ENGLAND: 306
(Gooch 99; Brearley 60 not out; Lillee 6–60)
AUSTRALIA: 477
(Chappell. G 114; Chappell. I 75; Laird 74; Border 63; Lever 4–111; Botham 3–105; Underwood 3–131)
ENGLAND: 273
(Botham 119 not out; Gooch 51; Lillee 5–78; Pascoe 4–80)
AUSTRALIA: 103 for 2
AUSTRALIA won by 8 wickets and won the series 3–0.

Centenary Test: at Lord's; August 28–30 and September 1–2 1980;   Australia won the toss

AUSTRALIA: 385 for 5 declared
Hughes 117; Wood 112; Border 56 not out; Old 3–91)
ENGLAND: 205
(Boycott 62; Pascoe 5–59; Lillee 4–43)
AUSTRALIA: 189 for 4 declared
(Hughes 84; Chappell. G 59; Old 3–47)
ENGLAND: 244 for 3
(Boycott 128 not out; Gatting 51 not out)

Bicentenary Test: At Sydney; January 29–31 and February 1–2 1988;   England won the toss

ENGLAND: 425
(Broad 139; Taylor 4–84; Waugh 3–51)
AUSTRALIA: 214
(Jones 56; Hemmings 3–53; Dilley 3–54)
AUSTRALIA 328 for 2
(Boon 184 not out; Marsh 56)

SHEFFIELD SHIELD AND COUNTY CHAMPIONSHIP WINNERS, 1945–2005

	Sheffield Shield		County Championship
1947	Victoria	1946	Yorkshire
1948	Western Australia	1947	Middlesex
1949–50	New South Wales	1948	Glamorgan
1951	Victoria	1949	Middlesex and Yorkshire
1952	New South Wales	1950	Lancashire and Surrey
1953	South Australia	1951	Warwickshire
1954–62	New South Wales	1952–58	Surrey
1963	Victoria	1959–60	Yorkshire
1964	South Australia	1961	Hampshire
1965–66	New South Wales	1962–63	Yorkshire
1967	Victoria	1964–65	Worcestershire
1968	Western Australia	1966–68	Yorkshire
1969	South Australia	1969	Glamorgan
1970	Victoria	1970	Kent
1971	South Australia	1971	Surrey
1972–73	Western Australia	1972	Warwickshire
1974	Victoria	1973	Hampshire
1975	Western Australia	1974	Worcestershire
1976	South Australia	1975	Leicestershire
1977–78	Western Australia	1976	Middlesex
1979–80	Victoria	1977	Kent and Middlesex
1981	Western Australia	1978	Kent
1982	South Australia	1979	Essex
1983	New South Wales	1980	Middlesex
1984	Western Australia	1981	Nottinghamshire
1985–86	New South Wales	1982	Middlesex
1987–89	Western Australia	1983–84	Essex
1990	New South Wales	1985	Middlesex
1991	Victoria	1986	Essex
1992	Western Australia	1987	Nottinghamshire
1993–94	New South Wales	1988–89	Worcestershire
1995	Queensland	1990	Middlesex
1996	South Australia	1991–92	Essex
1997	Queensland	1993	Middlesex
1998–99	Western Australia	1994–95	Warwickshire
2000–02	Queensland	1996	Leicestershire
2003	New South Wales	1997	Glamorgan
2004	Victoria	1998	Leicestershire
2005	New South Wales	1999–00	Surrey
		2001	Yorkshire
		2002	Surrey
		2003	Sussex
		2004	Warwickshire
		2005	Nottinghamshire

WHO GIVES A TOSS?

Who gives a toss about the toss of a coin at the start of the proceedings? Just how crucial is the flip of the coin in determining the subsequent proceedings? Let's take a look at the Ashes test matches since 1945 then. Well, the first obvious statistic to record is that Australia have won 85 tosses, while the England captains have only guessed correctly on 78 occasions, thereby reinforcing the Australian belief that the English are useless tossers. However, what is more noteworthy is the conversion rate of calling the coin correctly and then winning the ensuing test. Here one will find that the apparent advantage of choosing either to bat or field first isn't all it is cracked up to be, or at least if it is of supreme importance, then the team that decides whether or not to bowl first hasn't always made a sound judgement. Australia, for example, have won only 34 of their test matches after enjoying the luxury of choice at the outset. This represents only a forty per cent chance that an Australian success at the toss will be followed by triumph in the match itself. England cricket fans, grasping at all the comfort that they can muster, can thus console themselves that should Australia win the toss, post-war history has indicated that there is a 60% chance that they will not then win the match itself. However, the picture then looks bleak for England when one observes their success at converting successes at the toss into triumph in the test match.

Perversely, England have won only 19 of the 78 Ashes test matches between 1945 and 2005 when their captain correctly envisaged how the coin would be flipped. This means that there is a 75 per cent likelihood that England will not actually derive any advantage from the coin ritual! In summary, I can only conclude that anyone who jumps to conclusions that a winning toss will lead to a winning test, all I can state from the evidence presented to me is that all Ashes observers need not get too excited about this flipping coin!

AND FINALLY ...

The author would like to apologise to any celtic followers of the England cricket team who are mortally offended by the use of the England flag on the front cover. The author is aware that technically the team represents the England & Wales cricket board, that Cardiff is now an Ashes venue, and that several England players have hailed from Wales and Scotland. Sincerest apologies to any offended persons, though if you should choose to organise a protest rally, the publisher would be most grateful for the extra publicity.

ABOUT THE PUBLISHERS

If you are desperately trying to get a foot in the door and get your book into the public domain, you could do worse than submit a sample of it to ourselves, preferably on a disc and/or in PDF format. We are Parkbench Publications, PO Box 1081, Belfast, BT1 9EP. Unlike most publishers, we will not put your sample to the bottom of a pile and then glance at it several weeks later. You will receive a quick decision and your project will be afforded the respect that it deserves, which is uncommon amongst the major publishing houses that will not entertain you unless you have a cookery programme on Channel Four or appear regularly in OK magazine.

Alternatively, you can waste time circulating samples to the major publishing houses and wait literally months for their standard, tiresome 'good luck elsewhere' replies.

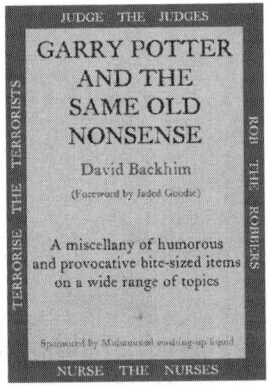

An Essential Guide to Music in the 1970s

by Johnny Zero

(courtesy of
Parkbench Publications)

This 360-page well of information contains the following:

Every Top 10 UK singles chart in the 1970s

The Number 1 UK album for each week

The Number 1 US album for each week

The Number 1 US single for each week

A top news story for each week

The concert highlights of each year

The sporting highlights of each year

The deaths of each year

The Oscar winners of the 1970s

Plus extra coverage of 120 notable recordings

Featured albums from Led Zeppelin, the Rolling Stones, Neil Young, Elton John, Bob Marley And The Wailers, Pink Floyd, the Eagles, Fleetwood Mac, Kate Bush, and Blondie

A
Concise
Guide
to
Eighties'
Music
by Karl Vorderman
(courtesy of
Parkbench Publications)

This fact-filled well of information contains songs from such acts as Madonna, The Smiths, Michael Jackson, UB40, Madness, The Pet Shop Boys, Queen, The Specials, George Michael, David Bowie, Debbie Harry, Duran Duran, The Housemartins, Cyndi Lauper, Bob Marley and The Wailers, New Order, The Pogues, The Pretenders, Public Image Limited, Roxy Music, The Stone Roses, The Stranglers, Paul Young, and lots more! This book contains:

- all the UK Number 1 singles and all the UK Number 1 albums
- all the US Number 1 singles and all the US Number 1 albums
- Major news stories and sporting highlights
- The Oscar winners and the bucket-kickers
- And lots more!

This compendium of statistics is a factual reminder of all the highs and lows experienced by the England football team from the end of the Second World War to the end of the Eriksson era. The national team has rarely been outside of the Top Ten ranked teams in world soccer, and yet for all the high expectations, there has been a recurring theme of under-achievement in the major finals of the World Cup and the European Championship. This *Complete Record* assembles every one of the 616 matches, all the players privileged enough to be selected for their country, and the club teams that they represent. There are many great victories to browse through as well as embarrassing setbacks to recall, from the glory of 1966 to the near misses of 1990, 1996, and 2006; from the humiliation against the USA in 1950 to the stunning triumph against Germany in 2001. This book is ideal for all you anorak England supporters who can look back in awe and regret at the achievements and failings of such legends as Finney, Matthews, Greaves, Charlton, Moore, Banks, Shilton, Clemence, Keegan, Hoddle, Robson, Gascoigne, Lineker, Owen, and Rooney, to name but a few.

PARKBENCH PUBLICATIONS

£9.99
€11.99
$14.99

ISBN 978 0 955575 6 7

ENGLAND FOOTBALL TEAM 1946 2006 JOHN BULL

England Football Team 1946–2006

A Complete Record

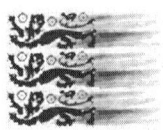

John Bull